# MULTICULTURAL FOUNDATIONS OF PSYCHOLOGY AND COUNSELING

Series Editors: Allen E. Ivey and Derald Wing Sue

# PSYCHOLOGY, POVERTY, AND THE END OF SOCIAL EXCLUSION

## Putting Our Practice to Work

## Laura Smith

### Foreword by Isaac Prilleltensky

Teachers College, Columbia University
New York and London

Published by Teachers College Press, 1234 Amsterdam Avenue, New York, NY 10027

Passages within this book have been adapted from my previous work, and I gratefully acknowledge the permission granted for their use by the original publishers.

*Published by the American Psychological Association:*
    Smith, L. (2005). Classism, psychotherapy, and the poor: Conspicuous by their absence. *American Psychologist*, 60(7), 687-696.
    Smith, L. (2009). Enhancing training and practice in the context of poverty. *Training and Education in Professional Psychology*, 3, 84-93.
    Smith, L., Chambers, D. A., & Bratini, L. (2009). When oppression is the pathogen: The participatory development of socially just mental health practice. *American Journal of Orthopsychiatry*, 79, 159-168.

*Published by Sage/Society:*
    Smith, L. (2008). Positioning classism within psychology's social justice agenda. *The Counseling Psychologist*, 36, 895-924.

*Library of Congress Cataloging-in-Publication Data*

Smith, Laura, 1960–
Psychology, poverty, and the end of social exclusion : putting our practice to work / Laura Smith ; foreword by Prilleltensky.
    p. cm. (Multicultural Foundations of Psychology and Counseling Series)
    Includes bibliographical references and index.
    ISBN 978-0-8077-5124-4 (pbk. : alk. paper)
    ISBN 978-0-8077-5125-1 (hbk. : alk. paper)
    1. Poverty—United States—Psychological aspects. 2. Marginality, Social—United States—Psychological aspects. 3. Poor—Services for—United States. 5. Cross-cultural counseling. I. Title. II. Series.
    HV4045.S65 2010
    362.5/860973—dc22                                                    2010011945

ISBN 978-0-8077-5124-4 (paper)
ISBN 978-0-8077-5125-1 (hardcover)

Printed on acid-free paper
Manufactured in the United States of America

17   16   15   14   13   12   11   10          8   7   6   5   4   3   2   1

*For Sean*

# CONTENTS

# FOREWORD

This is a liberating book written by a liberating author. In her writing, theorizing, and practice, Laura Smith wishes to free ideas from convention, psychologists from orthodoxy, and poor people from injustice. This book is an exquisite blend of phenomenology, critique, and practical hope.

Inspired by her own family vicissitudes, Smith dissects the phenomenology of poverty from the lived experience of marginalized people and from the perspective of psychologists trying to help. We quickly realize that poverty is not just about material deprivation, but about relative deprivation as well. It is about shame and self-derogation and exclusion. It is about doubting who you are and questioning the dignity of your own people. But it is also about questioning and doubting the cultural prescriptions that made you feel that way. This is where the phenomenology of the helper comes into play. For some psychologists, helping the poor is part of a charity ideology. For Smith, the charity model is inadequate, and she knows that psychologists who do not challenge it perpetuate it. We don't need charity, we need justice.

In this book you enter into the world of people who are poor. This is no removed discourse of their risk and protective factors. This is frustration and anger and disappointment, up close. Smith does not invite you to examine the life of the poor; she forces you to do it. And after you do it, you cannot help but question your practice. Whether you are a psychologist, a social worker, a counselor, a nurse, a psychiatrist, a teacher, or a community organizer, you will gain insights about the lives of the people you work with.

The helping professions have a long history of perpetuating oppression with the most caring of attitudes. Instead of helping people to organize for more resources and political power, we reduce the social complexity of their psychological pain to immaturity and defense mechanisms and we then blame them for missing appointments. We, agents of adjustment, have an occupational hazard: We ascribe individual intentionality to behavior that is enormously prescribed and proscribed by objective and subjective realities beyond the control of the individual whose intentionality we are judging.

If you wish to work with poor people, you would do well to read this book and understand how individual behavior is shaped and reshaped by material and perceptual contexts. This knowledge liberates us from constraining frameworks that reduce personal behavior to individual motivation. Our own behavior is much more prescribed and proscribed by social mores than we care to admit. Only after we acknowledge that our behaviors and thoughts are greatly determined by our social ecology can we begin to liberate ourselves from their constraining impact.

Once people who are poor understand that the world has been configured for them in oppressive ways, they can start the process of reconfiguring it. Once psychologists understand that their profession has been unwittingly supporting the status quo by redefining social injustice into personal inadequacy, they can forge bonds of liberation with the poor.

But after Smith's critique there is practical hope. In very pragmatic means, she reclaims psychology in ways that promote liberation and not justification of inequity. She defends the rights of the poor to get therapy when they need it, and the rights of the psychologist to deliver it whenever it is appropriate, and not wherever it is expected. Poor people need justice, but they need therapy, too. If they cannot afford the bus ticket to come to you, or don't have a winter coat to venture out, then perhaps you need to go and see them where they are. And if they don't need therapy, but instead need community organizing, then you can be instrumental in achieving that too. Whatever their needs, the message of this book is clear: We start where the clients are.

The passionate critique of this book is matched only by its passionate message of hope—hope that poor people and psychologists can work together to reinvent their relationship in liberating ways for both. This is what we can learn from Smith: You don't give in to orthodoxy and you don't give up. This is an inspired and inspiring book. May many helpers read it and become agents of justice instead of justification.

—Isaac Prilleltensky,
Erwin and Barbara Mautner Chair in Community Well-Being and
Dean of the School of Education at the University of Miami, Florida

# ACKNOWLEDGMENTS

The people who have supported and guided my work are truly too numerous to mention, but they include:

First and foremost, my mentor, Dr. Derald Wing Sue. I would never have had the idea to write this book, nor the confidence that I *could* do it, without your example and inspiration.

My amazing colleagues in the Department of Counseling and Clinical Psychology at Teachers College.

Meg Lemke, my editor at Teachers College Press.

My brilliant, passionate, and committed research team at Teachers College. You are my heroes.

Elizabeth Merrick, as always.

Carlos Montalvo, Andrew Baer, Rosío Gonzalez, Catherine Chanse, and all the West Farms interns.

The teachers and pathfinders with whom I have crossed paths over the years: Sandra Bernabei, Marjorie Silverman, Georgie Gatch, Richard Raskin, Steve Robbins, and Jack Corrazzini.

My family: Carroll Smith, Baska Smith, and their children and families, and especially my sister Leslie. Thank you for your patience, presence, and support now and in the past.

Most especially, endless thanks from the bottom of my heart to Sean Kelleher, the most wonderful partner and one-person cheering section that anyone could hope for.

# PSYCHOLOGY, POVERTY, AND THE END OF SOCIAL EXCLUSION

*Putting Our Practice to Work*

# INTRODUCTION

I have in my hands a little self-published book created in 1998 by a distant cousin of mine, Mark Smith. It is a collection of reminiscences written by our relatives about their lives in the mountains of West Virginia. They are stories of resourcefulness, poverty, simple pleasures, and getting by. "My One and Only Hair Dye Job" is recounted by my great aunt, Icy Belle Smith Gump. "Why I Don't Talk Much" is the contribution of Woody Smith. "Don't ever be ashamed of your people," said my grandfather to me at the kitchen table. "They worked hard all their lives."

How, in a world where poor Appalachian mountain people were shown to me as dysfunctional in-breeders or lazy moonshiners or the Beverly Hillbillies, was I to accomplish *that*? When my family left the little mountain town where I grew up to visit the relatives, I was determined to experience no connection to the images around me: the dirt roads, the rusty trailers, the skinny dogs and cats, the smell of coal smoke. My grandfather's house was furnished with seats from cars and trucks.

It was not until much later in my life that I appreciated other images of my people. Those images are anchored to a memory of my grandfather showing me something from his pocket, a small, worn card that he carried with him all the time. The card said, "Member, United Brotherhood of Carpenters and Joiners." I think now about that card and my grandfather's insistence on trooping us over to the local union hall to introduce us around. He had been poor all his life, but he had also, as he said, worked hard all his life. The worth of that work and the dignity of working people were strong in him.

The portrait that I am painting may be an unfamiliar one, because contemporary culture does not often present these concepts together: poor and strong; poor and working; poor and self-respecting; poor, yet receiving respectful consideration from the rest of society. And as this portrait comes into view, a sense of tragedy accompanies it: Where can poor people see such a portrait of themselves today?

Where can they see themselves as included within the circles of society and citizenship to which the rest of us belong?

If there is any segment of society that should be concerned with questions like these, it is those of us within the "helping professions" who have built our professional careers around understanding and facilitating human emotional well-being. We have a role to play in addressing poverty and social class, a role that complements the work of sociologists, political scientists, economists, and other social scientists involved in that work. As a psychologist, my frame of reference originates with that field in particular, which will be evident; however, as an applied psychologist, I am offering a perspective that is applicable across fields of social service practice. This book, then, is intended for practitioners, academics, and students within the mental health fields—psychology, counseling, social work, and psychiatry—who would like to implement considerations of social class and poverty within their own practice.

That intention can only be realized if we add new a perspective to our understanding of poverty, a perspective that will suggest new horizons of service and advocacy that go beyond sympathy, charity, and conventional treatment modalities. This perspective has its foundations in a conceptualization of poverty as more than just a lack of money—it positions poverty as the bottom of the social class hierarchy. Social class is understood, therefore, to be a dimension along which socioeconomic power, privilege, and disadvantage are inequitably distributed, so that people closer to the top have more privilege and people nearer the bottom have more disadvantages. This structural conceptualization represents a social justice framework for understanding the well-being of people at different points along the social class continuum, in the same way that we think of racism, sexism, heterosexism, and ableism affecting people differentially depending upon their specific group membership.

Pulling together concepts from topics as broad as social class, poverty, psychology, and mental health practice means there are many important elements within each that are not covered in a book like this. One of the things that this book is *not* is a comprehensive treatment of social class theory. Part of my goal is to present social class as a construct that is related to, but not the same as, more familiar variables such as socioeconomic status and income levels. In introducing this idea to mental health practitioners, I offer only an overview here. I am also working within the context of American poverty, rather than global poverty, which I do not address. Finally, even within an American context, poverty and social class share important, meaningful intersections with race, ethnicity, gender, sexual orientation, and (dis)ability—each of which merits extensive consideration beyond the parameters of my treatment. With regard to each of these limitations, I provide references for readers who want to gain a deeper under-standing of these issues.

Chapter 1 provides an overview of social class and introduces the way that I will be using this construct to reposition our consideration of poverty. What may initially seem like a small alteration in perspective will be shown to have far-reaching implications as the discussion proceeds through the remaining chapters. In Chapter 2, I explain more about what I mean by a social justice framework for social class. Within that framework, I define the operant form of oppression as *classism*, and I present examples of classism's impact on the lives of poor families. Chapter 3 traces themes within the extant psychological literature on poverty, including explorations of the mental health corollaries of poverty, the efforts of social and community psychology to draw attention to poverty's structural elements, and the history of practitioners' attention (or lack thereof) to poor clients.

The second half of the book begins with the voices of the poor themselves, as I move toward issues more specific to practice. Chapter 4 presents what poor people have had to say about poverty through their participation in interviews and narrative studies; I also weave in my own experiences as a psychologist in a poor community. I should note that whenever I mention interactions with com-munity members, I have altered or fictionalized some aspects of the descriptions to ensure anonymity. Chapter 5 focuses on the interface of classism and poverty with the work of mental health professionals. I describe how classist attitudes can play out in this work by presenting some encounters with my own classism, and then I suggest some strategies by which clinicians can address these issues within their own psychotherapeutic work or in their supervision of trainees. In Chapter 6, I make the case for mental health practice/action in poor communi-ties that goes beyond psychotherapy, and provide some examples of that.

Finally, in Chapter 7, I leave readers with some final thoughts about a new stance on poverty, which I believe can align mental health practitioners with broader forward movement toward economic justice. With these parting thoughts, the discussion will come full circle. I chose the words *social exclusion* for the book's title purposefully, and in the last chapter, I will elaborate on the idea of ending the social exclusion of poor families —of insisting on a new perspective on poverty that is incompatible with the relegation of the poor to the social margins. Is this within the purview of psychologists, therapists, and counselors? I think it is easy to assume that poverty, as regretful and sympa-thetic as we may feel about it, is a problem for someone else to solve. The fact is that our practice can and should contribute to the solution. What are we waiting for?

# 1

# WHAT IS SOCIAL CLASS?

> The closest most folks can come to talking about class in this nation is to talk about money.
>
> —bell hooks (2000, p. 5)

It seems like a simple question—yet many different things come to mind when we think of social class. Things like wealth (or lack of it), status and prestige (or lack of it), the pages of the newspaper where we see rich people dressed up for social events, words like *classy* and *trashy* and *low-rent*, the lords and ladies of English nobility, or the caste stratifications of traditional Indian culture. In this chapter, my aim is to present a particular formulation of social class that lends itself to a particular perspective on poverty, all intended (eventually) to frame out a particular approach to mental health practice in the context of poverty. I am not, therefore, suggesting that other approaches to social class and poverty are not useful. Social class is a multifaceted phenomenon, and a focus on different facets is appropriate for different purposes.

The purpose of my presentation is to provide a social justice grounding for social class—one that accounts for the ways in which social class is not just a question of different lifestyles or even just a function of money; it is also a question of structural power, privilege, and disadvantage. This perspective can illuminate the one-dimensional nature of much of our thinking about poor people and what constitutes "help" for them, a relevant consideration for helping professionals and policymakers—teachers, counselors, social workers, psychologists, grant-makers, legislators, and others—who include people living in poverty among those they serve. I will focus on the application of this perspective to the work of psychologists and other mental health practitioners, but it should be a short step to apply it to other professions whose work has bearing on the lives of poor families and communities.

## SETTING THE STAGE:
## SOCIAL CLASS AND MULTICULTURAL/SOCIAL JUSTICE COMPETENCE

As mental health professionals, many of us will have had multicultural training as part of our graduate curricula. Within multicultural training, we learn about the ways that forms of oppression such as racism, sexism, ableism, and hetero-sexism function to impact the emotional well-being and life chances of people in marginalized groups—people of color, women, people with disabilities, and the queer community. Certainly, as therapists, we believe that individuals have the ability (and responsibility) to take purposive action to improve their own well-being and to make the most of their life circumstances. What we learn, however, is that these individual stories and efforts play out within a sociocultural context in which privilege and disadvantage are not distributed equitably; rather, some groups have, overall, more access to power and resources, and more opportunities to use them, than do others.

In the United States, these power differentials have appeared historically, and continue to exist, with regard to a number of group identities such as race, ethnicity, gender, sexual orientation, and (dis)ability. The attitudes, policies, procedures, and taken-for-granted assumptions that catalyze relative advantage and disadvantage are often embedded so deeply within the societal status quo that we scarcely notice them, yet the evidence is all around us if we ask the right questions. Which groups make the majority of the corporate, financial, and political decisions in this country? Who owns most of the wealth? Whose lives and voices are most often represented in the popular media and other cultural narratives as important, credible, upright, admirable, strong, and *normal*? As a rule, the answers to these questions do not correspond to queer people, disabled people, women, and people of color. Notable exceptions to that statement definitely exist, but the broad implications of these general trends are nevertheless important for multiculturally competent professionals to understand with regard to their clients' experiences as well as their own biases and worldviews.

A basic part of my thesis is that social class constitutes another dimension of the spectrum of identities that we address as part of the multicultural/social justice agenda (Smith, 2008). Social class is more, therefore, than a matter of how much money you have. It signifies a spectrum of positions that is associated with differences in access to power and different assignments of social privilege. Correspondingly, life at the bottom of the social class spectrum presents challenges beyond that of material deprivation, although that is certainly a critical aspect of poverty. In making the argument that poor people contend with systemic biases that are associated with social stratification and more specifically with their positions at the bottom of the social class hierarchy, I am joining with sociologists, social psychologists, and other social scientists who have theorized about social class oppression. As such, the idea of class-based oppression is not a new one—it is simply not often integrated within discussions of applied psychology and mental health practice.

Within applied psychology, when the poor receive attention, it is often in reference to the mental health correlates of life in poverty, the provision of supportive or remedial services that address these corollaries, or charitable outreach. There is nothing at all wrong with any of these efforts *per se*; however, they sidestep structural aspects and sequellae of social class stratification. In fact, within this literature, social class itself is almost never actually referenced at all—rather, arguments are cast in terms of proxies for social class such as socioeconomic status (SES) or income level. My hope is to invite mental health professionals to stand in a different place as they consider their work with the poor—to step back and see themselves and their clients as occupying positions within a larger, interrelated social class structure. As they do so, I invite them to bring the same multicultural/social justice orientation that they apply to other group memberships to their understanding of that structure. Finally, I encourage them to consider a re-visioning of their practice in keeping with this new vantage point. Toward this end, I will present social class as a dimension of socially constructed identity and oppression on the order of race, gender, sexual orientation, and (dis)ability. Following the theorizing of social psychologists Bernice Lott and Heather Bullock (2007), I will refer to the corresponding system of class-based bias and discrimination as *classism* (to be explicated in the next chapter). Before I can move on to those discussions, however, it will be important to outline the sort of theoretical entity to which I am referring when I mention a social class group—something that this chapter will address and that applied psychologists do not usually tackle.

## THE SILENCE AROUND SOCIAL CLASS

### Understanding Social Class Means Moving Beyond an Individual Focus

There are probably a number of reasons that applied psychologists rarely talk about class stratification, and one of them is the context in which mental health professionals typically apply their practice. Most of our training prepares us for work that involves sitting with one client and applying theory and technique to the unwinding of that one person's individual history, that one person's feelings, and that one person's goals. As mentioned, multicultural and social justice approaches have insisted upon a modification of this state of affairs, in that these approaches to mental health theory and practice are grounded in a contextualized understanding of individuals' life circumstances and problems. Therapists who work from a multicultural/social justice framework, therefore, hear their clients' individual stories against the backdrop of the systematic privilege or oppression that accrues to their group, and that has shaped clients' journeys through life in ways that may be visible or invisible to them.

Even so, psychologists who study these group memberships are often most interested in studying the way that individuals feel or think about their own identities. This is true of social class: Among the very few psychological treatments that exist, some older studies (Centers, 1949) as well more recent work (Argyle, 1994; Liu, Soleck, Hopps, Dunston, & Pickett, 2004) approach social class primarily as a subjective phenomenon that has attitudinal and lifestyle-related derivatives. This is indeed an important aspect of social class; there is a subjective element to all sociocultural identities. White people and people of color may identify themselves more or less strongly with their own racial groups. Individual beliefs, meanings, feelings, and behaviors with regard to group memberships can be highly varied, yet they can be studied or clustered according to particular patterns, and those patterns themselves can be studied and described by researchers. That is certainly a valid, productive line of inquiry; it is simply a different project from mine. It is different from beginning with the question of where sociocultural power lies along a dimension of group membership.

When we begin with questions of power, privilege, and disadvantage, the subjectivity and relativism of our endeavor is reduced in that some groups *do*, objectively speaking, have more power and privilege than others, even when particular group members may not have beliefs that correspond to that actuality. For example, as a White woman, I may or may not *feel* White—I may tell you that I feel more Irish or Italian or Jewish or American, and as a psychologist, you may be interested in studying those self-perceptions and attitudes. I may or may not identify with the privilege that comes with my skin color; I may even deny completely that it exists. My feelings and beliefs, however, exist separately from the fact that a taxi cab just passed by a Black man who was hailing it and picked me up instead.

When psychologists begin with power and privilege, research questions unfold differently. They extend to such issues as the manifestations of privilege and disadvantage, the ways that they are perpetuated by individuals and by society, the extent to which these mechanisms are conscious or unconscious, the consequences of privilege or disadvantages in people's interpersonal and emotional lives, and how all of that affects and is reflected in psychological theory and practice. Such research questions invite psychologists to expand their scope beyond the individual stories and attitudes that are the traditional focus of individual practice.

## Cultural Roadblocks

The traditional individual focus of psychology is not the only hindrance to this discussion, however. In the United States, talking about social class and poverty is not a straightforward proposition. One of the cultural narratives surrounding our founding is that the New World was established to refute Old World caste systems and hierarchies. This was to be a country without kings and inherited class status, where every hardworking, common person participating in a national democratic process would have a voice and a vote that equals any other—and the notion of social class stratification does not coincide with this ideology. In addition, talking about social class means talking about possession of and access to money, power, and resources and how they are distributed, which can be tremendously uncomfortable for people. In a culture that assigns value to people according to what they can buy, people without money often feel deeply ashamed of their lack of purchasing power and work to conceal it. People with abundant purchasing power, on the other hand, may also feel disinclined to participate in conversations about money and power because the current system has brought disproportionate amounts of those assets their way.

Certainly, talking about other aspects of one's social location can be uncomfortable, too. Our identities according to race, ethnicity, gender, and sexual orientation also place us in groups that currently have either more or less power and privilege in society. There are differences, though, that make social class even more challenging and elusive. For one thing, it is assumed that one's group membership with regard to many of these identities cannot be helped. After all, people are just born into a racial group, or as men or women. The randomness of how one is born makes it easier to argue that discrimination on the basis of these chance events is unfair. People who are poor, on the other hand, may be tacitly assumed to have brought their predicament upon themselves. The cultural narrative sometimes referred to as the American Dream—that any individual who works hard enough can achieve economic success—also implies that if you are poor, it's because you did not pull hard enough on your own bootstraps. In other words, people are poor because they are lazy, or unmotivated, or not sufficiently talented.

These ideals continue to exert a powerful influence on the national psyche and, hence, upon our judgments of each other. National polls indicate that most Americans believe that their chance of moving up from one social class to another is actually greater than it was years ago, and that it is greater than it is in European countries (Connelly, 2005). Our attachment to this narrative has not, however, kept pace with social reality, as research indicates that American social mobility is flattening, and that families in many European countries and Canada actually have a greater likelihood of climbing the social class ladder than we do

(Corak, 2004). The title of Mazumder's (2005) analysis of the persistence of intergenerational income inequality telegraphs his results: "The Apple Falls Even Closer to the Tree Than We Thought."

## Conceptual Challenges: What Are the Different Social Classes, Anyway?

In general, we do not have shared, handy ways of thinking and talking about social class. By contrast, although language use is constantly evolving, the issue of which racial and gender groups exist and what to call their members does not hugely complicate a multicultural discussion of psychotherapy. Of course, all such sociocultural groupings represent oversimplifications, and universal agreement does not exist, for example, with regard to which groups are races and which are ethnic designations. Similarly, growing awareness of transgenderism and other intersections of sexuality and gender identity have added complexity to our understanding of the queer community. Nevertheless, most of the multicultural/social justice literature refers to group memberships such as *men* and *women*, or *Black* and *Asian*, and, for the most part, we know what they mean.

The situation is different when it comes to social class groups. The psychological literature may reference poverty, but usually it is as a condition of deprived living rather than as a location on the social class spectrum. A seemingly class-referenced descriptor that finds frequent use is *middle-class*, but it is typically employed to indicate a lifestyle that is assumed (rightly or wrongly) to be normative, or to refer to a person whose income falls near the numeric median for the United States—and, as will be explained, income brackets are not the same as social classes. Psychologists are certainly not alone in this regard; the language generally used to describe class groupings is notoriously ambiguous and wide-ranging (Baker, 1996). Descriptors include poor, low-income, disadvantaged, working-class, blue-collar, white-collar, wealthy, and upper-class. Class indicators (the criteria used to differentiate class membership) are similarly multitudinous and include such considerations as income, attitudes and beliefs, educational level, job prestige, power in the workplace, and distinctions between manual and physical labor. In fact, no classification system for a complex construct such as class (or any other sociocultural group) is completely without inconsistencies and gray areas; moreover, as Baker (1996) pointed out, class indicators are always inherently confounded in that they are integral aspects of the systems that they purport to describe. Nevertheless, as imperfect as our conventions of language will be, we can be deliberate in attempting to talk about social class itself as opposed to some its more familiar stand-ins, income and SES.

## The Limitations of Income Stratifications and SES as Proxies for Social Class

Given all this conceptual murkiness, what would be the problem with just dividing the population into segments based on their income levels or similar criteria, as in the use of socioeconomic status (SES) calculations? First, SES is not without murkiness itself. SES has its roots in seemingly clear-cut calculations like the Hollingshead Index of Social Position (Hollingshead & Redlich, 1958), which assigned class status scores based on a person's address, occupation, and years of education. Although all these characteristics are relevant to social class, Harvard epidemiologist Nancy Krieger and her colleagues (Krieger, Williams, & Moss, 1997) have punched conceptual holes in an unexamined reliance upon such indices as *substitutes* for social class. They reviewed data showing that, as a variable, income is confounded by problems such as the different socioeconomic implications of earned income versus dividends or interest, and the high short-term volatility of income levels within U.S. households. Similarly, educational attainment as a variable was shown to suffer from restriction of range and moreover does not correspond to the same life circumstances across gender, race, and/or age cohorts. The APA Task Force on SES (2006) also found SES to be unacceptably nebulous, reporting on problems of unreliability in measures of occupational status and the fact that income seems to be a less important measure of socioeconomic position than accumulated wealth.

Moreover, there is evidence that individual income is not related in a straightforward way to measures of well-being. Rather, society-wide income distributions also factor into the equation in that countries with greater income inequality, or the greatest relative gap between rich and poor citizens, appear to have higher mortality rates, though these findings are mixed (APA Task Force on SES, 2006). Conversely, the longest life spans are found in countries with the most social, economic, and political equity (Wilkinson, 1996, 2006). For example, in the United States, a country with the greatest income inequality in the developed world, demographic groups at the bottom of the economic spectrum have shorter life spans than people in other countries that are much more income-poor, such as India and China (Sen, 2008). Emotional well-being may also be a function of the width of a country's economic equity gap. Denmark, a country with one of the narrowest equity gaps in the world, is also the happiest, according to a study by the Organization for Economic Co-Operation and Development (Sherman, 2009).

For the purposes of the present discussion, the unreliable nature of SES and income as variables is not the only problematic aspect of reliance upon them as class indicators. The other substantive issue is that, if we wish to consider systematic inequities that are associated with social class, we require a framework for analysis that recognizes, rather than masks, power differentials—and this is precisely what is accomplished by parameters like SES. Creating class divisions according to SES sidesteps the issue of relationship to (or distance from) sociocultural power, and carries the implication that class-related experiences and oppressions are similar for people who fall within the same numerical SES stratification or income brackets.

For example, income brackets allow for the assumption that sociocultural forces operate with similar effect to enhance or diminish the life chances of a high school music teacher, a small business owner, a city sanitation worker, and a factory assembly line worker who each make $52,000 per year (Zweig, 2000). According to their incomes, they would all be considered middle-class, falling just above the 2007 U.S. median income of $50,233 (U.S. Census Bureau, 2008). Yet, without even speculating as to the different cultural stereotypes and attitudes that greet each of these individuals, it is clear that power relationships in the world of work—the socioeconomic world—differ among this group. Busy as they are, teachers exercise more freedom over the content and pace of their work lives than do factory workers, who are more likely to face exigencies such as limits on the number of bathroom breaks they may take, forced overtime, and layoffs of their entire workforce when an industry decides to relocate overseas. Small business owners may work longer hours than any of the other three, but at the end of the day maintain a different degree of socioeconomic power: They actually have access to a means of producing income, and are not constrained to sell their time and physical effort for whatever rate they can get in an economic system where wage increases can lag behind inflation (Ramachandran, 2005). Moreover, these four individuals' lives are affected differently by structural advantages such as the opportunity to benefit from tax writeoffs and disadvantages such as limits on the freedom to organize in the workplace—structures built in by a federal legislature that does not currently include extensive poor or working-class representation within its ranks.

Social class theory offers a framework that allows us to capture these systematic differentials of socioeconomic power and privilege. Social class constructs provide conceptualization and language that accommodate discussion of the fact that assets and disadvantages are *not* continuously distributed according to any numerical or statistical continuum. Instead, as sociologists David Grusky and Manwai Ku (2008) have explained, the economic landscape is understood to be "a deeply lumpy entity, with such lumpiness mainly taking the form of institutionalized groups (i.e., classes) that constitute prepackaged combinations of goods" such as wealth, political power, cultural knowledge, and physical health (p. 7). Moreover, we are witnessing an escalation in that lumpiness as the result of "the spectacular take-off in earnings inequality within the United States" since the 1980s (Weeden, Kim, Di Carlo, & Grusky, 2008, p. 249).

Researchers in the fields of public health and epidemiology have also worked to illuminate social class. British epidemiologist Michael Marmot (2006) has studied workplace freedom, stress, and status since the 1960s in association with the extensive Whitehall studies of British civil servants (Ferrie, 2004). These studies have demonstrated that, as stark as the differences are between health outcomes for the poor and the wealthy, the social gradient that includes classes between those extremes also corresponds to differential gradations of well-being. In particular, low levels of control and authority over decisions in the workplace were related to higher rates of sickness, heart disease, and mental illness; moreover, these relationships were shown to be independent of a range of individual characteristics. Noting that people in these working-class jobs—the porters, messengers, and other lower-level workers—were sicker, more stressed, more depressed, and died earlier than the supervisors and managers, Marmot likened social stratification itself to a public health problem. As studies like these reveal the characteristic assets and liabilities that come lumped together with each social class position, social class itself is brought to light as a pervasive phenomenon that can impact our circumstances, our minds, and our bodies.

Nancy Krieger has built upon work like Marmot's to theorize the ways in which people's bodies can be considered living ecosocial records of the assets and disadvantages of life at different social locations, a process to which she refers broadly as *embodiment*:

> Consider only: food insecurity and fast-food profiteering; inadequate sanitation and lack of potable water; economic and social deprivation and discrimination; physical and sexual abuse; ergonomic strain and toxic exposures; and inadequate health care—all leave their marks on the body. As do their converse: the security of a living wage, pensions for old age, and societal support for childcare; universal sanitation and sustainable development; safe workplaces and healthy cities; universal healthcare and immunizations; ant the protection and promotion of human rights—economic, social, political, civil, and cultural. (2004, p. 350)

She and her colleagues (Krieger, Williams, & Moss, 1997) have argued that what is needed is a comprehensive approach to the measurement of social class that incorporates people's structural location within the socioeconomic world. By way of example, they cite the work of sociologist Erik Olin Wright, who has developed measures of social class for use by social scientists and others. For example, Wright's Social Class Typology (1996) queries respondents about issues such as location in the employment/management hierarchy and opportunities to participate in workplace decision-making.

## APPROACHES TO SOCIAL CLASS ANALYSIS

In order to speak about the ways that privilege and disadvantage are distributed in this lumpy fashion among various social groups, we need theory and language to support the identification of groups of interest. Importantly, I do *not* imply that there is one and only one correct framework for doing so—in fact, many class stratification theories overlap or complement one another, and I will eventually employ language and concepts from more than one theory as the discussion proceeds. This part of the chapter will introduce class analysis—primarily the province of sociologists—in a very general way to mental health professionals who may not be used to thinking in such terms, and will leave us with some vocabulary that we can use afterward to reference social class locations. Readers who are interested in a thorough treatment of class analysis are encouraged to review Gilbert (2008), Grusky (2008), and Wright (2005) to get started.

### Foundations of Class Stratification Theory

So, if social class is not the same thing as SES, and if the task is to conceptualize a class system without using income brackets or similar criteria but instead with respect to power and privilege, what guidelines can we use to differentiate one class from another? Sociologist Dennis Gilbert (2008) suggested that consideration of three broad questions provides direction in this regard:

1. Economic basis. How do class distinctions arise from economic distinctions? And how, in particular, does economic change transform the class system?
2. Social basis. How are economic class distinctions reflected in social distinctions and social behavior?
3. Political implications. How does the class system affect the political system? How do economically dominant classes interact politically with the other classes in a society? (p. 10)

For Gilbert, examination of these questions highlights the significance of 10 variables to a discussion of social class: the economic issues surrounding *occupation, wealth, income,* and *poverty;* the social issues of *prestige, association, socialization,* and *social mobility;* and the political considerations of *power* and *class consciousness.* Within their configurations of social class categories and dynamics, class theorists attempt to account for the operation and interplay of some or all of these variables. These operations and their consequences result in the existence of certain groups with certain prepackaged combinations of social and economic "goods," to refer back to Grusky and Ku's (2008) "lumpiness" characterization. This statement will make more sense when we can see how it is represented within actual class stratification theories, so by way of illustration, I present thumbnail sketches of the approaches of two important class theorists, Max Weber and Pierre Bourdieu.

## Max Weber (1864–1920)

The influential German historian and political theorist Max Weber helped define sociology as a field with his theorizing on economic structures, social status, and cultural values. Weber considered the distinction between "property" and "lack of property" to be a primary basis for class groupings. In other words, one group is comprised of the people who own the means of economic production: They own the land, factories, technology, and other resources for producing goods, which can be sold for profit. The other group does not own any property or resources and has only one thing to sell: their labor, which the owners purchase for the cost of workers' wages. Weber conceptualized multiple classes to exist within these two basic areas. For example, people who own property can be differentiated as including those who can earn a living just from the financial returns from their property and holdings, as opposed to entrepreneurs and professionals such as lawyers and doctors who live by offering services. Non-owning people can also be understood to include different groups with different opportunities for success in the economic world, such as trained workers and technicians with formal credentials, and unskilled workers such as manual laborers.

Weber also theorized two other aspects of social stratification. In addition to *class*, Weber identified *status* and *party* as determining factors in the different *life chances*—or future opportunities and possibilities for success in life—that are experienced by different groups. *Status* referred to the social prestige or respect accorded to a particular group, and a *status group* is a community of people who observe similar conventions and consume similar goods and services. Weber described the relationship between these components in "Class, Status, and Party," which was published in a collection of his essays in 1948 (Gerst & Mills, 1948/2007). Status is therefore different from, but linked with, class in that people with similar incomes can afford similar styles of life, which are then associated with various levels of social honor:

> This honor may be connected with any quality shared by a plurality, and of course, it can be knit to a class situation: class distinctions are linked in the most varied ways with status distinctions. Property as such is not always recognized as a status qualification, but in the long run, it is, and with extraordinary regularity. (p. 187)

Status groups with high levels of perceived prestige are subjectively esteemed as superior to other groups, and they attempt to close ranks as much as possible to protect the exclusivity of their group. (Weber's notion of exclusionary closure as an aspect of social class subordination has been elaborated within some of the most current thinking about poverty, and we will revisit it later in the book.) *Party*, the third component of social stratification, refers to organizations of people who are striving for similar political goals:

> Whereas the genuine place of "classes" is within the economic order, the place of "status groups" is within the social order, that is, within the sphere of the distribution of "honor." From within these spheres, classes and status groups influence one another and they influence the legal order and are in turn influenced by it. But "parties" live in a house of "power." Their action is oriented toward the acquisition of social "power," that is to say, toward influencing a communal action no matter what its content may be. (Gerth & Mills, p. 194).

Weber, then, was interested in the ways that people's socioeconomic positions and the resources at their disposal resulted in different financial and personal options and opportunities—ultimately, different chances for success in life. Each of us has the opportunity to make the most of whatever resources come with our class positions, yet these positions present different groups of us with vastly different starting points, alternatives, supplies, and open doors.

### Pierre Bourdieu (1930–2002)

An intellectual and activist whose work spanned anthropology, education, art, philosophy, law, religion, media, education, history, and gender relations, French sociologist Pierre Bourdieu was one of the foremost social scientists of his time (Grenfell, 2008). Bourdieu's approach to social class addressed itself to the hierarchical relationship among class stratifications, but it was not based on a straightforward typology of class groupings. Rather, Bourdieu theorized that the positions occupied by groups within social space are functions of differential distributions of capital, which includes the dimensions of *economic capital* and *cultural capital*. Economic capital refers to financial resources, while cultural capital is culturally specific knowledge or competence that represents an asset to the holder. These dimensions can be envisioned as axes on a grid, along which various coordinates lie. Social groups find their coordinates—and so occupy more or less dominant positions—based on the *volume* and the *composition* of the capital in their possession. By way of example, the class positions of college professors and professional artists could be contrasted with the positions of industrialists and commercial employers (Weininger, 2005). Both groups of people are located in the upper portions of the class hierarchy, and have higher volumes of capital than secretaries and manual laborers, but the composition of their capital is different: The former has proportionately more cultural capital, and the latter has more economic capital. Bourdieu referred collectively to groups with the most capital as the dominant class or *bourgeoisie*, while groups at the other end of the spectrum were referred to as the *working class*. Bourdieu also made mention of the *petite bourgeoisie,* or *semi-bourgeoisie,* or middle-class categories that include people doing their best to affect the cultural tastes and consumption patterns that have been legitimized by the bourgeoisie's preference for them. Bourdieu also pointed out that, by "clutching at" these patterns and reproducing them, the petite bourgeoisie effectively renders them *déclassé*—so the bourgeoisie moves on to something else: "[L]egitimate culture is not made for him (and is often made against him), and . . . it ceases to be what it is as soon as he appropriates it" (1984, p. 327).

Bourdieu considered this class hierarchy to have enduring impact on the life circumstances of people at different locations in social space, and at the same time considered them to be theoretical rather than "real" social entities. To be real class groups, Bourdieu believed, members of a class need to consciously identify and organize themselves as such. Nevertheless, Bourdieu understood groups who share common locations in the social hierarchy to share common experiences, customs, opportunities, and challenges. Bourdieu's concept of *habitus* captures the lifestyle similarities that emerge as the result of a life lived at a particular social location. People's class-related similarities in outlook, values, habits, activities, and "a tacit sense of their place in the world" are closely related to their volume of capital, in that people at the same social location are more likely to be able to afford the same things and to live and socialize together (Crossley, 2008, p. 93).

Importantly, Bourdieu believed that lifestyle and taste are components of class-based domination and subordination—that class struggle arises not only from economically based conflict, but is also manifested within the field of cultural production. In his ethnographic work *Distinction: A Social Critique of the Judgment of Taste* (1984), Bourdieu dissected the functions of aesthetic consumption in demarcating and enforcing hierarchical relations between dominant and subordinated classes:

> Taste classifies, and it classifies the classifier. Social subjects, classified by their classifications, distinguish themselves by the distinctions they make, between the beautiful and the ugly, the distinguished and the vulgar, in which their position in the objective classifications is expressed or betrayed. (p. 6)

Moreover, although cultural producers such as artists and writers have a high degree of cultural capital, the entire field of cultural production occupies a subordinate position within the broader field of power, where economic and political capital trump everything else. Dominant economic classes, therefore, have the power to enforce cultural representations of reality that present their values, tastes, and way of life as natural, inevitable, and "right"—including representations of reality that legitimize their domination. Bourdieu referred to the enforcement of narratives and classifications that preserve the extant social hierarchy as *symbolic violence*, which he considered to be as real and as damaging as any other form of violence (Schubert, 2008). Bourdieu wrote evocatively of the insidious nature of the harm inflicted on subordinated groups through conventions of language usage, institutionalized educational practices, and the promulgation of consumerism. Through this emphasis on the symbolic aspects of social stratification, Bourdieu connected the oppressive consequences of class subordination with social domination according to race, gender, sexual orientation, and other social identities (Weininger, 2005).

## A FRAMEWORK FOR SOCIAL CLASS

Even from these brief glimpses into classic social theory, the operation of Gilbert's (2008) 3 questions and 10 variables is apparent in distinguishing different class groups from each other. Each theorist places a strong emphasis on the economic foundations of class hierarchies; Weber and especially Bourdieu also elaborated the ways that sociocultural factors such as status, lifestyle, and systems of thought figure prominently into the social class equation. Each was concerned with the ways that social class is manifested via issues of power and subordination in the political sphere. The workings of these social variables in the lives of individuals give rise to the parameters of the different class groups described by each theorist, in that people who share similar social locations are affected by these variables in similar ways. These effects are systematically, but not without exception, advantageous to people at some social class locations, and they are systematically, but not without exception, disadvantageous to people in others. These social locations do not describe perfectly delineated or mutually exclusive groups—areas of overlap and contradiction are easy to identify. Nevertheless, they provide a useful conceptual starting point by which we can consider class inequity as a form of sociopolitical dominance by which some groups systematically prosper at the expense of others, to use the words of the APA Task Force on SES (2006).

So, given that nearly every social class theorist uses different language to describe different groups, whose language will I be using? In my references to social class categories, my hope is to use language that invites the emphases of

Gilbert's (2008) 3 questions and 10 variables, but that is also handy and familiar enough that non-sociologists such as myself can employ it comfortably. Generally speaking, I am most influenced by Bourdieuian theory, but while Bourdieu's grid metaphor for class structure is richly descriptive, it does not easily translate into user-friendly terminology. Therefore, I will be borrowing from a few sources. First, two authors who have offered straightforward conceptualizations of social class structure with reference to existing power relations are Betsy Leondar-Wright (2005), a class activist, and Michael Zweig (2000), a professor of economics. Both emphasize socioeconomic foundations of class structure, and their formulations are quite similar. The following typology of class groupings combines elements from their work:

- *Poverty:* Predominantly describes working-class people who, because of unemployment, low-wage jobs, health problems, or other crises are without enough income to support their families' basic needs.
- *Working class:* People who have little power or authority in the workplace, little control over the availability or content of jobs, and little say in the decisions that affect their access to health care, education, and housing. They tend to have lower levels of income, net worth, and formal education than more powerful classes.
- *Middle class:* Professionals, managers, small business owners, often college-educated and salaried. Middle-class people have more autonomy and control in the workplace than working-class people, and more economic security; however, they rely upon earnings from work to support themselves.
- *Owning class:* People who own enough wealth and property that they do not need to work to support themselves (although they may choose to); people who own and control the resources by which other people earn a living. The owning class includes people who, as a result of their economic power, also have significant social, cultural, and political power relative to other classes.

This framework is my starting point, but I will modify my use of this language at times by referring to owning class people with idiomatic adjectives such as *wealthy;* I prefer the term *owning class* when I set out the framework because I think it conveys more precisely the distinction of this group. Next, I also find it useful at times to follow Gilbert's (2008) delineation within the middle-class group of the *upper middle class,* although this distinction is not terribly relevant to the subject of this book. These are highly educated, highly paid professionals such as doctors, lawyers, and business executives who can be distinguished from teachers, nurses, and lower-level managers (yet they still live on earnings from work). Finally, I consider Bourdieu's theorizing about cultural production, systems of thought, and symbolic violence to suffuse this entire framework, and my references to the cultural marginalization of subordinated economic groups bear the direct influence of his work.

## Clarifying Notes: About "Poverty"

Some other clarifying notes are in order with regard to this typology. First, when I use the word *poverty*, I do not refer to any specific numerical parameter such as the federal poverty threshold. In fact, different branches of the U.S. government use different criteria for such assignments; the Census Bureau derives its thresholds from a formula that incorporates family size and income, whereas the Department of Health and Human Services (HHS) creates different guidelines by adjusting those figures depending upon family size (U.S. Department of Health and Human Services, 2007a). Even then, the poverty guidelines underestimate the number of families who are struggling economically. The 2009 guidelines require that a family of four earn less than $22,050 per year to fall beneath the poverty line; therefore, a family of four attempting to live on $22,051 is not poor, according to this cutoff. Meanwhile, a basic *living* wage for a family of four anywhere is the country is estimated to be much higher, according to the Living Wage Calculator created by Penn State University. This tool was developed to calculate minimum costs of living for low-wage earners and their families according to essential food, child care, medical, housing, and transportation requirements in a variety of U.S. cities and counties, and is available online at www.livingwage.geog.psu.edu. In Akron, Ohio, the living wage needed to fully support the lives of two adults and two children for a year amounts to $55,432; in Chicago, it is $56,243; in Fairbanks, Alaska, it is $50,752.

My references to poverty and people who are poor indicate those living below or near such thresholds such that they do not have enough income to consistently support basic individual and family needs like shelter, food, clothing, and other requirements. Stein Ringen, a professor of sociology and social philosophy at Oxford, elaborated upon this way of conceptualizing poverty. Ringen (2009) characterized poverty as a broadly defined inadequacy of resources that also constitutes a moral problem:

> The problem of poverty manifests itself in the lives of persons and families as an enforced lack of basic material power to live as one wants or as reasoned fear that one might fall into that situation. It is to live under the dictatorship of material necessity without choice and control in one's daily life. That's what poverty *is*, it's about freedom and power and the lack thereof. (p. 7)

Next, why are people living in poverty described as predominantly working class? This is a crucial point both in terms of accuracy and in terms of countering classist stereotypes. One of the ways that we disassociate ourselves from acknowledgment of the attitudes and systems that help perpetuate poverty is to conceptually split poor people off from the rest of society by seeing them as essentially separate and different, an "underclass" of people who are chronically unable or unwilling to work (Zweig, 2000). In fact, the great majority of people who receive welfare benefits do so for a relatively short period of time; these tend to be working-class people who, because of low-wage jobs, health or child-care crises, layoffs, or unemployment are only a paycheck away from poverty (Ellwood & Bane, 1994).

## About the Working Class

Another point to underscore concerns the distinction between the working class and the middle class. Given that working-class people (such as skilled workers in unionized trades) may earn as much or more than people in some middle-class positions, and given the fact that fewer of these positions exist in a post-industrial world, how useful is it to consider the working class a separate social location? As argued by Beeghley (2008), the distinctions between these classes continue to be meaningful to our understanding of social stratification. Working-class occupations share important characteristics that, together, create a significantly different walk of life for these Americans as compared to their middle-class counterparts. As mentioned, working-class people have relatively little power or control over the pace and content of their work lives, and also contend with workplace conditions that are much more dangerous than those of middle-class people, whether it is because they are handling dirty or hazardous materials, operating powerful machinery, facing a potential collapse at a coal mine or a construction site, or simply working out in the weather all day. On top of all this, these workers have far less representation among city, state, and federal legislators than do middle-class people, and so have relatively little input into the decisions that affect their lives. These factors result in a substantively different range of life opportunities as compared to those in the middle and owning classes, which affirms our need to acknowledge their existence:

> These are the people who fix, haul, lift, scrub, shovel, help, and otherwise engage in potentially damaging exertions for a living. . . . Average middle-class Americans use electricity generated by coal that others have to mine, consume meat that others have to cut or grind, work in buildings that others have to build and maintain, and use paper made from trees that others have to log. Those "others" are working-class people. (Beeghley, 2008, pp. 228–229)

## SOCIAL CLASS MEMBERSHIP:
## A DIMENSION OF SOCIOCULTURAL IDENTITY

I have argued, then, for the usefulness of social class constructs to a discussion of socioeconomic privilege and disadvantage, and these are constructs that I will be using as I advance the discussion toward the work of mental health professionals. I want to conclude this chapter by noting the aspects of social class and poverty that, important as they are, will not be addressed here. First, the vast scope of culture, class, and poverty around the globe exceeds the parameters of this discussion, which takes place within an American context. For an introduction through a wider lens, the reader is referred to Carr and Sloan (2003), Marmot and Wilkinson (2006), Pogge (2007), and two books by Deepa Narayan and her colleagues (Naranyan, 2000; Naranyan, Chambers, Shah, & Petesch, 2000).

Next, social class intersects importantly with other forms of reference group memberships, such as race, gender, and sexual orientation. Consider, for example, the deep, historic intertwining of the American class structure with racism: Scholars who have analyzed the intersection of class and race have explained that White racism (and, indeed, Whiteness as a racialized social identification) originated with the need to rationalize the kidnapping and enslavement of Africans and the colonization of the African continent for the purposes of generating European and American wealth (Marable, 2000; Rodney, 1982). One of the legacies of this history is a vast contemporary racial wealth divide, with people of color owning less than a dime for every White dollar owned (Lui, Leondar-Wright, Brewer, & Adamson, 2006). Similarly, the profound economic deprivation of Native American communities continues to stand as a moral indictment of this country, with over a quarter of First Nation people living below the federal poverty line (U.S. Census Bureau, 2006). Poverty rates are nearly as high at 21% for another group of workers whose circumstances are perhaps the most precarious of all: undocumented immigrants (Passel & Cohn, 2009).

Gender intersects with class as well, operating so that women are 40% more likely to live in poverty than men. Of all adults living in extreme poverty (incomes less than half the poverty rate), 60% are women (Legal Momentum, 2003). The segregated nature of many forms of employment and the lower pay scales corresponding to work performed primarily by women contributes directly to these statistics (England, 2008). The race/class/gender intersection reveals some of the highest poverty rates in America (just under 40%), which belong to single African American and Latina mothers (National Poverty Center, 2006). Sexism, heterosexism, and class intersect in the elevated poverty rates of lesbians: Although gay men have poverty rates that are approximately equal to those of straight men, 24% of lesbians live in poverty as opposed to 19% of straight women (Albelda, Badgett, Schneebaum, & Gates, 2009). Transgender people also face high poverty rates (Transgender Law Center, 2009), high unemployment rates, and low earnings (Badgett, Lau, Sears, & Ho, 2007).

As the following chapters proceed to sketch out some of the overarching aspects of classism and poverty with regard to mental health practice, it is important to keep in mind the oversimplified nature of an overview of any form of oppression in isolation. I refer the reader to the excellent analyses of the intersections of race and class provided by Jill Quadagno (1994), Manning Marable (2000), Bill Fletcher, Jr. (2004), Melvin Oliver and Tom Shapiro (1997), and Meizhu Lui and her colleagues (2006). The triple intersection of race, class, and gender has been illuminated by bell hooks (1981, 1984, 2000) and Angela Davis (1983). Marcia Hill and Esther Rothblum's edited volume (1996) addresses gender and class with a focus on psychotherapy, and the intersections of sexual orientation and class have been explored by Amy Gluckman and Betsy Reed (1997), Julia Penelope (1994), Susan Raffo (1997), and in publications of the Williams Institute at the UCLA School of Law (www.law.ucla.edu/williamsinstitute/home.html). Finally, Lustig and Strauser (2007) and Stapleton, O'Day, Livermore, and Imparato (2006) are among those who have written about the intersections of poverty and (dis)ability.

# 2

# CLASSISM

Unfortunately, my first language—the English I learned to speak as a Southern low-income woman—is not seen as "equal." If I talk the way that comes most naturally to me, people judge me as being unintelligent or at least inarticulate.
—Linda Stout (1996, p. 118)

Now that I have introduced social class as a construct, I turn to the consideration of social class membership as a dimension of socially constructed identity and oppression on the order of race, gender, sexual orientation, and (dis)ability. This way of approaching social class membership begins with its correspondence to differential distributions of privilege and disadvantage in society, and how those distributions affect the life chances of individuals in different social class groups. This, in other words, is a way of understanding social class dynamics within a social justice framework, and I will begin the chapter by explaining what I mean by that. Within this framework, I follow social psychologists Bernice Lott and Heather Bullock (2007) in referring to the operant system of class-based bias and discrimination as *classism*. After presenting these concepts, I will offer examples of classism that are manifested in everyday life.

## A SOCIAL JUSTICE FRAMEWORK

In discussing social class and the circumstances of the poor, I have said that I work from a social justice framework (Smith, 2008; 2009). I will broaden the discussion beyond social class to incorporate other forms of oppression as I develop this statement. Social justice psychology itself has been explicated by a number of authors in recent decades (Goodman et al., 2004; Mays, 2000; Speight & Vera, 2004; Strickland, 2000), with most conceptualizations converging generally on a few central tenets. Along these lines, Speight and Vera (2004) described a social justice psychological perspective as requiring a willingness to address oppression beyond the traditional individualistic purview of applied psychology and an expanded notion of ethical duty that incorporates a responsibility to work for the liberation of oppressed peoples, explaining that "social advocacy is action linked with theory to alter the status quo" (p. 113).

These principles suggest a fundamental premise for a social justice framework (Smith, 2009; Smith, Baluch, Bernabei, Robohm, & Sheehy, 2003). This premise begins simply with the acknowledgment that the current societal status quo is characterized by an inequitable distribution of power, resources, and access to same. Moreover, these broad inequities can be described according to people's social identities: People in some racial, ethnic, gender, or other groups tend to have more power and resources across the board, and people in other groups tend to have less. Illustrations of these operations are not difficult to conjure up with regard to race and gender: Simply call to mind an image of the U.S. Senate floor, or a gathering of the CEOs of the Fortune 500 companies, or a meeting of the board of trustees of the American Medical Association. You probably do not know precisely who would be in those groups, but if your first impulse is to imagine that the faces represented there are mostly White and mostly men, you would be right.

This is in no way to deny that progress has been made in this regard—only decades ago, every *single* face in these groups would have been that of a White man, and this is no longer the case. Not only that, individual exceptions to these statements are well known to many of us, such as Oprah Winfrey, a wealthy, powerful media figure; Justice Sonia Sotomayor, who joined the U.S. Supreme Court in 2009; and General Eric Shinseki, a respected military leader, and, as of 2009, the U.S. Secretary of Veterans Affairs. Above all, the historic election of President Barack Obama signals the possibility of a future where equal distributions of power and disadvantage will be reflected across every dimension of identity. The reason that social justice considerations are relevant is that we are not there *yet*. The people in the rooms where power is held are still disproportionately White, male, and middle- or owning-class—and the people living below the poverty line are still disproportionately people of color and women (DeNavas-Walt, Proctor, & Smith, 2009). The people inside American prison cells are disproportionately people of color (U.S. Department of Justice, 2008). So are people without health insurance (Kaiser Commission, 2006). Children in lower-performing schools based on criteria such as class size, teacher experience and preparation, and outreach to parents are disproportionately children of color (Lee & Burkam, 2002). The list could go on.

The picture that emerges from statistics like these is not one that any person alive today created; rather, these systems of inequity are rooted in historical trends, conquests, and crimes (like the transatlantic slave trade) that long predate any of us alive today. Assuming that many, if not most, people today would state their opposition to those crimes and to inequality more generally, why do those statistics still exist? How is it that broad systems of inequity continue to characterize our cultural landscape after so many years, despite people's general good intentions and the success of exceptional individuals who defy the odds? The answer lies in the nature of privilege, the societal status quo, and the ideology that surrounds and maintains them. Isaac Prilleltensky, who has written extensively about psychology's role in supporting the status quo, explained the operation of deeply held social ideologies this way: "Every ruling group of an organized community requires the existence of cultural mechanisms designed to ensure, or at least facilitate, the perpetuation of its position" (1989, p. 796). These social messages and narratives are so much a part of our culture's worldview—our way of thinking about and relating to the world—that they require no deliberate support from us to in order to be perpetuated (D.W. Sue et al., 1998). According to Prilleltensky, they are automatic assumptions that have come to be taken-for-granted aspects of reality. They are assumptions that allow us to encounter the signs of an unequal status quo all around us and not be shocked by their injustice—assuming that we even notice them. Accordingly, a photograph of the assembly of the mostly White, mostly male CEOs of the Fortune 500 companies would likely strike us as unremarkable, whereas a photograph of the same event that showed a room filled with women would inspire some surprise—it would not correspond to our taken-for-granted assumptions about who rises to the top in the corporate world (and who does not). It would be similarly stunning to encounter a photograph of those CEOs' secretaries that presented us with a gathering of men. Such assumptions also allow us, if we do notice social inequities, to explain them away as being, for example, merely the result of other individuals' lack of ability or perhaps their unwillingness to work as hard as we do.

As people and as a professional field, we are all inevitably located within this sociocultural system—there is no way to step completely outside it. Not only are we within the system, the system is in us: It is the medium in which current professional fields were conceived and from which their practices evolved. We inevitably participate in it, therefore, even if unintentionally—*except when we take conscious, purposive action to the contrary*. Importantly, this implies that doing nothing is not a neutral position. When we choose to avert our gaze and leave oppression unacknowledged, we implicitly support inequity by helping to obscure it. That is, in fact, the only kind of support that is required from us for the status quo to roll on unaffected. All we need to do to support it is to not notice it, or at least not mention it if we do, and on it goes for another generation.

Building on this premise, the application of a social justice framework to any professional endeavor begins with the identification of dominant-culture assumptions and actions that are embedded within and perpetuated by a field's practices, even if unintentionally. Action toward the creation of new, socially just practices, policies, theories, and procedures can then be initiated and integrated within the field's activities and knowledge base. With regard to counseling and psychotherapy, this process leads to such considerations as the damaging impact of all forms of oppression on emotional and interpersonal well-being, the implications of relying on interventions that target the individual's "interior" while leaving sociocultural origins of distress unaddressed, and the ways that conventional psychotherapeutic roles and practices can reproduce power over relationships in the lives of clients from marginalized groups. Simultaneously, this perspective affirms that oppression may be the source of distress that brings people from marginalized social groups into treatment to begin with. In other words, oppression—as opposed to intrapsychic or interpersonal elements—may be the pathogen (Smith, Chambers, & Bratini, 2009).

A social justice framework does not, however, preclude the possibility that a client from a marginalized group might appropriately bear a conventional diagnosis or usefully receive conventional or medical treatments. Moreover, the application of a social justice framework to psychological practice or any other professional function does not transform the profession or the practice overnight. Changing worldviews, policies, and procedures at an individual level or as a discipline is much easier said than done, and must be understood as a work-in-progress. Nevertheless, the professional commitment to engage in that work-in-progress is a *sine qua non*, and gives us a platform by which we can refuse to join the "good people" in the quote from 18th-century Irish statesman Edmund Burke: "The only thing necessary for the triumph of injustice is for the good people to do nothing."

## LOOKING AT CLASSISM NOW

Now is a particularly appropriate time for mental health professionals to consider the class-related underpinnings of their theory and practice within a social justice framework (Smith, 2008). We are living during a period of our nation's history when the gap between the wealthiest Americans and the poorest has accelerated dramatically, a trend that has been called *economic apartheid* (Collins & Yeskel, 2005). Of course, there have always been "haves" and "have-nots," but never has the distance between the two been so great. For example, in the 30 years following World War II, economic growth occurred at roughly the same rate among every income group of Americans. Households across all earning brackets, from the wealthiest to the poorest, experienced an increase in income of approximately 90 to 100% during that time. This pattern of proportionate, across-the-board increases meant that the gaps between the wealthiest and poorest Americans remained relatively stable, even shrinking in size at times, during the three decades following the war—the rising tide truly lifted all ships.

## The Poor Get Poorer: The Emergence of Two Americas

However, this trend shifted dramatically in the 1980s, after which time only some ships were lifted while others sank, regardless of what the tide was doing. Since 1979, the average income of the bottom fifth of American households has increased by only 9%, while the average income of the wealthiest 1% of households in America has skyrocketed by 201% (Collins & Yeskel, 2005). As the result of these trends, approximately 10% of the U.S. population owned 70% of all American wealth (such as savings, home equity, consumer goods, stocks, bonds, and real estate) by 2001; *1% of the population owned almost 40% all by itself.* Among the 90% of the population left with the other 30% of the wealth, 17.6% (or one in six households) had zero or negative wealth—that is, they owed more than they had. Simultaneously, the pay received by CEOs was supplemented dramatically: In 1970, the average gap between a company's highest-paid employee and the average-paid employee was 28 to 1, whereas in 2006 that gap was 369 to 1 (Henry, 2006). Correspondingly, for the first time in the magazine's history, the 2006 *Forbes* listing of the 400 wealthiest Americans was comprised entirely of billionaires (Miller & Serafin, 2006).

As the group at the bottom of the economic spectrum—people living in poverty—has broadened, it has begun to include more people who contradict common stereotypes of who the poor are. For example, it increasingly includes people with jobs. In 2003, a quarter of all American workers could be described as working poor; that is, they earned poverty-level wages (Tait, 2005). The Working Poor Families Project (WPFP), a national initiative supported by the Annie E. Casey, Ford, Joyce, and C. S. Mott Foundations, came to similar conclusions, estimating that one out of four families with children have incomes so low that they cannot meet their families' basic needs—even though the adults in these families worked 2,552 hours per year in 2006, the equivalent of one and a quarter full-time workers per family (WPFP, 2006). Housing is becoming one of those basic needs that low-wage workers cannot afford: As of 2005, an adult working full-time at minimum wage could not afford a one-bedroom apartment anywhere in the country at the fair market rent level established by the U.S. Department of Housing and Urban Development (National Low Income Housing Coalition, 2005).

These startling findings go hand in hand with a report by the National Coalition for the Homeless (2005) that as many as 25% of people inside U.S. homeless shelters had jobs. Shelters are also more frequently counting people in families among their populations; the number of homeless shelter residents who were members of homeless families rose 9% in 2007, from about 473,000 to 517,000 (Koch, 2009). The homeless also included a greater proportion of people outside the big cities, as the proportion of homeless people in rural and suburban shelters jumped from 23% of all shelter residents to 32% in 2007 (Koch, 2009). Meanwhile, the title of a 2009 paper by University of California Berkeley professor Emmanuel Saez tells another story: "Striking It Richer." In this report, Saez described the continuing boom in the proportion of national income claimed by the very wealthy. In 2007, the top 10% of all earners took home half of all American income, a level that is "higher than any other year since 1917 and even surpasses 1928, the peak of stock market bubble in the 'roaring' 1920s" (p. 2). Accordingly, the Roaring 2000s have seen the emergence of trends such as the luxury customization of jumbo jets for the private hauling of "not only pampered passengers and their entourages, but also, in some cases, their Rolls Royces and racehorses" (Sharkey, 2006). Not surprisingly, the United States now stands as the most economically unequal nation in the developed world (Fischer, Hout, & Stiles, 2006). We often hear the United States referred to as the wealthiest nation in the world; perhaps it is more accurate to call it the nation with the richest rich people.

While the capitalist economic system of the United States is certainly the vehicle that has permitted the remarkable growth of the equity gap, a critique of its escalation is not reducible to merely an indictment of capitalism. We have been a capitalist country since our nation's founding, but as indicated earlier, something *different* is happening now. Since the 1980s, increasing proportions of wealth and income have steadily trickled away from the largest mass of citizens and *up*, producing a tiny, ever-wealthier group of owners at the top and a growing, ever-poorer group of Americans at the bottom. Our collective willingness to avert our gaze as our countrymen and women head for the homeless shelters has become so glaringly apparent that even leading capitalists have commented on it. John Bogle, the founder and CEO of the investment management company The Vanguard Group, has written of what he calls the recent "pathological mutation" within American capitalism (2006, p. 1). In his opinion, we have moved away from a business ethos built on trust and toward "a new 'bottom line' society whose attributes include grossly excessive executive compensation and stock options, part of an enormous transfer of wealth from public investors to the hands of business leaders, corporate insiders, and financial intermediaries" (p. 1). The result, according to Bogle, is "greed, egoism, materialism, and waste" (p. xvi), manifested by a failure to allocate enough funding for causes such as poverty-reduction and education, coupled with a massive misuse of the world's natural resources.

## But What About the Recession?

It is clear that as the stock market dipped in 2008, the value of owning-class people's financial portfolios (along with the 401(k)s of middle-class people) dipped, too. Economists are mixed, however, as to whether this downturn will reduce the *proportional* discrepancy between the rich and poor. Some economists expect that inequality will decrease, while others predict that, unless Washington makes structural changes to regulate executive pay and change the tax structure, the equity gap will continue unabated (Davis & Frank, 2009; Leonhardt & Fabrikant, 2009). In the meantime, no one is happy to see the value of their assets decline, and Paul Sullivan, a *New York Times* writer who covers financial matters from the perspective of the wealthy, has documented the impact that the downturn has had in the lives of the super-rich. The wealthiest Americans, Sullivan reported, are focusing on maintaining cash assets, reining in the intrafamily handling of their inheritances, and potentially scaling back philanthropic donations (2009a). Along these lines, Sullivan quoted the president of a wealth management firm who shared the advice that he was giving to his affluent clients: to live their lives in the way that they always have, but to tone it down a bit (2009b). This executive even gave an example of how he was taking his own advice:

> He bought his dream car, a Jaguar XKR, before the market crash but then felt uncomfortable about it. "I didn't like the way it made me feel, but not enough that I was going to get rid of the car," he said. So he made light of it with a vanity plate to recall better times: "PRE LEHM." (p. 2)

FYI, that's pre-Lehman Brothers, the financial services firm that declared bankruptcy in 2008. Yet less than a year later, happier days had returned to the banking industry. By July 2009, Goldman Sachs was back on track to "dole out bonuses that could rival the record paydays of the heady bull-market years"—which their CEO acknowledged as "something of a P.R. challenge" (Bowley, 2009, p. 1). By October 2009, other major financial firms like J. P. Morgan Chase had joined in Goldman's good fortune. Simultaneously, middle-class and poor working Americans were contending with image problems of a different kind as the economic crisis sent fresh streams of them to the homeless shelters in the wake of mortgage foreclosures. "These families never needed help before," said Larry Haynes, executive director of Mercy House in Santa Ana, California. "They haven't a clue about where to go, and they have all sorts of humiliation issues. They don't even know what to say, what to ask for" (Goodman, 2009, p. 1). The jobless rate had climbed to 9.8% by October 2009 (U.S. Department of Labor, 2009), and those people who managed to hold on to jobs saw their wages cut at the highest rate since the Great Depression (Uchitelle, 2009).

At the time of this writing, the recession is a little over a year old, and as mentioned, it is too soon even for economists to forecast what its outcome will be. In the meantime, it seems that the story of the economic downturn is still the story of two Americas.

## PUTTING IT ALL TOGETHER:
## SEEING CLASSISM WITHIN A SOCIAL JUSTICE FRAMEWORK

The stage is now set for a more extended definition of classism, and I use Heather Bullock's and Bernice Lott's definition of this term (Smith, 2008). Bullock (1995) defined classism as "the oppression of the poor through a network of everyday practices, attitudes, assumptions, behaviors, and institutional rules" (p. 119). Lott and Bullock (2007) elaborated this definition further as encompassing *institutional classism*, through which social institutions and their policies and procedures function to perpetuate the deprivation and low status of poor people, and *interpersonal classism*, which refers to individual prejudice, stereotyping, and discrimination.

Because cultural narratives shape our ability (or inability) to see the existence of social class, the examples of classism that are all around us often manage to evade notice—which is true of other forms of oppression as well, of course. Understanding classism begins with learning about the circumstances of life in a social class that does not enjoy economic power, but it does not end there (Smith, 2008). Understanding classism also means identifying the taken-for-granted social mechanisms that place obstacles in the paths of poor and working-class people, a subtle, often invisible bias that gives rise to the cliché "the rich get richer and the poor get poorer." In reviewing the following examples of classism, it is useful not only to consider the classist elements of each, but also to question the attitudes, biases, motivations, and fears that allow many of them to hide in plain sight. These examples include the cultural invisiblity of poor people; negative attitudes toward the poor; classist microaggressions; educational, healthcare, judicial, and environmental inequities; and issues related to living wages and labor organizations.

### The Cultural and Institutional Invisibility of Poor and Working-Class People

Writing in 1970 about perceptions of the poor, Harvard professor of sociology Lee Rainwater explained that the predominant way of seeing the poor is to not see them as part of society at all: "The central existential fact of life for the lower class . . . is that their members are not included in the collectivity that makes up the 'real' society of the 'real' people" (p. 10). Decades later, Bernice Lott (2002) struck the same note, describing the primary characteristic of classism as "cognitive and behavioral distancing from the poor," a response that renders the poor invisible in many interpersonal and institutional contexts.

Writer Dorothy Allison (1994), who was raised in poverty, observed, "My family's life was not on television, not in books, not even in comic books" (p. 17). Social psychological research bears out her perception that the poor rarely make appearances within mainstream media (e.g., Bullock, Wyche, & Williams, 2001). Perhaps one of the best examples of the taken-for-granted invisibility of poor people in the mainstream U.S. cultural experience is the widespread astonishment at the depth of American poverty revealed in the aftermath of Hurricane Katrina, which struck the Gulf Coast in 2005. Eugene Robinson (2005) made this point in his *Washington Post* column: "After seeing who escaped the flood and who remained behind, it's impossible to ignore the shocking breadth of the gap between rich and poor. It's as if we don't even see poor people in this country anymore, as if we don't even try to imagine what their lives are like" (p. 3).

## Negative Attitudes and Beliefs Toward the Poor

When the poor do command our attention, it is often in an unfavorable way. Writing about the year she spent working in minimum-wage jobs, Barbara Ehrenreich (2001) experienced with surprise the contemptuous attitudes that are often directed toward poor and working-class people. Wearing her maid's uniform, she reported, "I used to stop [at the supermarket] on my way home, but I couldn't take the stares, which were easily translatable into: what are *you* doing here?" (p. 100).

The social psychological literature supports Ehrenreich's experience (Lott, 2002): Participants in one study (Cozzarelli, Wilkinson, & Tagler, 2001) endorsed traits such as *lazy, stupid, dirty*, and *immoral* more often for poor people than for middle-class people; in another (Hoyt, 1999), the most common stereotypes listed for poor people were *uneducated, lazy, dirty, drug/alcohol user*, and *criminal*. Not surprisingly, these attitudes are reflected in and perpetuated by media representations of poor people, as analyzed by Bullock, Wyche, and Williams (2001). These authors demonstrated that when the poor do appear in mainstream media, it is most often via daytime reality shows such as *Jerry Springer* or police live-action programs where they are seen as dysfunctional, unruly, promiscuous, and/or drug users.

I have detected the operation of these attitudes in some of my own work. My colleagues Alizah Allen and Rashidah Bowen and I were interested the associations that exist between class membership and perceptions of misbehavior (Smith, Allen, & Bowen, 2010). These perceptions are relevant for therapists in that, unchecked, they may influence the ways that we hear, interpret, and evaluate our clients' disclosures. Participants in our exploratory, Internet-based study were presented with a list of 174 actions, infractions, and crimes derived from the crime-seriousness literature, and were asked with which social class categories they most associated each action. Our results showed that when an infraction could only have been committed by a member of a certain class category, participants associated it with that position. For example, in order to commit the infraction *embezzling money from the company that one owns*, one would most likely have to be wealthy to begin with, and such actions were indeed associated with the wealthy. Only the poor were considered most likely to commit actions like *painting graffiti in public places*—actions that could conceivably be committed by people at *any* class position. These findings speak to a general tendency to think of the poor as being more unruly and irresponsible than members of other classes and the relative ease with they come to mind as the perpetrators of assorted actions and infractions.

As negatively as the poor may be regarded, the addition of welfare to the picture can inspire outright disgust. Again, social psychological research supports this contention. For example, Henry, Reyna, and Weiner (2004) found that study participants responded more unfavorably to funding services for people on welfare (and toward those people *themselves*) than they did to funding for the poor more generally. Findings like these indicate first and foremost that we think we know who people on welfare *are*, as though there is something enduring and essential about them—despite the fact that an estimated half of new welfare recipients receive benefits for only 2 years or less, and about 75% receive it for 5 years or less (Bane & Ellwood, 1994). Attitudes toward welfare also exemplify the interweaving of classism and racism: Clawson and Trice (2000) found that when magazine stories focused on negative poverty-related topics such as the so-called "cycle of dependency" among welfare recipients, the poor people in the pictures were more likely to be Black.

## Classist Microaggressions

Negative attitudes toward the poor leave their traces within ordinary, unexamined experiences and language use—in fact, once we become aware of them, we can see that everyday interactions and popular culture are replete with class-based messages and slights (Smith & Redington, in press). These incidents correspond to the derogatory verbal, behavioral, and environmental messages that psychologist Derald Wing Sue and his colleagues have described as racial and cultural *microaggressions* (e.g., D. W. Sue et al., 2007). Although the perpetrators of microaggressions are often unaware of the implications of their behavior, poor people who are exposed to classist microaggressions are usually able to detect that they are being insulted, even if politely. Having transitioned from a working-class youth on a hog farm to a privileged college campus in an urban area, Chaney (1994) wrote of the unconscious symbols and rituals that her new peers used to signal class membership. "Table manners," Chaney observed, "seem to evoke some of the ugliest class righteousness" (p. 174). Evans (1994) described the impact of an off-hand comment by a friend who was a dental student:

> "What kind of parents wouldn't provide their children with something as important as dental care?" I grow quiet as I think of my childhood, of not having gone to the dentist until I was in my mid-teens, of having teeth pulled because they were too decayed to fill. . . . Shame washed over me as I realize that I am the type of person the dental student is talking about, shame that my parents couldn't manage money better, shame that there wasn't more money to manage . . . [but] I keep my mouth shut, for my mouth is one of the places that I carry evidence of my poverty. (p. 163)

Similarly, the recent economic recession has seen a burgeoning of articles and television programs on middle-class people experimenting with frugality. An MSNBC report, for example, featured a mother who set out to see if she could feed her family of four on a food budget of $100 for a week. She concluded by wondering, "Could we do this again? Probably. But I don't think we would. . . . The next week I spent more than ever, to make up for feeling deprived" (Fulmer, 2008, p. 3). In a post on the website Democratic Underground, a woman who had lived in poverty expressed her frustration at the coverage of these middle-class people who were "roughing it," conveying the microaggressive nature of such presentations:

> I know these types of stories are aimed at those recently experiencing a budget crunch, but the effect . . . at least to me . . . is trivializing what it is like to really struggle. . . . The people doing these "human interest" stories are always so relieved to be done with their "challenge" and go back to regular life. When do the thousands of Americans living below the poverty level get to be done with their "challenge"? (Democratic Underground, 2008)

## Educational Inequities

An equal valuing of the educational experiences of all children, whether they come from wealthy families or poor, should mean that each American child is provided with an equal share of the educational resources available to the nation's families. Yet, the gap between the educational opportunities of children from poor families and their wealthier peers continues to widen (Anyon, 2005; Fine, 1990). As documented by Jonathan Kozol (2005), students in poor communities attend schools that have fewer computers, fewer library books, fewer classes, fewer extracurricular opportunities, and fewer teachers than students in more affluent neighborhoods. Students who attend public schools in poor communities are more likely to be taught by poorly paid, uncertified teachers; the average salary of schoolteachers in poor communities is $43,000, while the salaries of teachers in wealthier school districts can range from $74,000 to $81,000. Correspondingly, less money is spent per student in poor neighborhoods, a gap that spans from $8,000 per student on the low end to $18,000 per student in wealthier neighborhoods (Kozol, 2005).

Michelle Fine and her colleagues have described the "civic lessons" that students are learning as they negotiate these inequitable systems (Fine, Burns, Payne, & Torre, 2004). Young people in poor communities, they write, sustain personal damage as the decaying buildings and deficient resources speak to them about their value to the rest of us. Through the presentation of focus group data, the voices of schoolchildren themselves attested to the hurt:

> It make you feel less about yourself, you know, like you sitting here in a class where you have to stand up because there's not enough chairs and you see rats in the buildings. . . . So in all honesty, it really makes me feel bad about myself. Obviously, you probably can't understand where I'm coming from, but it really do. And I'm not the only person who feels that. It really make you feel like you really less than. And I already feel that way because I stay in a group home because of poverty. (p. 2199)

Even those poor students who receive adequate preparation for college-level work will subsequently face financial obstacles that few can surmount: In a report called "Losing Ground," the National Center for Public Policy and Higher Education documented that the costs of a college education are escalating at a rate higher than both inflation and family income, lowering the rates of attendance by low-income students while "those from middle and high-income families continue to attend college in record numbers" (National Center for Public Policy and Higher Education, 2002). As a result, higher education, rather than representing a social equalizer, actually functions to catalyze the equity gap:

> College graduates have received steady pay increases over the past two decades, while the pay of everyone else has risen little more than the rate of inflation. As a result, despite one of the great education explosions in modern history, economic mobility—moving from one income group to another over the course of a lifetime—has stopped rising, researchers say. (Leonhardt, 2005, p. 1)

## Health-Care Inequities

Here in the wealthiest country on earth, it is not surprising that more money is spent on health care than anywhere else in the world, as was reported by the annual United Nations Human Development Report in 2005. What is startling, however, is the extent to which poor Americans have been left behind as medical innovations and expenditures have advanced: Among poor people and people of color, the UN reported that health indicators are worse in the United States than in some developing countries. Infant mortality, for example, has increased for the past 5 years and is now equal to that of Malaysia. The *New York Times* described the health risks of poverty and the inadequacy of health care for poor people in a series of articles on class that was later combined into a book, revealing the dynamics behind the fact that "upper-class Americans live longer and in better health than middle-class Americans, who live longer and better than those at the bottom" (Scott, 2005, p. 19). Class, it was reported, is associated with everything from risk factors for chronic illnesses to quality of care, access to care, availability of social and financial support during illnesses, relationships with doctors, and overall stress level.

And how do those at the bottom of American class structure fare? Belle, Doucet, Harris, Miller, and Tan (2000) affirmed that "[p]overty is associated with elevated rates of threatening and uncontrollable life events, noxious life conditions, marital dissolution, infant mortality, many diseases, violent crime, homicide, accidents, and deaths from all causes" (p. 1160). The differences between the health status of the poor and the affluent is so stark that a single street that divides two neighborhoods can distinguish a rate of disease that is 20 times higher on the other side, as is the case where Harlem borders the Upper East Side in New York City. Kleinfield (2006) observed life across East 96th Street:

> A few things to notice. On Third Avenue, around the corner from the art shop, a banner outside McDonald's proclaimed, "$1 Menu." Down the way, plastered on Burger King, "New Enormous Omelet Sandwich. It's Huge." At KFC, a sign boasted, "Feed Your Family for Under $4 Each." The art-shop gatherers sometimes talked about 96th Street, the tangible southern divide of a neighborhood and of a disease. Go north of 96th Street and you enter a constricted world laden with poverty. Go south and you find promise and riches, thin not fat, the difference between East Harlem and the Upper East Side, the difference between illness and health. Go north and the chances of bumping into a diabetic are maybe 20 times greater than if you go south. For the Upper East Side, according to the health department, has the lowest prevalence in the city, about 1 percent. In East Harlem, people sometimes have to choose between getting their diabetes medication and eating. They sometimes share their pills, cut them in half and take half-dosages. They improvise. Everywhere blare the signals that the best meal is the biggest meal. (p. 4)

## Disparities in the Judicial System

Under this heading can be found one of the clearest examples of classism: bail. Mentioned casually in television reports and newspaper headlines, this overt form of discrimination operates blatantly as the poor remain in prison cells while wealthier people accused of the same crimes go home. More generally, millions of Americans are priced out of the civil legal process for the vast majority of their legal concerns, according to Rhode (2004). Despite the fact that the United States positions itself as a leader in human rights, America's provision of access to justice for poor and working-class people is considerably less that that of citizens in other developed countries; the U.S. allocates only about a sixteenth of what Great Britain budgets for civil legal assistance, a sixth of what New Zealand provides, and a third of what some Canadian provinces guarantee. Rhode (2004) went on to quote President Jimmy Carter's 1980 comment on this state of affairs: Although the U.S. has "the heaviest concentration of lawyers on earth, no resource of talent and training is more wastefully or unfairly distributed than legal skills. Ninety percent of our lawyers serve ten percent of our people. We are overlawyered and underrepresented" (p. 369).

Above and beyond these specifics, American University philosophy professor Jeffrey Reiman (2007) has argued that the criminal justice system itself is classist at the deepest levels of its operations. According to Reiman, the criminal justice system keeps the threat of crime within public awareness with its focus on rising and declining crimes rates—and in so doing, also functions as a smoke screen to distract us from where the most serious crimes originate. The system accomplishes this by portraying crime as the misdeeds of the poor. Poverty can indeed be a source of crime (which is different from a *cause* of crime, says Reiman) in that it leaves people in positions where they have fewer legal alternatives for meeting legitimate needs. This scenario associates poverty with crimes like burglary, theft, and selling drugs, along with all the other street crimes that are the contents of the typical police blotter. These are not, however, the crimes that cause the most death, destruction, and suffering in our country. Those crimes, according to Reiman, derive from the actions of class elites via corporate fraud, hazardous working conditions, the creation of toxic pollutants, profiteering from unhealthy or unsafe products, and risky high-level financial services ventures where the American public ends up bearing the consequences of the risk. By defining crime in the popular imagination as street crime, and by promulgating images of criminals as poor people (especially poor people of color), the system protects the interests of the powerful as it "deflects the discontent and potential hostility of Middle America away from the classes above them and toward the classes below them" (p. 4).

### Environmental Injustice

Classism and racism operate so that waste tends to flow toward communities with weak response capacity (Heiman, 1996), and in urban areas, this means that garbage dumps, bus depots, trash-burning plants, and other pollution-producing operations are predominantly located where poor people and people of color live. In economically depressed rural areas like the central Appalachian mountain region, it means that local families contend with the effects of strip-mining and its most extreme form, mountain-top removal (MTR). Through the use of MTR, coal companies access underlying coal deposits by literally blasting off the tops of the Appalachian Mountains, a cost-cutting, profit-enhancing method that has already resulted in the decapitation of some 300,000 acres of mountain area in West Virginia alone (Vollers, 1999). Nearby valleys and streams are filled in with everything from the blast that is not coal, while the coal-washing process leaves behind vast slurry ponds of coal sludge, a tar-like mixture of soil, water, and the toxic chemicals used in coal processing. There are more than 700 slurry impoundments in the United States, many of which are considered to be at risk for failure because they are built on or near underground mines. On October 11, 2000, a 72-acre, 2.3 billion–gallon impoundment near Inez, Kentucky, failed. A torrent of slurry was released into the surrounding countryside, ruining property, destroying drinking water systems, and killing animal and aquatic life. Although the U.S. Environmental Protection Agency declared it the worst environmental disaster in the history of the Southeast (U.S. Environmental Protection Agency, 2001), this catastrophe in one of the poorest counties in a poor region of our nation received little national media attention.

Environmental injustice in the Appalachian Mountain region extends to working conditions inside the mining operations themselves. West Virginia alone has been the scene of literally hundreds of fatal mining disasters over the last century. One of the most recent of these took place in January 2006, at which time the Sago Mine in Sago, West Virginia, exploded, trapping 13 miners underground. Twelve of them died. The mine owners, Anker West Virginia Mining, had racked up 270 safety violations over the previous 2 years, with government records showing that the owners knew about and failed to correct many of them. "[T]he $24,000 in fines paid by the Sago managers last year constituted little more than the cost of doing business," suggested a 2006 *New York Times* editorial, which went on to state:

> Just as Hurricane Katrina forced Americans to look at the face of lingering poverty and racism, this mining tragedy should focus us all on another forgotten, mistreated corner of society. . . . The dozen dead miners deserve to be

memorialized with fresh scrutiny of the state of mine safety regulation and a resurrection of political leadership willing to look beyond Big Coal to the interests of those who risk their lives in the mines. (p. 4, 6)

West Virginia continues to wait for this memorialization as another iteration of the same headlines unfolds there: The worst mining explosion in 40 years has left 29 miners dead as this book goes to press in 2010. Massey Energy Company, the owners of the Upper Big Branch Mine, had accumulated 1,342 safety violations since 2005 (Mufson, 2010). During that time, they have paid out the largest settlements in the history of the coal industry in association with their guilty pleas (Urbina & Cooper, 2010).

## The Absence of National Attention to an Unlivable Minimum Wage

Without people working in minimum-wage jobs to carry it along, everyday life in America would come to a standstill. Most of us in the middle or owning classes rely regularly upon these people, who are all around us—working in child care, taking care of our elderly, cleaning our offices, serving us food, taking away the dishes and washing them, cutting the grass, and delivering the flowers. They are behind the counters in stores where we shop, they sell us tickets to the movies, and they change the sheets on our hospital beds. Setting aside the question of whether or not we personally would like to clean offices or change hospital beds, most of us would agree that *someone* needs to do those things. Yet our society does not seem to be noticeably disturbed by an arrangement in which the adults who perform these necessary jobs cannot earn enough money to support their families. After years of stagnation, the raising of the federal minimum wage to $7.25 (effective July 24, 2009) is a welcome advance, yet the economic survival of minimum-wage workers continues to be precarious. The increase will still not lift low-wage workers and their families out of poverty; I refer readers again to Penn State's living wage calculator, which provides estimations of a living wage for cities and counties around the country (http://www.livingwage.geog.psu.edu). For example, in Oakland, California, a living wage for a single adult *with no children* is $11.23 per hour; in Norfolk, Virginia, it is $9.30.

The consequences for poor working people who try to survive in these jobs are clear. Less obvious are the benefits and comforts that concurrently accrue to those of us in the middle and owning classes: We can afford to buy more products and services more cheaply when employers do not pay employees enough to live on. In a statement to Congress regarding the 1938 Fair Labor Standards Act, in which he advocated the establishment of a minimum wage, President Franklin D. Roosevelt had something to say about such acquisitions: "Goods produced under conditions which do not meet a rudimentary standard of de-cency should be regarded as contraband" (quoted in Grossman, 2006).

## The Deprecation of Labor Organizations

This example of classism has much in common with negative attitudes to-ward poor people in general, yet is significantly different in that it strikes more particularly at the ability of poor and working-class people to come together to participate in this country's democratic style of discourse and decision-making. Most of us take for granted the right of middle- and owning-class people to organize and advocate for concerns that relate to their own or their business's welfare—chambers of commerce, professional associations, lobbying groups, and think tanks are just a few of the many examples. However, when poor and working-class people organize to participate in workplace negotiations and decision-making they are not greeted with the same casual acceptance. Such organizations, which comprise labor unions, provide the sole avenue by which working-class people can have a voice in workplaces where they do not own or control resources, have authority in the content or availability of jobs, or occupy roles in the corporate power structure.

Certainly, no one likes to be inconvenienced when a labor union goes on strike—but a strike represents the only opportunity for working people to bar-gain with the single thing of worth that they have: the value of their bodies showing up to do the job. Yet the vehemence of negative public reaction and media reporting to even talk of a strike is conspicuous. The *New York Times* reported that when the New York City Transport Workers Union opened a web log for public comment on their strike of 2005, they were forced to quickly shut it down again when it became "clogged with messages comparing the workers to monkeys and calling them 'you people'" (Cardwell, 2005, p. 3), demonstrating the simultaneous infusion of racism into public reaction to this group of work-ers, most of whom are people of color. Along these lines, Zweig (2000) discussed the fact that unions are most often either ignored or attacked in the media; Leondar-Wright (2005) cited examples of union members being stereotyped as "rednecks" (p. 59). An August 2005 Harris Poll confirmed these sentiments, finding that a majority of U.S. adults surveyed (68%) rated labor unions nega-tively (Harris Interactive, 2005).

My point is not that particular extant labor unions represent the ideal configuration of such organizations. In fact, many union members themselves polled by Harris indicated dissatisfaction with their union's performance; 60% of union households, for example, agreed that unions today are more concerned with fighting change than with trying to bring about change. Rather, my emphasis is on the negative attitudes that commonly surround a type of organizing that is in good accord with the best democratic values of our nation—again, the same values that are commonly put into practice by members of other classes who organize to protect their interests. Moreover, organizations of working people have initiated many valued and taken-for-granted aspects of the American social contract. These include such humane innovations as the ending of child labor and the establishment of the 40-hour (as opposed to the unlimited-hour) work week. Yet, a nation that prizes the rights of the common person has allowed unions to be weakened nearly out of existence, with union density in the United States dropping to 12% in 2005 (Shaiken, 2007). Cultural acceptance of (or turning a blind eye to) the devaluing and undermining of working people's right to have their voices be heard seems contradictory in a country that prides itself on democracy and the idea of a level playing field.

## THE IMPLICATIONS OF SEEING CLASSISM

The mental health professions have benefited greatly from the scholarship of multicultural psychologists and their impact on therapists' preparation to work with diverse populations. As part of our training, we have had the opportunity to learn about the damaging effects of systemic oppression in the lives of these clients, and also about the impact of our own biases on the ways that we respond to clients and hear their stories. For example, researchers have demonstrated that therapists may overdiagnose psychotic disorders in their Black clients (Barnes, 2004; Pavkov, Lewis, & Lyons, 1989), perceive female clients as hyperemotional and male clients as hypoemotional (Heesacker et al., 1999), and see bisexual clients as having problems with intimacy (Mohr, Israel, & Sedlacek, 2001). Most often, however, classism and classist attitudes are not considered alongside racism and sexism in graduate training curricula (and it should be noted that heterosexism and especially ableism also often receive short shrift in this regard). *Seeing* classism provides a starting point for practitioners who would like to examine the class-based cultural attitudes that they have internalized so that they can bring the fullest measure of humanity to their practice.

On a broader level, seeing classism adds a missing piece—social class—to most social justice formulations, providing a platform by which we can begin to identify the cultural attitudes and practices that support the relegation of poor people to the cultural margins. Given the examples of classism cited above, it is not difficult to understand how this marginalization is enacted—how it actually comes to pass that the rich get richer and the poor get poorer. Again, exceptions to that rule certainly exist, and we celebrate the stories of men and women from poor families who succeed against the odds. It is the *length* of the odds, and the well-being of the many Americans who do not defy them, and our participation in maintaining those circumstances, that are at issue.

This issue raises the question of what kind of country we want to live in. If we choose to think of nations as businesses, and businesses as entities that prioritize the bottom line above all else, then perhaps poverty becomes a side-issue to be managed insofar as it affects the bottom line. As I mentioned previously, this way of thinking is what John Bogle, founder of The Vanguard Group of investment funds, sees as having led to "the pathological mutation" of modern capitalism that undermined the nation's financial strength, ultimately resulting in the stock market bubble of 1997–2000 (p. 3). Bogle, then, tied contemporary bottom-line, profit-motive priorities to a dangerous weakening of our economy, drawing parallels between these cultural changes and the fall of Rome. This idea dovetails with pragmatic arguments for addressing poverty that have to do with long-term cost-cutting on behalf of the American taxpayer. Michelle Fine (Fine et al., 2001) has argued, for example, that it is more cost-effective to provide access to college education within prisons—thus better preparing inmates for participation in our legal economy—than to reincarcerate the same people years later. Similarly, addressing the chronic, toxic stress encountered by children living in poverty could help forestall health problems and learning deficits whose remediation must be funded down the road (Harvard Mahoney Neuroscience Institute, 2009). In addition to these pragmatic concerns, I believe there is a moral imperative.

Those of us living our lives in the middle and owning classes do not exist in a vacuum. Our class locations and experiences are part of a larger system—a system that is working relatively well for *us*. Yet, we cannot sustain this system all on our own. We all *require* the participation of people throughout the economic spectrum to make our society go. We need people to be doctors, and also people to keep the hospitals clean. We need people to start companies, and also people to operate the cash registers. Since society requires the contributions of workers in low-wage jobs, it seems only fair that we should also ensure that they can earn enough to live decently. Moreover, we in the middle and owning classes are winners in an economy that does not offer enough jobs for every American adult to have one—rather, the configuration can be compared to a game of musical chairs, where, inevitably, some of us will have nowhere to sit when the music stops (Rank, 2004).

Yet, what about the initiative and hard work that we may have invested in the attainment of our middle class or owning class positions? My intention is not to diminish the value of anyone's work. Indeed, for those of us who have not inherited wealth, our own effort is definitely part of the equation, and that effort is something that we can be proud of. Yet, as I have discussed, effort alone is not enough to keep increasing numbers of families in this country out of the homeless shelter. Other people are also working hard, but cannot lift their families out of poverty; other children also have big dreams, but are not at schools with the resources to make those dreams a reality; other people have medical conditions that need not have derailed their lives, but because of a lack of health care, they have.

This is when our moral compasses come into play: What are the ethical implications of living well in the midst of a basic unfairness of things? I feel certain that the great majority of us have moral compasses that point toward a leveling of the playing field, which is exactly what is suggested by Marymount University's recent surveys of shoppers (Marymount University, 1999). In 1995 and 1996, 86% of survey respondents indicated that they would pay an extra dollar on a $20 garment for a guarantee that the garment was made under fair working conditions. Furthermore, 56% said that fair labor tags would be helpful to them in identifying these goods and the retailers that sell them. I am convinced that, even if there will always be people who have *more*, most of us want to know that the women and men around us have *enough* to make decent lives for their families—enough food, safe places to live and work, health care for their families, and good schools for their children. When we buy a shirt or a sofa or a glass of wine, we want to know that our ability to afford it is not a function of the poverty of someone else who made it or served it or cleaned up after us.

# 3

# POVERTY IN PSYCHOLOGICAL SCHOLARSHIP

It is not necessary to search the scientific literature for evidence that water runs downhill.

—George Albee (1996, p. 1132)

Given the haziness around social class within psychological thought, it is not surprising that psychological researchers have helped elucidate some aspects of class and poverty while leaving others largely unexamined. Rather than present this scholarship according to chronology or psychological specialty, I present it here according to three interwoven themes—three lines of inquiry that have been explored contiguously and contemporaneously, but that reflect different vantage points on poverty. The first theme concerns psychologists' documentation of the varieties of harm that are associated with life in poverty, whether physical, emotional, cognitive, or developmental. This vantage point has been the most typical for psychologists to assume. The next theme emerges from the work of psychologists who have focused their attentions more broadly on the structural elements of poverty. This theme has roots in early social justice and liberatory models of psychological well-being, and has been explicated most substantively by community and social psychologists. The literature in this area sheds light on poverty as the bottom rung of the social-class ladder, and on how that subordinated position is manifested within the individual and cultural experiences of the poor and perpetuated by mainstream academic psychology and mental health practice. The third theme derives from the practice-related scholarship. Applied psychology has a history of ebbs and flows with regard to clients who live in poverty as practitioners have struggled to understand their work (and often their treatment failures) with poor clients. This literature converges sporadically with the previous theme: At times, practitioners have made use of structural perspectives, and at other times have seemed to close their eyes to poverty altogether.

## POVERTY HURTS PEOPLE

A literature search of mental health and poverty returns primarily studies of poverty's undesirable psychological and health-related corollaries. Although it represents a proportionately small amount of all psychological research, this literature is resoundingly conclusive: Poverty is terribly bad for people's mental health. Men, women, and children who live in poverty have been found to experience profoundly negative outcomes along every imaginable dimension, with rates of psychological distress, physical illnesses, and mortality itself showing strong, consistent relationships with poverty (Adler et al., 1994; Belle, Doucet, Harris, Miller, & Tan, 2000; Scott, 2005).

### Counting the Ways that Poverty Hurts

Among the most robust and frequently pursued findings regarding the damaging effects of poverty is that people living in poverty experience depression and related psychological symptoms at higher rates than the rest of us (e.g., Blazer, Kessler, McGonagle, & Swartz, 1994; Brown & Moran, 1997; Bruce, Takeuchi, & Leaf, 1991; Hobfoll, Ritter, Lavin, Hulsizer, & Cameron, 1995; Siefert, Bowman, Heflin, Danziger, & Williams, 2000; Williams, Takeuchi, & Adair, 1992). Jeanne Miranda and her colleagues have been important contributors within this area, helping to confirm the linkages between poverty and depression, calling for more attention to the mental health needs of poor women (Miranda & Green, 1999) and studying treatment outcomes among poor clients (Miranda, Azocar, Organista, Dwyer, & Areane, 2003). Similarly, Salomon, Bassuk, and Brooks (1996) found higher levels of depression among mothers on welfare as compared with women generally, along with higher levels of substance abuse and post-traumatic stress (PTSD) symptoms. Vogel and Marshall (2001) also identified high rates of PTSD and partner violence in the lives of low-income women. Among poor women, some had even higher rates of depression than the rest: Those who were homeless (Banyard & Graham-Bermann, 1998) and those without enough to eat evidenced the most distress (Heflin, Siefert, & Williams, 2005).

Health psychologists, whose expertise involves the contributions of psychology to the understanding of health and illness, have studied poverty's relationship to mental health and the mechanisms by which it diminishes well-being through mediators such as reduced access to health care and increased exposure to stress and environmental hazards. Barefoot et al.'s (1991) national survey of 2,536 adults showed that low-SES people had higher scores on a measure of hostility associated with unfavorable health outcomes. Seeman et al. (2004) analyzed longitudinal data for 1,313 participants that included assessments of physical and cognitive performance, health status, and other behavioral and psychosocial characteristics. Their results indicated that a portion of the increased mortality seen among low-SES participants was derived from a higher cumulative burden of physiological dysregulation—or the increased "biological wear and tear" (p. 1994) that comes with a life in poverty. Gallo and Matthews (2003) presented a psychological framework to explain the mechanisms by which the emotional factors associated with low SES can contribute to socioeconomic health disparities. Their model, called the *reserve capacity model*, proposed that lower-SES environments are characterized by greater exposure to stress, which is associated with more negative and less positive emotions among people living there.

Developmental psychologists and others have examined many of these same issues in the context of their impact on the development of children. Bradley and Corwyn (2002) provided a general overview of the associations between SES and children's well-being. Similar to reviews of such findings for adults, the deleterious effects of poverty upon the development of children reads like a laundry list of everything that can go wrong: Low-SES children are more likely to experience growth retardation *in utero*, to be born prematurely, and to have birth defects, fetal alcohol syndrome, and AIDS. They are more likely to have cavities, high blood lead levels, iron deficiency, stunted growth, sensory impairment, and to have accidents and die. They manifest more symptoms of psychiatric disturbance and maladaptive social functioning. Similarly, Evans (2004) contributed a conclusive analysis from the perspective of the depleted, dangerous environments in which poor children grow up: "The air and water poor children consume are more polluted. Their homes are more crowded, noisier, and of lower quality. Low-income neighborhoods are more dangerous, offer poorer municipal services, and suffer greater physical deterioration" (p. 77).

Seeking to understand why children in poverty might be affected so negatively, psychologists have pondered the impact of poor adults' parenting styles. McLoyd (1998) reviewed the literature in this area, documenting the strong pattern of findings that attest to the deleterious effect of "parental dysphoria and harsh, inconsistent parenting" among the poor (p. 195). Researchers who have continued to examine this area since McLoyd's (1998) review include Bradley, Corwyn, McAdoo, and Coll (2003), who analyzed data from a large-scale national survey of families performed between 1986 and 1994. Their results indicated that poverty was associated with parenting styles along multiple dimensions, including parental responsiveness, parental teaching, the display of affection from the mother, and significant contact with the father—poor children were found to receive less of all these. Swick (2008) discussed the obstacles that homeless people face in being good parents to their children, including a lack of resources, poor personal development, social isolation, the lack of role models, and the degrading ways in which they are viewed by others.

Psychological research, then, has established and continues to re-establish a conclusion considered to be ironclad over 20 years ago:

> The correlation between social class and prevalence of symptoms of psychological disorder is one of the most thoroughly documented relationships in epidemiological research. So consistent are these findings, with so few exceptions, that we will assume this relationship as given. (Allen & Britt, 1983, p. 149)

Nevertheless, scholars continue to publish example after example of this axiomatic trend, finding, for example, that the development of poor children's oral reading fluency is not as good as other children's (Crowe, Connor, & Petscher, 2009). Children in poverty are not able to gain cognitive skills as quickly as children from more affluent families, and these deficits are already in evidence at age three (Ayoub et al., 2009). People living in poverty also have higher blood pressure than other people (Thomas, Nelesen, Ziegler, Natarajan, & Dimsdale, 2009).

Along the way, some researchers broaden their gaze to encompass the societal parameters of poverty as they interpret these results. Farber and Azar (1999) critiqued the proliferation of literature attributing poor children's behavioral and academic difficulties to their dysfunctional parents and teachers. Such interpretations, Farber and Azar contended, fail to factor in the ongoing, literal threats to survival with which parents and children in poverty are contending, and also corresponded to the scapegoating of urban welfare mothers, women whom mainstream society finds easy to cast as inferior "others." Salomon et al. (1996), who studied depression among the poor, noted that their findings were "both critical to welfare reform efforts and profoundly disturbing. The low-income mothers in this study lead extremely difficult lives. American families are more vulnerable than ever, but poor families headed by women face extraordinary challenges" (p. 521). Also documenting the high levels of depression that accompany poverty, Siefert et al. (2000) stated straightforwardly that "the real experiences of poor women's lives are absent from public discourse. The present findings support the need for programs and policies that reduce environmental risk factors for major depression among welfare mothers" (p. 517). Miranda and Green (1999) tied their findings directly to a call for welfare reform.

Other researchers called for more attention of a different kind. Highlighting the role of cognitive-emotional factors in mediating the association between SES and health, Gallo and Matthews (2003) recommended "further studies that adopt a more integrative approach to examining the roles of psychosocial factors" in poor people's distress so that clinicians can create interventions to target them (p. 41). Similarly, Ayoub et al. (2009) suggested that we help poor children by intervening in their homes: "Supporting parent–child interactions and enhancing cognitive and language stimulation in the home may be effective at supporting the cognitive skill development of children in poverty" (n.p.). Bradley and Corwyn (2002) pointed out that, although researchers have identified many of the variables that link SES with children's well-being, we do not yet know the details how those variables may interact with each other. "A more complete understanding of the child's home environment will require an even more detailed mapping of those exchanges and conditions," they advised (p. 1865).

The very firm foundation of findings that documents the multifaceted physical, emotional, cognitive, and behavioral damage exacted by poverty is valuable to social scientists, policymakers, activists, mental health practitioners, and others who would like to advocate on behalf of poor families—this mountain of evidence supports claims that Americans living in poverty are in need of national attention to their situations. This foundation, then, provides an essential platform on which we can stand in support of economic and social justice for people of all classes. In general, however, something is missing—and it is not something that more of the same kind of data can supply. Certainly, accumulating of more of the same kind of data is something with which we could busy ourselves for untold years to come. Psychologists could go on documenting the devastations of poverty using different kinds of constructs and instruments. Given the research record thus far, existing or newly constructed depression scales or anxiety scales will likely continue to find high levels of depression among people living in poverty. Elaborate statistical models of the various ways that these scale scores relate to each other can be hypothesized and tested. Children in poverty can again and again be shown to be lagging behind children from affluent families in important ways. Poor people can continue to be found to be sicker and to die earlier. Poor parents can continue to be shown to experience higher levels of stress, which affects the ways that they parent their children. Mental health professionals can propose and develop parenting skills workshops and other kinds of interventions to be administered to poor people—*if* this well-worn path is the one to which we choose to confine ourselves in our approaches to poverty.

## What Is Missing from This Picture?

As mentioned, the development of the foundation of evidence regarding poverty and well-being is valuable. If we care about poverty, we can only be happy that researchers have devoted time and effort toward its explication—yet there is something unsatisfying about consideration of this documentation. In his book *Blaming the Victim*, first published in 1971, William Ryan provided direction as to what this something might be. Ryan described an approach to the investigation of social problems that actually operates to support national denial that a particular issue *is* a social problem. Instead, problems such as poverty are investigated and palliative measures proposed as though they are problems of individuals. Most often, these investigations do not convey outright, old-fashioned condemnation of the poor as being constitutionally inferior. In fact, such research can even have a humanitarian flavor, in that the authors are not claiming that the poor were born sicker and less intelligent; rather, these deficits are acknowledged to be the unfortunate result of environmental stresses. This allows the researcher, according to Ryan, to

> concentrate his charitable interest on the defects of the victim, condemn the vague social and environmental stresses that produced the defect (some time ago) and ignore the continuing effect of victimizing social forces (right now). It is a brilliant ideology for justifying a perverse form of social action designed to change not society, as one might expect, but rather, society's victim. (p. 8)

The proposed remedies that arise from such analyses, Ryan continued, have a "terrifying sameness" about them (p. 8). Ryan gives such examples as the development of "compensatory educational programming" to support students in poor communities (rather than improving the adequacy of public schooling in poor communities) and programs to "strengthen" families of color (rather than working to eradicate racism). These dovetail neatly with psychological research that ends by suggesting that what is needed is, for example, more detailed mapping of poor people's home environments.

George Albee (1996)—prevention psychologist, social justice advocate, and former APA president—remarked on the state of psychological attention to poverty:

> It is not necessary to search the scientific literature for evidence that water runs downhill. Nor do we require elaborate epidemiological studies to validate the observation that economically exploited groups are regarded as inferior, even subhuman, by the exploiters. And it is clear that these groups have higher rates of both physical illness and mental/emotional disorders. (p. 1132)

What is needed, he argued, are interventions that target these problems at their sources: prevention programs that "include efforts at achieving social equality for all," noting that "such efforts threaten the status quo and so are not part of the prevention agenda" (p. 1132).

Albee put his finger on the missing piece. Establishing the evidentiary basis for the supposition that poverty is destructive to well-being has the potential to be helpful the work of policymakers and others who hope to address economic injustice. On the other hand, when nearly all the attention is focused on elaborating the individual particulars of the destruction and very little is focused on the injustice, the body of literature as a whole has the effect of distracting us from social forces and social change. In fact, it is easy to distract us "helping professionals" in this particular way. With the best of intentions, most of us intuitively conceptualize "help" as help to an individual, since most of us have been trained in delivering helpful interventions to individuals and most of us are employed in the implementation of such help and/or the training of others to do so. A deliberate, conscious, rethinking of social class and poverty can allow us, however, to supplement this orientation with the piece that often goes missing: the integration of a desire to work helpfully with individuals within a commitment to address the sociocultural context of individuals' distress. Prevention psychologists like George Albee, along with social psychologists, community psychologists, and others who work from a social justice framework, have been influential in bridging psychological theory with sociocultural considerations of poverty, power, and oppression. They align themselves with Albee's refusal to ignore the social context of the suffering of the poor, and so provide a counterpoint to the body of literature that conspicuously ignores such structural elements. In the following section, I will profile this line of work, beginning with Albee and including its roots in social justice and liberatory approaches.

## FOUNDATIONS OF ECONOMIC INJUSTICE
## IN SOCIAL AND COMMUNITY PSYCHOLOGY

I have borrowed a phrase in the title of this section from one of the most outstanding contributions yet made by psychologists to a class-based explication of poverty and its implications for our field—*Psychology and Economic Injustice* by social psychologists Bernice Lott and Heather Bullock (2007). By the time one has finished the first few pages of this book's introduction, Albee's (1996) missing pieces are no longer missing. Pointing out psychology's general neglect of issues of social class, Lott and Bullock emphasize that it is social class and emphatically *not* SES that they are addressing, in that "social class, unlike socioeconomic status, focuses attention on socially constructed aspects of social standing" and connotes differences in power within the economic system (p. 3). Already we can see that we are now talking about a system—all of *us*, not just *them*; we are talking about a hierarchy in which the poor occupy a certain position, and so do we. The authors go on to preview their discussion of some of the consequences of this system for poor and working-class people, such as the increased demands of wartime, given that three quarters of all soldiers come from poor and working-class homes (Halbfinger & Holmes, 2003). Documentation of the devastating impact of poverty is presented, but it is not left primarily at the level of the individual—instead, the scope of the presentation is widened to show society's role, and ultimately, our own role, in this state of affairs.

In addition to conceptualizing poverty as part of a societal system, Lott and Bullock's (2007) introduction invites another, related dimension into the discussion. Their questions not only concern the myriad and characteristic injuries caused by poverty, although Lott and Bullock do present those data. Their questions go deeper, to get at what British epidemiologist Michael Marmot called "the causes of the causes" (2006, p. 2)—the social forces that create the life circumstances that create the symptoms. What are the policies, procedures, attitudes, and other mechanisms that keep poor people at such a disadvantage? And again, from a structural perspective, how do we—as middle-class or owning-class people, as professionals, as researchers, as mental health practitioners, as caring observers, as well-intentioned helpers—play our parts in maintaining that system? In raising these issues, Lott and Bullock are contemporary voices within a distinguished psychological lineage of scholars who were talking about poverty and social justice before social justice psychology had that name.

## Early Voices on Psychology and Poverty: George Albee, Isaac Prilleltensky, and Ignacio Martín-Baró

Although never a part of psychology's mainstream, a tradition of scholarship within psychology has long called for attention to the circumstances of people living in poverty and other marginalized social locations. One of the most influential and persistent early expositors of this perspective was the prevention psychologist and former APA president mentioned above, George Albee. Beginning in the 1960s, Albee illuminated the classist underpinnings of conventional psychological practice, mincing no words in the process. In a 1969 article entitled "Who Shall Be Served?" Albee blasted the accepted wisdom of the day that the best places for psychological training were medical settings: "The damn trouble is that these 'best places' do not concern themselves with the *real* problems of serious emotional disturbance" (p. 4), which he explicated as the human consequences of an unjust, dehumanized society. Neither were these the settings, Albee contended, where psychologists were likely to be encouraged to explore the relationship between poverty, social injustice, and emotional well-being:

> It is not polite to attack the American establishment-supported forces which enforce discrimination, to point to the industry-funded lobbying that opposes any tax increase to improve the lot of the poor, to point to the responsibility of the White majority for racism. . . . These are not gentlemanly middle-class things to do. It is certainly not done in "the best places." (p. 5)

The passage of nearly 30 years found Albee undeterred in locating the origins of mental disorder in "a pathological social environment" that included poverty (p. 1130):

> Many mental disorders result from the stresses associated with poverty; from the physical and sexual abuse of children; from child neglect, social isolation, and exploitation; from the low self-esteem associated with involuntary unemployment; and from low social status, being female in a patriarchal society, being African American in a society dominated and controlled by Caucasians, or being gay in a homophobic world. The key concept is that the stress engendered by these experiences leads to behavior that is socially disapproved. And we label these patterns of behavior *mental illnesses.* (p. 1130)

In 1989, Albee served as the external reviewer for the dissertation of a graduate student who would go on to join him in the analysis of psychology and social injustice: Isaac Prilleltensky. This dissertation was the basis for the landmark 1989 article "Psychology and the Status Quo," in which Prilleltensky systematically deconstructed the little-questioned, ideological, class-based assumptions at the heart of the field, assumptions that are derived from and that help perpetuate an unjust status quo. Deeply held premises such as individualism and male supremacy, along with practices such as the testing movement and medical-model diagnostic conventions, attest to psychology's sociocultural embeddedness; our simultaneous claim to be value-free and scientifically neutral further conceals the actions of the field to support existing power relations. Moreover, Prilleltensky pointed out that psychologists' class socialization had prepared them not to object to (or even detect) this state of affairs: "It should not be forgotten that most social scientists belong to a social class whose political and economic interests are usually in accordance with those of the dominant sectors" (p. 796).

That same year, hundreds of miles away, Latin American psychologist Ignacio Martín-Baró was murdered by the Salvadoran army, having devoted his life and his career to El Salvador's poor. Martín-Baró had merged his training as a psychologist with liberation theology and the revolutionary pedagogy of Paulo Freire (1970) to create one of the most explicit and powerful statements of social justice psychology to date. Like Prilleltensky, Martín-Baró understood mainstream psychology to be inseparable from the social, historical, and political perspectives of the dominant social classes from which it had emerged, and that to operate from its premises among the poor was to perpetuate their oppression. Rather, a psychology of the people—a liberation psychology—must abandon false, self-serving psychological abstractions of humanity and begin with the people themselves in their socioeconomic contexts:

> Have we ever seriously asked what psychosocial processes look like from the point of view of the dominated instead of from that of the dominator? . . . What would mental health look like from the place of a tenant farmer on a hacienda, or personal maturity from someone who lives in the town dump, or motivation from a woman who sells goods in the market? This is not a matter of thinking for them or bringing them our ideas or solving their problems for them; it has to do with thinking and theorizing with them and from them. (1994 p. 28)

The work of these three psychologists—Albee, Prilleltensky, and Martín-Baró—are indispensable foundations for mental health practitioners seeking a way to theoretically ground their work in a class-based conceptualization of poverty. Add the name of an educational theorist—Paulo Freire—and we have a list of the best mentors that we could hope for in understanding the interface between social class dynamics, poverty, and psychological practice. Their influence continues to be felt, particularly but not exclusively, within scholarship in community and social psychology.

## Community Psychology

Consonant with Albee's and Prilleltensky's influence, community psychologists have investigated many of the ways that poverty as a dimension of community ecology impacts its members, encompassing variables such as community social capital (Caughy & Ocampo, 2006), violence (James, Johnson, & Raghavan, 2003, and work and welfare dynamics (Yoshikawa & Seidman, 2001). Sousa and Rodrigues (2009) discussed the ways that community-based interventions themselves have the potential to be disruptive to the well-being of poor communities in that they may be positioned as replacements for people's natural helping networks. Homelessness has received more attention from community psychologists than from any other psychological specialty, with Paul Toro and his colleagues notable among them. Community psychologists have studied homelessness with regard to issues such as prevalence rates (Tompsett, Toro, & Guzicki, 2006), the maintenance of personal dignity within shelter life (Miller & Keys, 2001), and the community services most utilized and most needed by homeless people (Acosta & Toro, 2000). Victoria Banyard (1995) interviewed 64 homeless mothers to learn about their coping skills and daily survival strategies. Describing an interwoven web of stressors—shelter-related issues, child-disciplinary concerns, financial problems, and being viewed negatively by others—the women reported coping strategies that included confronting problems, locating social support, enduring patiently, thinking positively, and thinking about their futures and their children.

Given the ecological, macrolevel perspective of community psychologists, it is perhaps not surprising that powerful statements regarding the operations of oppression in poor and marginalized communities have come from members of that field. In 2008, Prilleltensky's concept of psychopolitical validity (2003) was the topic of a special issue of *The Journal of Community Psychology*. In proposing this concept, Prilleltensky challenged psychologists to engage questions of power more directly in their work on behalf of oppressed. As a construct, *psychopolitical validity* embodies the inseparability in Prilleltensky's theorizing of wellness and liberation: To be psychopolitically valid, interventions should 1.) promote knowledge and awareness of oppression and power dynamics, and 2.) produce action toward liberation in personal, interpersonal, and/or structural domains. Addressing poverty and "economic colonialism" (p. 132) among other forms of oppression, Prilleltensky's (2008) message to practitioners is that if your interventions are not incorporating these elements, then your interventions are not accomplishing your social justice intentions (and they may even be adding to the problem): "[M]any community psychology interventions, however well intentioned, do not alter structures, but rather help their victims. Along a continuum of amelioration to transformation, our actions contribute primarily to the former and only peripherally to the latter. Hence, the need to concentrate on political action" (p. 130).

## Social Psychology

As indicated by my introduction of this part of the chapter, social psychologists have led the way in bringing attention to the injuries sustained by the poor as the result of class-based structural oppression. Social psychological research has revealed the negative stereotypes of the poor that are often held by individuals (Bullock, 1995; Cozzarelli, Wilkinson, & Tagler, 2001) and by society at large (Lott, 2002). Lott captured the essence of society's stance regarding the poor this way:

> I propose that a dominant response [to the poor] is that of distancing, that
> is, separation, exclusion, devaluation, discounting, and designation as "other,"
> and that this response can be identified in both institutional and interpersonal
> contexts. In social psychological terms, distancing and denigrating responses
> operationally define discrimination. These, together with stereotypes (i.e., a
> set of beliefs about a group that are learned early, widely shared, and socially
> validated) and prejudice (i.e., negative attitudes) constitute classism. (p. 100)

Lott (2002) based her analysis on the research of social psychologists to whom I referred in Chapter 2, including Cozzarelli, Wilkinson, and Tagler (2001). In that study, participants were more likely to attribute negative characteristics (such as *dirty, violent, unmotivated,* and *promiscuous*) to the poor, and more likely to attribute positive characteristics (such as *healthy, friendly,* and *intelligent*) to the middle class. Lott and Saxon (2002) asked their research participants to consider information about a hypothetical target woman who was described as a candidate for vice president of the parent-teacher organization at her child's school. Regardless of ethnicity, when the target was described as working-class, she was rated as cruder, more irresponsible, and less suitable for the job than when she was described as middle-class. Susan Fiske (2007), a social psychologist and neuroscientist, investigated automatic prejudicial responses to the poor using MRI technology. Fiske discovered that these responses go beyond prejudice: Apparently, many of us do not see the homeless as human at all. She found that when research participants were shown the photograph of a homeless man, their brains' activation patterns included areas that are "reliably implicated in disgust toward nonhuman objects such as garbage, mutilation, and human waste" (p. 157). At the same time, their brains demonstrated none of the responses that are associated with the perception of another human being. "These areas simply failed to light up," reported Fiske, "as if people had stumbled on a pile of garbage" (p. 157).

Straddling social psychology and human development, Deborah Belle has called for research attention to the struggles and resiliencies of poor women and to the ways that practitioners can best serve them (1990). Belle's important 2003 article with Joanne Doucet framed with striking clarity the idea that living in the context of oppression can make people sick. Belle and Doucet spelled out the material hardship, chaotic life events, societal and interpersonal powerlessness, diminished status, and outright discrimination that led them to call poverty itself "depressogenic" (p. 109). Michelle Fine and Lois Weis have worked across the boundaries of social psychology and educational policy (Fine & Weis, 2003; Weis & Fine, 1993), documenting the crises visited upon poor urban youth in the forms of underresourced schools, high-stakes testing, classist and racist tracking practices, and a society that depicts them as "the *cause* of national problems . . . the *reason* for the rise in urban crime, as *embodying* the necessity for welfare reform, and of sitting at the *heart* of moral decay" (p. 1). Along with other colleagues such as María Elena Torre, Yasser Payne, and April Burns, Michelle Fine's participatory action research projects bring to light the movement of "poor and working class bodies . . . from communities to incarceration" (Torre & Fine, 2005, p. 571) and the psychological violence perpetrated again poor urban students in the form of crumbling buildings, negligible supplies, and unqualified teachers:

> Poor and working-class youth of color are reading these conditions of their schools as evidence of their social disposability and evidence of public betrayal. These young women and men critically analyze social arrangements of class and race stratification and come to understand (but not accept) their "place" in the social hierarchy. Like children who learn to love in homes scarred by violence, these young women and men are being asked to learn in contexts of humiliation, betrayal and disrespect. It would be inaccurate to say that youth are learning nothing in urban schools of concentrated poverty. Neither fully internalizing this evidence nor fully resisting it, these children are learning their perceived worth in the social hierarchy. This profound civics lesson may well burn a hole in their collective souls. (Fine, Burns, Payne, & Torre, 2004, p. 2194)

## PRACTITIONERS AND THE POOR

The third theme that I will draw from the psychological literature on poverty emerges from the vantage point of mental health practitioners. A thread of dialogue with regard to poor clients has been faint but discernible within psychological practice for over 50 years (Smith, 2005). At some points, this dialogue has been reminiscent of the individually focused perspective described in the first section this chapter; at other times, it has advanced the structural contextualization of poverty advocated by Albee, Prilleltensky, Lott, and Bullock.

The dialogue begins at a place of overtly unfavorable opinions regarding the presence of the poor among psychotherapeutic caseloads. The unsuitability of poor people for treatment was discussed openly among mental health professionals during the first half of the 20th century. A widely held opinion during the 1950s and 1960s was that most poor people did not have the skills to engage in the therapeutic process, were unlikely to benefit from it, and dropped out prematurely in any event (Graff, Kenig, & Radoff, 1971; Heitler, 1973). Lorion reviewed the research from that period in 1974, finding that therapists often perceived poor clients as hostile (Hollingshead &

Redlich, 1958), crude in language and behavior (Affleck & Garfield, 1961), and a waste of supervisory time (Baum, Felzer, D'Zmura, & Shumaker, 1966). Correspondingly, researchers found higher class status to be reliably associated with acceptance into psychotherapeutic treatment (Jones, 1974).

## A Surge of Support for Poor Clients: The CMHC Movement

Discourse regarding psychotherapeutic treatment for the poor was affected in some quarters by the advent of the community mental health center (CMHC) movement in the 1960s. As described by Albee and Gulotta (1997), the Joint Commission on Mental Illness and Health delivered a report to Congress in 1961 that outlined the overwhelming demand then being placed on public mental hospitals. Two years later, President John F. Kennedy advocated for federal funding of mental health research and the construction of 2,000 CMHCs nationwide began.

As CMHCs began to open their doors during the 1970s, a new, more culturally aware interpretation of poor clients' treatment difficulties began to emerge: Perhaps the problem lay with middle-class therapists who were not inclined toward working with poor clients and who held out little hope for a beneficial prognosis. Lorion (1973) offered such an assessment, pointing out that no empirical demonstration of a relationship between SES and treatment outcome had ever been presented, and suggesting that therapists seemed to be seeking to rationalize their disengagement from the poor. In a review published the following year, Lorion (1974) suggested that therapists' negative attitudes could be important contributors to treatment failures with poor clients, and he lamented the lack of supervisory techniques for addressing these biases. "Therapist-centered problems," he concluded, "do not justify decisions not to treat. Rather, they should be considered as training-supervisory problems that can be overcome by recognition and discussion" (Lorion, 1974, pp. 351–352). Similar conclusions were reached in another review article published the same year by Jones (1974), and again by Siassi and Messer (1976), who concurred with the view that "there has been a misplaced emphasis on the role of the patient in attempting to explain negative therapeutic reactions of the lower class patient" (p. 32).

## Shifting Attention

The 1970s, then, had seen a relative surge of support for a perspective summed up by Karon and VandenBos (1977): When therapists have the skills and awareness needed to understand class-related attitudes and issues, then "psychotherapy with the poor patient is no different from good psychotherapy with anyone" (p. 169). Shortly thereafter, however, came what Albee (1996) described as "the counterrevolution" (p. 1132). During the 1980s, psychologists' attention shifted away from concern with the psychological consequences of poverty and other forms of inequality and toward the biology, neurology, and genetics of mental disorders. While this so-called medical model was gaining in prominence, federal support for the CMHC movement waned as the Reagan administration began to scale back funding for CMHCs in the 1980s. Of the 2,000 CMHCs planned for construction, only 750 had been established, and they were now struggling for their economic survival (Humphreys & Rappaport, 1993). Nevertheless, during the 1980s and 1990s, a degree of attention to the issue of psychotherapeutic services for the poor was maintained among specific groups of psychotherapists.

## Feminist Psychology

By the early 1980s, feminist thinkers and social critics such as Davis (1983), hooks (1981; 1984), and Lorde (1984) were effectively challenging mainstream feminism on its claims that it represented the experiences of all women—rather, they argued, it was concerned primarily with the experiences of middle-class, White, heterosexual women. As part of this movement, feminist psychology began its own process of self-examination and, in so doing, became a source of advocacy for services to poor clients and the development of class-related cultural competence among therapists. Denny (1986) asked whether poor women could "benefit from, or even survive feminist therapy" (p. 51) as she systematically explored classist bias in feminist psychotherapeutic theory and practice. In the coming years, this effort would be advanced by psychologists such as Brown (1990) and Reid (1995), the latter stating that poor women had been "shut up and shut out" (p. 184) of mainstream psychology as a whole.

## Family Systems Therapy

Family therapists and others who work from a systems or structural perspective, who attempt to "view families within a larger social, economic, and political framework" (Mirkin, 1990, p. xiii), use an approach that, by definition, affords an opportunity to consider poverty as it affects psychotherapeutic treatment. Family systems therapists, accordingly, helped bring attention to the issue of psychological practice with poor clients. Presenting systems theory as providing a basis for more meaningful treatment formulations for poor clients, Inclan and Ferran (1990) proposed a conceptualization of the problems associated with poverty that uses clients' relationships with the mainstream work world as a starting point. Brown and Parnell (1990), Minuchin (1995), and Boyd-Franklin and Bry (2000) have all described applications of a family systems approach to psychotherapeutic work with clients living in poverty; Aponte (1994) and Minuchin, Colapinto, and Minuchin (1998) contributed books entirely devoted to the topic. Among these authors, Aponte is notable in emphasizing the importance of therapists' own awareness and preparation with regard to their work with the poor.

## Psychoanalysis

Given their "reputation for elitism" (Altman, 1995, p. xiii), psychoanalysts might not be expected to figure in a discussion of psychotherapeutic treatment for poor clients; nevertheless, a number of analysts have challenged the field of psychoanalysis to broaden its scope (e.g., Moskowitz, 1996; Siassi & Messer, 1976; Thompson, 1989; Trevithick, 1998). Pérez Foster (1996) wrote of psychoanalysis's "secret shame" (p. 3): clinicians who claim to prize the value of all human life yet have virtually excluded poor and culturally diverse people from treatment. Altman's (1995) comprehensive explication addressed the classism and racism that are embedded in psychoanalytic theory and practice and described the use of a three-person model for psychoanalytic practice that incorporates the influence of social systems. Focusing on countertransferential issues, Javier and Herron (2002) suggested that psychotherapists not only have trouble relating to poor people, but they also resist such connection defensively. Highlighting the social and political dimensions of poverty, the authors explained that

> most therapists are middle class, so it might be argued that they are too separated from upper class patients to understand them sufficiently, but that is unlikely. Middle-class people frequently wish for more, and often try to achieve it. . . . In contrast, therapists have no interest in being poor, and despite social conscience, do not seek to identify with the poor. In essence . . . the potential for disruptive countertransference is high and prone to override egalitarian and altruistic desires as well. (2002, p. 9)

## Community-Based Practice

Schnitzer (1996), a practitioner in an urban state-funded clinic, wrote about the themes that she had observed within psychotherapists' "clinical stories" (p. 573) about the poor. In relating these stories or anecdotes, Schnitzer explained, clinicians can be heard to reveal more about their approach to their work than they do when they are speaking deliberately and with the appropriate professional jargon. The stories that Schnitzer heard most frequently clustered around three clinical storylines. The first—*They don't come in*—raises questions about the unreliability and irresponsibility of poor clients. Stories of the second variety—*They're so disorganized*—imply euphemistically that that poor clients suffer from cognitive shortcomings, while *They don't care* stories center on depleted moral and ethical standards among poor families, with poor mothers frequently appearing as the main characters. Schnitzer noted that these stories parallel national cultural narratives, which are currently dominated by characterizations of the poor as undeserving due to their moral and intellectual shortcomings: "These characteristics are seen as personality traits, or at least as deeply ingrained habits, and taken to be the starting point for the social and economic factors that create the environment of the impoverished class" (p. 576).

## Practice-Related Scholarship Since 2000

At the turn of the millennium, practice-related research in psychology presented two faces regarding the poor. On the one hand, contributions to the literature suggested that poor people had again receded into the background of psychological concern. Saris and Johnston-Robledo (2000) summarized the results of their PsycLIT database content analysis in the title of their article "Poor Women Are Still Shut Out of Mainstream Psychology." Similarly, Lott (2002) identified "the near invisibility of the poor in psychology" (p. 6), Javier and Herron (2002) interpreted a "fear of the poor" (p. 26) among therapists, and Furnham (2003) observed that "the most important topics in poverty research have been almost totally neglected by psychologists" (p. 164). Moreira (2003) deplored the growing tendency worldwide to relegate mental health treatment for the poor to hospitals and psychiatrists, a trend that she called "the medicalization of poverty" (p. 81). S. Sue and Lam (2002) included social class in their review of psychotherapeutic treatment outcomes for diverse cultural and demographic groups. With regard to poor clients, they observed that "despite the important influence of socioeconomic status on an individual's life, this variable has been widely ignored" (p. 414), and that the most that can be reliably gleaned from the literature is that poor clients are likely to drop out of treatment prematurely. "It seems that there are still biases and stereotypes that psychologists have with regard to this population," the authors concluded (S. Sue & Lam, 2002, p. 414).

On the other hand, better intentions were also being articulated within the field. The American Psychological Association (APA) adopted a Resolution on Poverty and Socioeconomic Status in 2000, in which the APA stated that "poverty is detrimental to psychological well-being" and charged psychologists with the responsibility to "treat and address the needs of low-income individuals and families" (APA, 2000, p. 23). The proposition's 17 resolutions challenged psychologists to address poverty, classism, practitioner competence and training, and public policy, clearly portraying a field in service to all segments of society. A task force was subsequently convened within the APA specifically to examine the implications of SES for psychological theory and practice, eventually resulting in the establishment of the APA Office on Socioeconomic Status.

## Counseling Psychology

This was a momentous time for the applied specialty of counseling psychology, and an unfolding of events positioned counseling psychologists to align their practice with the structural assessments of poverty articulated by prevention, social, and community psychologists. With sentiment coalescing at the 2000 National Counseling Psychology Conference in Houston, social justice assumed a prominent position within discussions of professional identity and direction within the specialty (Fouad et al., 2004), an identity that built on the foundations of counseling psychology's history of attention to culturally contextualized practice more generally (Smith, 2008). In 1981, APA Division 17 president Allen Ivey created a committee charged with the development of multicultural counseling competencies, and appointed counseling psychologist Derald Wing Sue to lead it. Sue's research on multicultural counseling had already spanned the previous decade (e.g., D.W. Sue & S. Sue, 1972; D.W. Sue & Kirk, 1975) and had specifically identified culturally incompetent practice as oppressive (D. W. Sue, 1978). The committee's 1982 report was eventually endorsed in adapted form as the APA's Multicultural Guidelines on Education and Training, Research, Practice, and Organizational Development for Psychologists (APA, 2002).

Counseling psychologists did not stop at the Multicultural Guidelines, however. Derald Wing Sue (2001) advised the specialty not to limit their attentions to the consulting room:

> In truth, psychologists have played a minimal role in the formation of public policy because they have failed to understand how systemic forces affect people and because they have been averse to becoming active in the social and political arenas (D.W. Sue, Parham, et al., 1998). They can no longer be only concerned with individual change but must use their knowledge and skills to improve conditions in the world for all groups. (p. 811)

Toporek, Lewis, and Crethar (2009) described the work of the American Counseling Association to build on the foregoing efforts through the establishment of specific advocacy competencies for counselors. These competencies begin at the level of advocacy on behalf of individual clients, but broaden to encompass systems advocacy, the education of the general public with regard to oppression and its impact, and social/political advocacy. Within this focus on social justice, attention to social class has begun to appear in the counseling psychology literature, although it is still scarce. For example, the comprehensive *Handbook for Social Justice in Counseling Psychology*, edited by social justice scholars Rebecca Toporek, Lawrence Gerstein, Nadya Fouad, Gargi Roysircar, and Tanya Israel (2006), is significant for its provision of detailed examples and case studies of social justice practice. The economic barriers and hardships faced by various groups are mentioned at several points in the book, and the circumstances of poor people in the United States were the central themes of 3 of its 36 chapters.

Those counseling psychologists who have made notable contributions with regard to social class begin with William Liu, one of the earliest and most prolific applied psychologists to address it. Liu (2001) presented a social class worldview model according to which multiple subjective economic cultural experiences are possible, and has also presented case vignettes (2002) to demonstrate the use of this model within counseling practice. Moreover, Liu and his colleagues were instrumental in spotlighting psychology's general lack of substantive attention to social class (Liu, Ali, Soleck, Hopps, Dunston, & Pickett, 2004). Nadya Fouad and Michael Brown (2000) discussed the relationship between perceived social standing and psychosocial development, while Judy Daniels, Michael D'Andrea, and their colleagues wrote about counseling interventions with homeless children and their families (Daniels, 1995; Daniels, D'Andrea, Omizo, & Pier, 1999). In their conceptual presentation of social privilege, Black and Stone (2005) included a section on what they called SES privilege, and offered the unusually forthright observation that "oppression of the disadvantaged maintains the comfort, convention, and convenience of the status quo and ensures an underemployed, unemployed, and service class of persons" (p. 249).

Counseling psychologists who focus on vocational issues have addressed the implications of poverty for the career development process (e.g., Heppner & O'Brien, 2006; Heppner & Scott, 2004; Juntunen et al., 2006). The work of vocational psychologists David Blustein, Ellen Hawley McWhirter, and their colleagues has been particularly comprehensive, and addresses social class directly via its associations with power and privilege. Blustein et al. (2002) began with a contextualized discussion of economic inequity as they presented an analysis of narrative data illustrating the ways that social class operates within the vocational experiences of young working-class adults. Their results indicated that more affluent participants valued personal satisfaction, access to external resources, and high levels of career adaptability within their vocational plans, whereas the working-class participants saw work primarily as a way to survive economically. Blustein, McWhirter, and Perry (2005) theorized a comprehensive integration of social class with career development theory, social justice tenets, and Prilleltensky's (1997) emancipatory communitarian approach to create a "truly inclusive psychology of work" (p. 312).

A recent edited book, *Advancing Social Justice through Clinical Practice* (Aldarondo, 2007) describes the ROAD (Reaching Out About Depression) project. This project represents a compelling practice-based line of inquiry interweaving practice, social class, and poverty that evolved from the work of Lisa Goodman and her colleagues (Goodman et al., 2007). A collaboration with a group of low-income women, the ROAD project is a grassroots program that combines support, advocacy, and community organizing on behalf of poor urban women who are struggling with symptoms of depression. As part of one of its components, the Advocacy Resource Team, graduate student counselors partner with women from the community who are involved in the overall project as either participants or workshop facilitators. The partners then work flexibly together for about 9 months to facilitate progress toward participants' own goals. The model by which the pairs work together is called Feminist Relational Advocacy (FRA), an approach with roots in feminist therapy (Goodman, Glenn, Bohlig, Banyard, & Borges, 2009). In its explicit incorporation of social action, the ROAD project signifies a revolutionary turn in psychologists' conceptualizing about what sorts of experiences might be healing for people living in the context of oppression, and I will have much more to say about this in Chapter 6.

## THE CAUSES OF THE CAUSES

Too much of the psychological literature treats the devastations that accompany a life lived in poverty as though they exist in a sociopolitical vacuum. This is not to suggest that these researchers are unsympathetic to the plight of the poor. Rather, they simply do not address (or, often, even mention) the social, cultural, and political context of poverty—and there are far-reaching implications to presenting the problems that poverty causes without mentioning the causes of the causes. As I noted earlier, oppressive status quo ideologies get passed along from decade to decade precisely because the good people do nothing—they look the other way, they avert their gaze from the sociocultural origins of oppression, they maintain the silence that surrounds it—and they explain this as a "neutral" moral and political stance. As we have discussed, however, there is no such thing as neutral place to stand with regard to the perpetuation of inequity. Silence supports it, identification counteracts it, and action begins to change it. The more we insist upon an explicit cultural framework for any consideration of poverty, the more our work will align with social action for economic justice. Moreover, psychological research could be truly instrumental in helping to identify and dismantle oppressive attitudes. What are the attitudes, stereotypes, and other psychological gymnastics that enable us not to see class-based oppression for what it is? Psychologists have been active in bringing to light the pervasive racism and sexism that suffuse contemporary consciousness, and we can apply these same skills to the analysis and dismantling of classism.

# 4

# IN THEIR OWN WORDS: QUALITATIVE EXPRESSIONS OF LIFE IN POVERTY

We believed that if we could simply tell people what was happening to very poor people, someone would put a stop to it. . . . How do you make public what so many people more powerful than you are trying their damnedest to keep secret?

—Welfare mother Theresa Funicello (1993, p. 22)

In the previous chapter, I described psychological approaches to the study of poverty; in this chapter, I hope to convey aspects of poverty with more immediacy by drawing upon qualitative studies of poverty by journalists and social scientists who listened to the voices of people living in poverty through extended series of interviews and conversations. Their reporting represents these conversations through extensive use of verbatim quotations, as well as through the reflections and experiences of the reporters themselves. For example, social worker Jill Duerr Berrick and her research team interviewed more than 400 poor women across California over the period of a year for the study she described in the book *Faces of Poverty* (1995). Sociologist Mark Rank (1994) collected data over a 10-year period in the state of Wisconsin for *Living on the Edge: The Realities of Welfare in America.* Journalist David Shipler (2004) interviewed poor people across the country over six years, sometimes dozens of times each, for *The Working Poor: Invisible in America.* Most of these studies included both male and female participants, although a few included only women, such as Berrick's; all included participants of every race, although only a few incorporated racial differences within their analysis, as Michelle Fine and Lois Weis did in their book *The Unknown City: The Lives of Poor and Working-Class Young Adults* (1999).

Given the fact that poor people currently have little in the way of a public platform by which to tell their stories, studies such as these provide a crucial window into the lived experience of poverty in America. Yet, even when the data are so rich and naturalistic, a cautionary note is in order. Mitchell Duneier, a sociologist who spent 7 years documenting the social world of sidewalk vendors in New York, explained that even the most scrupulous devotion to methodological parameters does not guarantee that objective truth will be revealed, and that researchers never know when trust has been established with their participants, or even exactly what it would look like if it were. In his book *Sidewalk* (1999), Duneier reminded readers "Like all observers, I have my subjectivities" (p. 14), explaining that

> One of the greatest strengths of firsthand observation is also its greatest weakness. Through a careful involvement in people's lives, we can get a fix on how their world works and how they see it. But the details can be misleading if they distract us from the forces that are less visible to the people we observe, but which influence and sustain the behaviors. (p. 10)

Duneier immersed himself more than most within the world that he studied—during the period of his work, he spent time scavenging and selling magazines on the street alongside his interviewees. Yet Duneier advises us that nothing that we see, even firsthand, is *all* there is—powerful sociohistorical forces are at work to shape everything that we see in others and everything about how we interpret it. We can never separate ourselves from that context, and researchers who interview people across divides of class and race can never "take off" those identities and differences. Students of their work cannot, either. Reading through data like these, we need to keep in mind that whether the results seem to confirm or disconfirm our assumptions about the poor, those evaluations are refracted through the lenses of our own social class and racial identities.

With those qualifications in mind, I present four themes that emerge from these portraits of life in poverty—four broad areas that seemed to be echoed in the words of many of the participants and to cut across the reporting by the authors who interviewed them. These themes illustrate both what poor people share with other Americans and the extent to which the poor are excluded. I will interweave my commentary on these themes with occasional examples of how I encountered these aspects of community life as a practitioner working in a poor community. These themes concern poverty as 1.) life without basic necessities, 2.) an ongoing condition of chaos and crisis, 3.) a stigmatized social position, and 4.) the location of deep, persistent ideals regarding work and family.

## LIFE WITHOUT THE BASICS

Probably the most intuitive aspect of poverty, and one about which people in every qualitative study have spoken, is the sheer survival-related deprivation of food, shelter, health care, and other basic requisites of daily life. Most of us in the middle class have never had to face the reality of literally having no food in the house and the complete absence of any money with which to purchase any. Mark Rank (1994) asked Carol, one of his interviewees, whether she ever ran out of food at the end of the month. This scenario is a familiar one to people living in poverty because food stamps are usually not enough by themselves to provide adequately for a family until the next month arrives with its new supply:

> CAROL: Yeah. All the time.
> Q: How do you manage?
> CAROL: We've got a food pantry up here that they allow you to go to two times a month. They give you a little card. And in between those times, we find other food pantries that we can get to. We've gone to different churches and asked for help all the time. And we get commodities at the end of the month. Cheese and butter. And we usually get one item out of it, which helps an awful lot. (p. 55)

Two couples interviewed by Rank described their end-of-the-month survival strategies. One couple described financing groceries by collecting aluminum cans from the ground and selling them; the husband in another couple said, "That's the main reason that we're always going to University Plasma. That's the main reason. . . . If the bills weren't a problem, we wouldn't go every week like we do" (p. 56). Selling blood to the plasma center was key to meeting the monthly bills and still providing food for the family.

Shipler (2004) described the bind in which his interviewees found themselves: The issue was not that food for the family was seen as less important than other bills; it was that food was the only bill that was at all elastic. Rents are fixed and the electricity bill is fixed—so the ability to buy food for the family became a function of what was left after these fixed expenses had been met. The impact of these circumstances on children is clear; Shipler described the visits of impoverished parents to malnutrition clinics in Boston, where doctors outlined the cognitive deficits and immunological damage that they observed in poor parents' children. The parents, however, were suffering as well:

> To be the mother or father of a malnourished child is a most painful price of poverty. Feeding a child is the most intimate responsibility, closest to the heart

of a parent's duty. Other essentials feel less controllable. Even the most frugal mother cannot reduce the rent, but when she runs out of money for adequate food, she often blames herself for mismanagement . . . her inability to nurture a child seems a final failing at the core. (p. 207)

These interviewees were describing what the federal government calls "food insecurity," and it is an increasingly common landmark of American poverty, having recently reached its highest levels since being tracked (DeParle, 2009). Feeding America, the nation's largest hunger-relief organization, reported that one in eight Americans currently relies upon them for food, with 36% of the households whom they serve having at least one working family member (Mathematica Policy Research, 2010).

The spaces that poor people occupy also represent and exacerbate their deprivation. Poor communities often feature barren stretches of small, run-down businesses and lack the conveniences that middle-class people take for granted in daily life, such as large grocery stores and discount variety stores. In fact, a new milestone was reached in one of the poorest American cities, Detroit: It now has not a single major chain supermarket anywhere within city limits. As residents are forced to rely on small corner stores, which are more expensive and more restricted in their offerings, the numbers of food stamp applications and visits to food pantries have exploded (Hargreaves, 2009). These depleted communities can be also constant sources of anxiety and danger. Sondra, one of the women interviewed by Katherine Newman and Victor Tan Chen for their book *The Missing Class* (2007), put it simply. "Our neighborhoods are poison," she said, describing the drug trade and the accompanying violence that had taken over her Brooklyn neighborhood and claimed the life of her son (p. 17).

For people living in poverty, home offers little respite from these realities. Katherine Newman (1999) spent two years with the participants in her study, meeting them at home, at work, and at school. She painted a picture of the home where she met one of her interviewees, a 22-year-old man named Jamal and his wife, Kathy. Although the outside of the building looked like a poorly maintained but livable property, this impression ended at the front door:

> For at least a decade, the building has been broken up into separate living quarters, a rooming house with whole families squeezed into spaces that would not even qualify as bedrooms in most homes. Toilets, such as they are, sit at the end of a dark hallway. Six families take turns cooking their meals in the only kitchen and argue with one another about the provisions they have squirreled away in the refrigerator they share. The plumbing breaks down without warning—the bane of everyone's existence. Most rooms sport windows that are cracked and broken, pieced together by duct tape that barely blocks the steady, freezing draft blowing through on a windy evening. (p. 3)

Peter Davis (1995) experienced these communities as geographical, economic, educational, and psychological "pens" that American society creates for the poor so that it does not have to acknowledge the circumstances of their lives. Spending time at a Salvation Army soup kitchen with some of his interviewees, Davis found himself "dying to get out of there," encountering thereby his own participation in this strategy: "I understood my own need to have the very poor in pens where I didn't have to be confronted by them, by their discomfort that can so easily make my comfort uncomfortable" (p. 70).

Of course, many people who slip into poverty are not fortunate enough to have even these roofs over their heads, sometimes choosing to sleep in hallways, parks, subways, and cars rather than brave the often violent, drug-ridden, rodent-infested, and otherwise unsanitary conditions of many homeless shelters. Ian Urbina (2006), writing for the *New York Times*, conveyed the voices of people who were "living in their last major possession":

> After being evicted from his apartment last year, Larry Chaney lived in his car for five months in Erie, Pa. As he passed the time at local cafes, he always put a ring of old house keys and several envelopes with bills on the table to give the impression that he had a home like everyone else. While Michelle Kennedy was living in her car with her three children in Belfast, Me., she parked someplace different each night so no one would notice them, and she instructed the children to tell anyone who asked that they were "staying with friends." Last year, William R. Alford started keeping a car cover over the station wagon where he sleeps. "I originally just had drapes, but the condensation on the inside of the windows was a dead giveaway," said Mr. Alford, who has been homeless here in Fairfax since May 2005 (p. 1).

I often heard people in the community where I worked speak about these kinds of living conditions. At first, I was not sure how to interpret the things that clients dropped into their conversations; for example, early on, a young man mentioned in passing that he shared his bed with his grandmother. As a therapist coming from a middle-class setting, alarm bells went off for me: *what?* Inappropriate boundaries within the family's relationship structure? As time went by, however, I came to see these circumstances for what they were: My clients often had no good choices regarding where to sleep. Five adults to a room, 11 in a basement, sleeping in a parked car, sleeping in the hallway of a building, sleeping outside, sleeping on the subway, moving from a couch in one friend's apartment to another, interspersed with stints in the homeless shelter. There were simply no physical spaces for them to occupy other than these.

Another necessity that the poor are without is basic health care for themselves and their families. One of Katherine Newman's (1999) interviewees, Kyesha, described the bind she was in once she found work in a fast-food restaurant. A diabetic, she now made too much money to qualify for Medicaid for herself, although she could get it for her child. Yet she had no benefits at work and no extra money to see a doctor. Her only recourse, when her skyrocketing temperature told her that her insulin levels were too high, was to spend hours in an emergency room waiting for an insulin shot: "I just got Medicaid for my son. They said that I made too much at [the fast-food restaurant] to get Medicaid. I said, 'One-fifty a week . . . shit.' I guess I have to be completely broke to get medical assistance" (p. 31).

The disabilities that result from a lack of health care not only derive from poverty, they help perpetuate it. One of Shipler's (2004) participants, Caroline, was able to obtain an entry-level position at a large discount store working the night shift. Seen by her co-workers as friendly, hardworking, and punctual, she hoped to move up at some point to a slightly higher-level position where she could earn a wage that would lift her out of poverty, and prevent the slide back into welfare that characterizes the histories of many low-wage workers. She applied for job after job within the company and watched as others were selected to fill them, suspecting that part of the reason she was not being selected might be that she looked older than she really was. "My age shows on me terribly," she said, commenting that people often thought she was her daughter's grandmother (p. 52). Shipler thought about the implications of his interviewee's comments:

> The people who got promotions tended to have something that Caroline did not. They had teeth. Caroline did not have teeth. If she had, she would not have looked ten years older than she was. But her teeth had succumbed to poverty, to the years when she could not afford a dentist. . . . Caroline's was the face of the working poor, marked by a poverty-generated handicap more obvious than most deficiencies but no different, really, from the less visible deficits that reflect and reinforce destitution. If she had not been poor, she would not have lost her teeth, and if she had not lost her teeth, perhaps she would not have remained poor. (p. 52)

Other deprivations of poverty tend to perpetuate poverty as well. One of my clients, a 20-year-old living in a shelter, took part in an application program designed by a bank to identify candidates for bank teller positions in its branches. The program, which lasted several days, included personality inventories and tests of mathematical ability as well as more standard types of interviews. Preliminary results were promising: My client told me excitedly that he had received the highest composite score in the group on the battery of inventories. Yet, ultimately, he was passed over for a position. When he asked for feedback, he was told that the bank's administrators were disappointed that he had not chosen to dress more professionally for the formal interview. My client told me that he had worn what he considered to be his best outfit: black pants and a black Tupac Shakur T-shirt, ironed for the occasion. It did not occur to the administrators, obviously, that if they gave this talented young person a chance to earn a living, he might have more choices in what he wore to work.

## CHAOS AND CRISIS

When people are scraping to survive on a month-to-month basis, it does not take much to send them careening toward disaster. Many of the life-disrupting crises that befall the poor are uncommon in the lives of more affluent people, such as being evicted from one's home; others may happen to us and are inconvenient but do not completely derail our lives, such as having the car break down. The resulting precariousness of life, and the possibility of being plunged into chaos at any given moment, is another one of the hallmarks of life in poverty. Summarizing the experiences described by his interviewees, Shipler (2004) commented:

> [B]eing poor means being unprotected. You might as well try playing quarterback with no helmet, no padding, no training, and no experience, behind a line of 100-pound weaklings. With no cushion of money, no training in the ways of the wider world, and too little defense against the treats and temptations of decaying communities, a poor man or woman gets sacked again and again—buffeted and bruised and defeated. When an exception breaks this cycle of failure, it is called the fulfillment of the American Dream. (p. 5)

Because of the literal precariousness of their living and health situations, I saw people in poverty adopt crisis management as a way of life. My clients seemed to hang on by their fingernails from day to day, always expecting the other shoe to drop and making the best of things in the meantime. These expectations were adaptive in that they enabled people to survive the disruptions that were more the rule than the exception. The downside was that my clients were at a loss when it came to making plans for the future—and how could it be otherwise? They certainly understood the benefits of looking ahead, but were without confidence or evidence that their plans would bear fruit and thus be worth the trouble—expecting the unexpected, after all, had been the lesson that their lives had taught them. Mark Rank (1994) captured this aspect of his interviewees' lives with the phrase "one day at a time" (p. 93). One of his interviewees, Ruth, spoke of the futility of making long-range plans:

I take one day at a time. One day at a time, that's what I'm doing. 'Cause every time I make a plan, or doing something, you know, it always turns—always something a little different. One of the kids will get sick or somebody real close to me will get sick or something, something happens. So I said, from now on I just live one day at a time and see what happens. (p. 93)

As chaotic events toss people in poverty from crisis to crisis inside communities without resources or safety nets, some of the residents become living reminders of the depths to which people can plunge. Katherine Newman's (1999) participant Kyesha spoke of the sobering confrontations that she had daily with the young people with whom she had grown up. Working at a fast-food restaurant, Kyesha now saw them among the street-corner men who lingered outside:

Kyesha and Tyron grew up in the same housing project, not far from the [restaurant] where their paths cross these days. They played together when they were little, but long ago lost touch. By the time Tyron had resurfaced as a street-corner man, Kyesha had forgotten all about him. She recognized him, though, the first day he came into the restaurant and ordered a meal. His history was written all over his face and tattered clothes. . . . Encounters like this happen all the time in Kyesha's world. . . . For Kyesha, these chance meetings are filled with lessons. They are daily reminders of the ease with which she could have found herself on the other side of the counter, waiting for a handout. (p. 24)

The chaos also includes the unpredictable violence that characterizes vulnerable communities. Michelle Fine and Lois Weis (1999) described their participants' persistent messages regarding the life-shaping impact of violence in their lives. Although experiences of violence were communicated by participants across race and gender, the expressed nature and location of the violence did not. Poor White men talked about street violence, and identified men of color as its cause. African American and Latino men, however, spoke of state-initiated violence, such as police harassment, the flight of money and jobs from poor communities, and the disproportionate arrest and incarceration of men of color. Women of color contributed experiences of state-initiated violence, too, but poor women of all races told primarily stories of domestic and relationship violence. This one, from Fine and Weis's participant Tamar, is an example:

TAMAR: He was doing all the screaming and punching and she was the one doing all the crying, so you could tell. And I called the cops and said, bring, you know, can you send me a car, there are kids involved, the man is hitting, and I said please hurry up, and I was polite. . . .
MUN [the interviewer]: Did the police come?
TAMAR: Yeah, they came. They came in less than three minutes. If it wouldn't have been for me, forget it.

MUN: How did that make you feel?

TAMAR: It gave me flashbacks of me. And I wish that when they heard me screaming, somebody would have called the cops or knock on my door and tell me if I'm all right, they don't do that. (p. 126)

My clients were affected deeply by the crowded, crumbling, dangerous, isolated conditions in which they lived, and frequently spoke about that directly. One young man, who was one of five adults living in a single room, talked about the mounting, frightening frustration that he experienced at having no space in the world where he could relax. Certainly, home did not represent any kind of sanctuary, given the close proximity of four other tense, quarrelsome adults who were no happier to be crowded together than he was. However, being outside was no better because the community was the scene of drug transactions and gang violence, and most people ventured outdoors only when they had to. My client and I talked about the fleeting urges that he had to scream, or to hit someone. Other people came to ask for help with PTSD-like symptoms after having witnessed murders. One woman dreamed constantly of the friend that she had seen stabbed. A man's brother died in his arms after a shooting. Another young man described growing up with adults who held guns to his head and pulled knives at home. He had begun hearing a voice in his head saying, "Stand up for yourself!" Along these lines, it is not a stretch to imagine the emotional and physical consequences to poor families of the ongoing effort to survive the jolts and freefalls of life in poverty. Jill Berrick's interviewee Darlene put it simply: "I'm heart-battered," she said (1995, p. 90).

## STIGMA AND EXCLUSION

One of the less tangible yet most pervasive and damaging consequences of poverty is the stigmatization and social marginalization that accompany a position at the bottom of the social class spectrum. Poor people readily read the signals that they receive regarding their devalued status. One of Rank's (1994) participants, Janice, described a common scenario that is initiated by the use of food stamps:

You really do have to be a strong person to be able to use food stamps and not get intimidated by how people treat you when you use them. And even then it's still hard. You feel people's vibes, you know, in the line. And the checkout people are almost without exception rude, unless you really get to know them. And I always feel like, "God, I'll be glad when I don't have to use these." (p. 137)

Interviewees across studies described the extent to which public service bureaucracies themselves are the settings of rude treatment. Participants in Michelle Fine and Lois Weis's (1999) interviews provided examples:

BEATRICE: No, they treat you so down. They treat you so low. So low. It's like they're too good to be bothered with people like . . .

MERCEDES: You want to know what they did to me once? I was at welfare with my little baby now. And I went to this . . . lady and I was like, "Listen, right now I don't have a place to stay. My father won't take me back. . . ." "Well, honey, all I can tell you is to beg, borrow, and steal." What? Now if I woulda went and did that . . .

BEATRICE: The thing is, it's hard. When I first moved here, we had to go to welfare, and that was when we first started here . . . you just walked in and you got all these nasty looks. When you come from an abusive situation, and you gotta go to welfare. That negative feeling, plus the negative feelings that you get in there. Because you expect that you're gonna go into the office and you swear that you're gonna be treated nicely, decently. Show some type of courtesy that you are somebody. No, they treat you like garbage there, too. (p. 225)

Poor mothers spoke of the lengths to which they would go to try to disguise their poverty on behalf of their children and thereby rescue them from being shamed and ostracized. I saw this frequently in the community where I worked, and also heard the disapproval masked as surprise in the remarks of middle-class observers: "She's on welfare? Her son's sneakers cost more than mine!" The point that is missed here is that as middle-class people, we might or might not enjoy the extra status that we associate with the display of expensive purchases, but we do not usually feel compelled to display a particular kind of item to validate our general citizenship and *social personhood*—those memberships are self-evident. For poor mothers, living in the projects in isolated communities, the desire to rescue their children from cultural exile is a desperate one. Adrian Nicole LeBlanc (2003) described a participant's budgeting procedures, which stipulated that anything left after the bills went to clothing for her little girls, since children's sloppiness could be seen as "evidence of failure, of poverty winning its battle against you" (p. 145). Along these lines, one of Rank's (1994) interviewees, Denise, commented:

My oldest daughter, she graduated from middle school. And she told me last year that she did not want to receive the hot lunch program because the children made a difference. So I had to scrape for the last couple of years while she was in middle school and try to make ends meet so that I could send her with a dollar or two dollars every day. Which is a big chunk out of our budget. . . . But rather than see her mistreated, or have her friends sit away from her, this is what I had to do. (p. 139)

And poor children have learned long before middle school how the rest of society sees them. In her qualitative study of 24 poor children between the ages of 5 and 13, social worker Susan Weinger (1998) showed her young interviewees photographs of two homes. One was a suburban ranch-style house with a lawn, and another looked like the homes in the kids' neighborhood, which Weinger described as having "junk in the yards, chained dogs, smashed fences, unsafe steps, torn screens, boarded-up windows, sheets for curtains, peeling paint, and litter that blows across yards into the streets" (p. 103). She asked the children to talk about the families that might live in the two houses. How did they think *other* people would describe the people living in the poor house? Twenty-two of the children believed that people would be disapproving of this family, and would see them in ways that included:

> "Messy," "dirty," "stupid or something because they ain't got a lot of money," "crazy cause they are poor," "ugly, nasty, disgusting, digging in their nose," "put knees on chairs, never tell people thank you," "not good people," "do drugs and just go around and steal trucks and steal cars," "don't take care of their family," "mean—could slap or punch somebody," "that they are gonna be troublemakers or something like that when they grow up," "mean, cruel, and unkind". (p. 108)

The children's words painted a different picture of how they themselves saw the family inside the poor house:

- They need money, they need paint, maybe a job. (p. 112)
- They might not have a lot of food because they gotta pay for the house payments and stuff. (p. 105)
- Somebody might just take their house away because they didn't pay rent. (p. 106)
- Maybe their parents are in the hospital and they don't know about it. (p. 106)
- [The child inside might be thinking] What will happen to me when I grow up? Will I have any friends? Will I graduate and who will I be when I grow up? (p. 107)

And what about life in other house? "They have beds. And sheets," said one child. "They can feed their children" (p. 106). Another conveyed a wishful childhood vision of the good life: "(They could ask their friends) to come over and if they want a popsicle—they would just go in their refrigerator and get a popsicle" (p. 106).

Life as a stigmatized outsider to mainstream culture produces self-perpetuating problems of its own, such as a lack of knowledge of the middle-class codes and soft skills that help people get ahead—what Pierre Bourdieu called *cultural capital*. These skills include basic elements of workplace protocol, such as on-time arrival, calling ahead when you are sick or otherwise unable to come to work, and otherwise notifying co-workers of your whereabouts. I encountered this in the students with whom I worked in an internship program. Part of the program involved securing internship experiences with local businesses, all of which began with an interview. One young woman had a series of reasons for not being able to attend her interview, which was rescheduled several times after she simply no-showed when the appointment time arrived. She was incredulous at my suggestion that she call the employer in such cases to cancel, and was mortified by the idea of leaving a voicemail message if the employer did not pick up the phone. I was incredulous that she was incredulous. What were ordinary interpersonal interactions to me seemed drastic and audacious to her. Shipler (2004) pointed out that it is unreasonable to expect that employers would not be annoyed by such behavior—of course they would be. However, he also quoted an employer who had a more nuanced perspective:

> [S]omething deeper may be going on, as Ann Brash observed. Having descended into poverty after growing up in middle-class comfort, she felt a smothering sense of worthlessness that gathered around her like a heavy cloak. "People who don't call when they can't come to work probably don't think they're important enough to matter," she explained simply. "It's more than low self-esteem, it's invisibility." (p. 129)

When they are able to obtain work, poor people and low-wage workers often continue to face a no-win situation. As unemployed people, and especially as people on welfare, they are the targets of undisguised disgust within American culture. They are exhorted to get a job as a way of exiting this devalued status and contributing to society, and to consider any work preferable to the indignity of not working. Yet low-wage work itself is utterly devalued and stigmatized. What is even worse is that it can also leave poor workers' families in a more dire economic predicament than they were in before, in that the minimum wage that poor workers receive is not enough to live on, yet it makes them ineligible for many of the medical and food-support benefits upon which their families depend. So, not only are these poor workers not able to surmount the stigma of poverty, they are in many ways poorer in material respects than when they were unemployed.

Katherine Newman (1999) observed the workings of this double-bind in the lives of her interviewees, several of whom worked at a fast-food chain that she called "Burger Barn." Among her participants, part of the stigma was manifested in the casual rudeness of customers. One participant, Natasha, said:

It's hard dealing with the public. There are good things, like old people. They sweet. But the younger people around my age are always snotty. Think they better than you because they not working at Burger Barn. They probably work at something better than you.

Another participant, Roberta, summarized her experiences:

The customers? Well, I had alcoholics, derelicts. People that are aggravated with life. I've had people that don't even have jobs curse me out. I've dealt with all kinds. Sometimes it would get to me. If a person yelled out [in front of] a lobby full of people, "Bitch, that's why you work at Burger Barn," I would say [to myself], "I'm probably making more than you and your mother." (p. 90)

## VALUES AND HOPES

The final theme that emerged for me from qualitative studies of the experiences of the poor had to do with the life-directing values that they expressed, and the hopes and dreams that they had for the future. I was struck both by the ways that these were shaped by poverty, and also the ways that they sounded like the same values embraced by Americans of every class.

Every study that I read provided evidence to debunk a widespread myth about the poor: that they do not wish to work. No author disputed the fact that there are *some* poor people who are content not to work, and that there are, moreover, some poor people who game the welfare system in order to secure benefits. Many interview participants also commented on this reality, and I have encountered it myself. I would simply add that there are people of every class who do not care to work and/or who find ways to game the system. For example, a U.S. Senate subcommittee recently determined that the wealthiest Americans are defrauding the government via high-level tax schemes of at least seven cents out of each dollar paid by honest taxpayers for a total theft of $70 billion per year (Johnston, 2006). I say "by at least that much" because the subcommittee also concluded that the cheating that they were able to uncover was just the tip of the iceberg. "The universe of offshore tax cheating has become so large that no one, not even the United States government, could go after all of it," concluded the senator who helped head up the investigation, Carl Levin of Michigan (Johnston, 2006, p. 5). Certainly, no one approves of such schemes by owning- or middle-class people, yet upon discovery, people in these classes are not uniformly stigmatized as lazy cheaters in the same way that poor people often are. We receive such news as the bad behavior of a few, not a typical characteristic of all people who share their social location. Yet the latter is precisely what many of us have internalized about the poor.

Along these lines, Newman (1999) discussed the work ethic that she observed among poor workers in the fast-food industry. Earning a minimum wage that did not lift them out of poverty, and working in a stigmatized job that brought them rude treatment from customers and mockery from their friends, these workers were "scraping the bottom of the employment barrel", as Newman described them (p. 113). In spite of this, their dedication to mainstream American-Dream values was underscored by their comments about what kept them going back to "Burger Barn" every day, as evidenced in a remark by Danielle:

> Regardless of what kind of work you do, you can still be respected. Ain't saying I'm ashamed of my job, but I wouldn't walk down the street wearing the uniform. . . . Guys know you work there will say, "Hi, Burger Barn." I ain't gonna lie and say I'm not ashamed, period. But I'm proud that I'm working. (p. 100)

Fine and Weis's (1999) participants made similar points. They affirmed overwhelmingly the value of education as a means of self-development and as a way to get ahead, yet participants of color were also skeptical about the about the chances that their educations could actually convert to a career. The authors affirmed the realism of their interviewees' doubts, citing national data indicating that White male high school dropouts employed full-time have approximately the same incomes as Black female college graduates with full-time jobs. Yet the commitment to work persisted, as suggested by the analysis offered by Fine and Weis's interviewee William:

> You got a lot of people in my neighborhood that's dealing in drugs and they're making money and they're comfortable, so it's hard to say what could change them. But the people that's having the problems, and just having hard times, can't find jobs. . . . Jobs. Some kind a, you know, you ask people what they want to do, they want to work. (p. 32)

One of Berrick's (1995) interviewees, Rebecca, wished for the experience, identity, and fulfillment of work as much as she wanted the income that it could bring. Talking about what she would do if she were suddenly rich, which she interpreted as being the recipient of $40,000 a year, she said:

> I'd still want to work. I don't know how much. But it would be boring not to work. I want to always do something, like work with kids. But if I could do anything, at least for a little while, I'd like to be an archeologist and go dig bones. That would be so fun. If somebody gave me $40,000 a year, I might do that. (p. 86)

Marta, one of Rank's (1994) interviewees, explained that, having been divorced by her husband and left with three young daughters, she had had no choice but to go on welfare to feed and clothe the children. Yet even her knowledge of this necessity did not mitigate the shame that she felt for needing public assistance, and she hoped someday to make amends for accepting it:

> And the hope that I have is . . . (*sigh*) after I start workin', I'll pay the state back somehow. I keep track of everything I get from them. And I already know how much I received last year from them. And this year . . . And this is the hope that I have. To know that I do not owe anything. That if ever someone asks me, "Did you ever receive welfare?" I say, "Yes. But I paid it back. It was a loan that I got." That's my hope, pretty much. (p. 99)

Finally, parenthood emerged within the stories of poor interviewees as both a higher calling and a saving grace. This theme is a fit with my experience: I remember two young women who had met because both lived in a nearby shelter for homeless teen mothers. Although they dreamed of careers that would take them far beyond the shelter, each insisted that she was not sorry that she had had a baby as young teen. Both of them said that their sons had helped them get their priorities straight, become more future-oriented, and "be less wild," as one of them put it. I did not know quite how to take this in. Having babies at age 14 and 15 was not compatible with the goals that the young women described—they had both dropped out of high school. Was this their way of rationalizing what seemed to be a misstep, now that there was no going back?

What I did not understand is what Kathryn Edin and Maria Kefalis (2005) learned from their conversations with 162 poor women: that life before children can be a lonely struggle against the chaos, deprivation, violence, failure, hopelessness, and sense of shame that are part of life in poverty:

> The redemptive stories our mothers tell speak to the primacy of the mothering role, how it can become virtually the only source of identity and meaning in a young woman's life. There is an odd logic to the statements mothers made when we asked them to imaging life without children: "I'd be dead or in jail," "I'd still be out partying," "I'd be messed up on drugs," or "I'd be nowhere at all." These mothers, we discovered, almost never see children as bringing them hardship; instead, the manage to credit virtually every bit of good in their lives to the fact that they have children—they believe motherhood has "saved" them. (p. 11)

In an unpredictable world where many things seemed to be beyond their control, men and women alike reported parenthood to be an anchoring connection to each other and to the baby, even when the men were not part of the mother's or the child's daily life. Babies brought their mothers the possibility of relational intimacy, and the opportunity to give and receive love openly. They introduced new meaning to life, and imposed a welcome demand for order and planning. And they were a source of joy. "I didn't know I could *be* so happy!" said Lenise, one of the participants in the study (p. 43). Kyra, a teenager, reported that her son gives her "something to look forward to. Like when I don't even have enough energy to get out of bed in the morning . . . I know I have to. When I turn over and look at him, it's like I'm trying to give him a better life, so I gotta get up and I gotta do" (p. 172). Similarly, Alison, who had been a heroin addict, said:

> There was nothing to live for other than the next day getting high. [My life had] no *point*, there was no *joy*. I had lost all my friends—my friends were totally disgusted with me—I was about to lose my job, [and ] I ended up dropping out of college. . . . Now I feel like, "I have a beautiful little girl!" I'm *excited* when I get up in the morning! (p. 172)

## REFLECTING ON THESE STUDIES

When I went to a poor community to work as a psychologist, I had not read any of the studies whose results I present here. Certainly, I knew that life in poverty was hard, as we all do, and I felt a great deal of sympathy for people trying to survive those hardships. Yet, there were a hundred large and small things that I did not understand about community members and their lives. I have mentioned some of them in the course of this discussion, and I will return to them in the next chapter, but there are literally countless more.

I remember the brief flurries of amazement when people described having missed out on important appointments, events, or opportunities because they did not have money for *one* subway ride. Visiting the GED classes, I assumed without a second thought that the distracted-looking students that I observed were most likely just the ones who were uninterested or for some other reason checked-out, like kids in my school—and I am sure that some of them were. Then one day, one of them fell out of his desk. "Probably hasn't eaten for a while," said one of teachers matter-of-factly. She was connected to the community grapevine and knew his family's circumstances. She dispatched a co-worker to go to the store for a bagel. I also remember marveling at the kids' ability to seem impervious to even the coldest winter weather. (I might have even commented about this to a co-worker.) Here it was January, and they came to school wearing sweatshirts—they didn't bother with coats at all. That's what it means to be young, I thought. Then one day, one of the young women came into my office in a down jacket. "Hey!" she said delightedly, taking it off and showing it to me before hanging it on my coat rack. "I've never had a big warm coat before!" She had received it from a coat drive.

The fact that people are literally without food and coats in American cities may sound obvious, but, in my ignorance, I was surprised by it. I learned layers and layers of lessons from these and other interactions as I was repeatedly thrown back on my assumptions about who poor community people were and what my work with them might be like. The barriers to moving beyond this ignorance have been formidable, and I will return to them in the next chapter.

# 5

# PSYCHOTHERAPY AND TRAINING IN THE CONTEXT OF POVERTY: BARRIERS AND GROWING EDGES

[Y]ou don't care if you eat dirt, but you'll take a lot of crap to make sure that your kids get what they need. My therapist couldn't understand that. . . . In her life, there has always been enough for everybody and that's a big difference.
—Bonnie Chalifoux (1996, p. 30)

Generally, the professionals operated with a healthy dose of myth-tainted information but virtually no direct experience of poor people.
—Welfare mother Theresa Funicello (1993, p. 62)

Many therapists will never work with a person living in poverty, as poor people do not frequently appear within the caseloads of mental health practitioners in private practice. Yet, poor clients are seen by independent clinicians who accept Medicaid, and by therapists or therapists-in-training in hospital outpatient clinics, community health centers, and similar settings. In my opinion, conventional psychotherapeutic modalities are not the only or even necessarily the best vehicles by which to offer mental health interventions in the context of poverty, an idea upon which I will elaborate in the following chapter. Nevertheless, these interventions are standard in the settings in which most of us currently practice and train, and I believe that such services can be improved for the benefit of poor clients when therapists understand the implications of classism within their work.

What classist barriers should therapists be on the lookout for as they practice in the context of poverty? And how can they and their supervisees improve the effectiveness of their practice with poor clients? In this chapter, I will apply the previous discussions to psychotherapy practice and training. I begin with a discussion of cultural competence around social class by describing my own encounters with classism during my work in a poor community (Smith, 2005). Afterward, I discuss some areas for training and continuing education that clinicians can apply to their own practice or to their supervisory work with therapists-in-training.

## EXPLORING CLASSIST ATTITUDINAL BARRIERS TO PSYCHOTHERAPEUTIC COMPETENCE

When middle-class therapists go into poor communities to work, they can expect to encounter characteristic obstacles to the best implementation of their practice. Among these obstacles are attitudinal barriers associated with their own lack of class-related awareness. Working as a psychologist in a community center located in one of the nation's poorest urban neighborhoods, I experienced such barriers repeatedly. They came in the form of blind spots, classist stereotyping, and feeling overwhelmed. I should note that I was not only a middle-class psychologist in a poor neighborhood, I was also a White psychologist in a mostly Latino and African American neighborhood, so my attention to cultural competence around race and ethnicity was equally vital, as was the necessity to identify personal and professional barriers that related to my own racism. Fortunately, supervision and guidance have been available to me with regard to those issues: Since graduate school, I have benefited from the rich multicultural counseling literature (e.g., Carter, 1995; Ivey, D'Andrea, Ivey, & Simek-Morgan, 2002; Ponterotto, Casas, Suzuki, & Alexander, 2001; Sue, D. W. & Sue. D., 2007), from explications of Whiteness as an identity (e.g., Helms, 1990; McIntosh, 1988), and from many workshops, seminars, and focused supervisory experiences. In fact, in our community center, staff members attended training sessions on racism, and we had weekly meetings for the sole purpose of enacting antiracist principles in our work.

Analogous opportunities for training and professional development with regard to classism are not readily identifiable, nor had I ever even thought of seeking them out. In retrospect, the class-related attitudinal barriers that I have encountered can be described according to four overlapping themes.

1. *Poor people are forced to contend with so many overwhelming day-to-day problems that they have no use for what a psychologist can offer; what they need is assistance with identifying important basic resources and problem-solving.* This attitudinal barrier, which was one of the earliest that I encountered in myself, is

essentially classist while containing a grain of truth. The truth is that the poorest clients withstand existences that are so tumultuous, precarious, and bleak that discussions of concrete survival strategies must indeed be part of the work. For example, a young man from the community had fallen behind on the rent he paid for a single unheated room and, having hidden from his landlord for months, now had to decide where to go. We discussed such grim alternatives as the notoriously unlivable Emergency Assistance Unit (the first stage in the shelter system) or living in his friend's parked car, which he had done the last time he was homeless. We spent many hours following the trail of phone calls, office visits, lost faxes, and missing files that eventually led to temporary public rent assistance, a meaningful outcome that brought profound relief. Yet, when the young man spontaneously assessed the usefulness of his counseling experience months later, what he emphasized was the opportunity to talk about loneliness, relationships, and the problems in his family and their impact on him—the same sorts of issues, obviously, that people everywhere in society explore. Space and time in which to introspect, analyze obstacles, and consider alternatives were not available in his life. "I needed something like this," he said. (Loneliness, by the way, is an issue that I heard mentioned frequently in the course of my work; the first individual client I ever had in this community was a 23-year-old man who sat down, looked at me, and said, "Nobody knows me, miss.")

Do I imply that having someone to talk to compares with the importance of having a roof over one's head or takes the place of advocating for the policy changes that will put roofs over more people's heads? Absolutely not. My point is that, time after time, I was thrown back on my own implicit assumptions about the poor. I realized that, knowing their lives are difficult, I had effectively reduced their existences to the surmounting of those difficulties, dehumanizing them in the process. I would have never have given credence to the more blatant misperception held among some service providers that poor people are incapable of insight (Lott, 2002), but I would have said (and have said) that what poor and working-class people need is economic opportunity and social justice. Given the enormity of that need, what does a psychotherapist have to offer? The answer is that, along with a commitment to "support public policy and programs that ensure adequate income . . . for poor people and all working families" (APA, 2000, Resolution 10), psychotherapists can offer poor people what they offer everyone else: an opportunity to become differently and more fully conscious of their feelings and actions, to be more aware of the societal forces at work in their lives, to imagine and reach for new goals, and to do so within the parameters of a safe interpersonal alliance. When I have been willing to learn and be clinically flexible, I have seen again and again that poor people make the same use of such opportunities that middle-class and wealthy clients do; the difference is that they are otherwise forced to devote much more of their energies toward securing the basics of existence.

2. *Poor people contend with so many overwhelming day-to-day problems that psychologists who work with them can experience their own interventions, even when helpful, as diminished in significance.* This barrier overlaps with or perhaps underlies the one described above. My first misperception had been that poor people would have little capacity to use psychological services because the circumstances of their lives are so difficult and taxing. As that assumption was discredited through experience, I noticed a disquieting new doubt creeping into my awareness—that my services did not seem quite as valuable or potent as they had before. When I had a mostly middle-class and wealthy clientele, I was working with people whose distress, relatively speaking, was proportionately more available to my interventions. When people have reasonably comfortable lives in which the basics—food, shelter, health care, personal safety—are in place, the relief of psychological conflicts or symptoms can leave them feeling quite well. Life cannot be perfect for any client, of course, and it is the clients themselves who actualize the changes that produce relief—the psychologist does not take credit for that. Nevertheless, a psychologist treating a middle-class client has the opportunity to facilitate a therapeutic effort that returns the client to a largely satisfactory life. This, in turn, leaves the psychologist feeling efficacious, and all parties are suitably gratified. This moment is experienced differently when one's client lives in poverty. Even when they have made the best possible use of psychological services, poor clients frequently depart the office to resume a difficult life of sobering obstacles that a psychologist cannot touch. Against the backdrop of these obstacles, I found myself arriving at session's end feeling unproductive and disoriented, even when the work seemed to help with a client's particular emotional concern.

A conversation with a 65-year-old community member helped me make sense of this impasse. This senior citizen had been a participant in the center's internship program, which included a focus on interpersonal and sociocultural awareness, so we had shared many discussions of such topics. As we talked about psychology's lack of service to poor people and my work in the center, he observed that, indeed, what poor people require for survival are major changes such as the institution of a living wage and improvements in public education. However, he also believed that to conclude that psychological services were therefore not worthwhile in poor communities was classist and that my feelings of diminished importance in the face of poor clients' unremitting struggles were "[my] issue." As I thought about it, I realized that the issue was that my sense of my own effectiveness and worth as a professional was shaken by the persistent presence of pervasive, elemental, and often dire systemic problems that my clients and I could not alter in the course of our work together. Some portion of this confusion, I believe, comes from disappointment and frustration related to our good intentions to be helpful; some of it comes from the jolt to our professional self-concept that occurs when we repeatedly fail to see clients return to lives that are largely satisfactory. A third factor is that these encounters force psychologists to confront the different positions that they and their clients occupy in society, a barrier in and of itself, as I will describe next.

3. *Working in a poor community takes away the comfort of not knowing how poor people live.* Most of us who are middle-class or wealthy only occasionally brush up against the reality of poverty in this country. Often, this is an indirect encounter: I might, for example, feel sincerely moved by a book or news account, by the sight of a homeless person on the street, or by an afternoon spent volunteering in a soup kitchen. Feeling genuine sadness for the deprivation I had seen, I could return to the relative comfort of my existence. The poor, of course, were still all around me, busing tables, cleaning offices, unpacking truckloads of flowers outside florists' shops, and delivering take-out food, but now they melted into the familiar structures of my life. I was free to pay the delivery man and have dinner without necessarily giving much thought to the world he went home to.

Working in a poor community undermines the ignorance that contributes to this bliss. Aponte (1994) observed that one can be "dragged down by the emotional and family devastation, the educational failures, criminal convictions, and domestic violence that so often pervade poor families that are losing or have lost hope, meaning, and purpose" (p. 10). Not all poor families have lost hope: Daily, I met community members who remained courageous, spirited, and loving in the face of tremendous hardship. I also saw, daily, people being crushed beneath the weight of society's ills and failed systems: racism; persistent involuntary unemployment; jobs that do not pay a hardworking adult enough to live on; emergency rooms bursting with people who have no place else to turn for health care; deteriorating public housing; overcrowded, underresourced schools; unpredictable eruptions of violence among both acquaintances and strangers; inconsistent police presence and protection; streets where gang members openly sell drugs, but where there are few places to buy groceries or clothing. These people see us every day, when they turn on their televisions or come to our neighborhoods to wait tables or clean homes. We rarely see them—and we do not want to.

I do not imply that this avoidance is conscious. Javier and Herron (2002) suggested that this distancing is the result of unconscious fear of identification with the poor and negative stereotyping, and I agree. I believe that we avert our gaze from the poor as an unconscious way of preserving our ability to enjoy our relative good fortune amid an unequal distribution of resources. When we from the middle class go into poor neighborhoods to work, we must admit into consciousness a vivid comprehension of the disparity between our lives and theirs. Once we have done so, it is difficult to conjure up the oblivion that previously sheltered us from this awareness, and any unexamined assumptions that may have reassured us—that the poor lead contented, uncomplicated lives or that people are poor because they do not wish to work or that each of us has what we deserve—are suddenly exposed to daylight and lose their power. It becomes impossible not to know that a few subway stops away from cafés full of smiling middle-class faces is what amounts to a third-world country.

The parallels between class privilege and skin color privilege and the pressures to avoid awareness of them are clear. As McIntosh (1988) wrote:

> For me, white privilege has turned out to be an elusive and fugitive subject. The pressure to avoid it is great, for in facing it I must give up the myth of meritocracy. If these things are true, this is not such a free country; one's life is not what one makes it; many doors open for certain people through no virtues of their own. These perceptions mean also that my moral condition is not what I had been led to believe. (p. 9)

Psychologists are, of course, not immune to such pressures, and psychology as a field does not stand apart from the sociopolitical power structure: Cushman (1990), Prilleltensky (1994), and Sampson (1993), among others, have written about professional and academic psychology as both products of and bolsters to the status quo. Such pressures make their influence felt on psychologists as individuals and collectively as a discipline and can be understood as hindrances to service to the poor.

4. *Conventional psychological services are neither familiar to nor widely accepted in the cultures of many poor and working-class communities, so that even poor people who could benefit will not be likely to use them.* This is another barrier with a basis in reality that demands conceptual, technical, clinical, and personal flexibility in psychologists who face it. In my career, I had been an unequivocal supporter of the importance of multicultural competence, and, in this community, my theoretical commitment was put to the test: It quickly became apparent that I would need to be flexible, culturally competent, and innovative all day, every day. Community members who met me were congenial and welcoming; none, however, rushed to claim any of the week's worth of 50-minute hours that I made available. I had expected this on an intellectual level, yet now I felt uncertain about how to proceed. I had never realized the extent to which the conventional parameters of mainstream psychological practice reassured me of my competence

and professional identity; now, as I began tentatively to consider reshaping the way that I worked with people to better fit their needs, the ghosts of old supervisors whispered dangerously in my ear.

The comfort and confidence that my former supervisors and I derived from these parameters should not have surprised me, as the culture of the psychologist's office is the culture of Whiteness and class privilege (Javier & Herron, 2002). Operating within the confines of that culture, I felt at home, and using the techniques, guidelines, and customs that my clients and I had tacitly agreed on assured me of my professional fitness. Outside that culture, I initially felt unanchored and a bit directionless, as my new clients did not seem to be playing by the rules that I was used to. Community members were friendly but politely uninterested in speaking with me on the basis of my being an impersonal professional stranger with expertise that related to mental dysfunction. My schedule book, which had filled so quickly in independent practice and counseling centers, lay empty on the receptionist's desk.

I continued to hope, however, that there was a way for me to be useful on behalf of this community. I believed that I had skills to contribute, but I seemed to need a different understanding of *how* to contribute them. Clearly, the answer was not to keep trying to do the same things in the same way, but what new approaches could I try? I consulted openly with community members on these questions, and the responses that I received encouraged me to move out of my office to become more involved in the life of the community. This included being more broadly involved with the alternative high school that the community center operated. The more I participated in center, school, and community events, the more participation I received in my own interventions, which I began creating after asking people what kinds of things they would like to work on, and in what formats. I presented workshops and classroom discussion groups on topics like peer pressure and the interface between societal stereotyping and emotional well-being. I developed a discussion group on the "holiday blues" as poor families told me how it felt to be surrounded by ads showing Christmas trees ringed with mountains of presents, holiday tables piled with food, and new cars in the driveway with giant red bows tied around them. I offered a media literacy workshop for teenagers in which we examined the ways that corporate entities and the entertainment industry were teaching them to see themselves and their community. I partnered with one of the center staff members to conduct a young people's discussion group about teen fatherhood.

Gradually, people began to drop by my office to talk, and then they began to schedule times to follow up. Some clients scheduled appointments weekly; most came less frequently than that; a few stopped by to touch base almost daily during weeks of crisis. Others suggested the initiation of new interventions and groups: After 5 months of individual meetings, one woman ventured, "I know now that I want to be able to talk to other people like me, people who have been mentally ill and homeless. People who nobody loves." Many community members had contact with me through center programming exclusively. The unclaimed time in my schedule had disappeared.

As I mentioned earlier, I offered community members essentially the same opportunities that I offered clients in middle-class settings. I was clearly *not* doing conventional psychotherapy, however. A number of descriptors represented my professional functions: counseling, psychoeducation, prevention psychology, community psychology. This effort eventually felt integrative rather than directionless; it is also in good accord with multicultural psychologists, who have long contended that the conventional roles and behaviors of psychological practice are "culture bound and potentially unhelpful and oppressive to culturally different clients" (D. W. Sue et al., 1998, p. 81).

Discovering and confronting these classist barriers has been just one aspect of the process of self-understanding and accountability that began during those years. It is a process that not only changes us as professionals, it changes us as people: For many of us, once we begin to see the structural workings of oppression, we can never *not* see it again. Once we begin to notice the ways that sociohistorical systems—racism, classism, sexism, heterosexism, ableism—have shaped our everyday thoughts and behaviors, it becomes difficult to coast along as though our good intentions absolve us of responsibility for them. My learning curve continues to be steep and multifaceted, and I have had the chance to continue it by extending it to my supervisory work with trainees in the context of poverty. In the next section, I offer five areas for growth that have been important to that work and my own learning.

## ADDRESSING CLASSISM AND POVERTY
## WITHIN PSYCHOTHERAPY AND SUPERVISION

I hope that sharing my experiences can guide practicing therapists in thinking about the potential influence of unexamined classist attitudes in their work—but I also believe that there are ways that we can shape the training of new therapists to incorporate class awareness from the beginning as we continue to educate ourselves. Currently, there is little in the way of graduate curricula focusing on social class and the cultural preparation of therapists to work in the context of poverty, and the development of such coursework will be an important step in helping to address the corresponding gap in the mental health field's knowledge and skill base. However, the creation and implementation of new coursework at the graduate level will not be possible for every training program, and it can be a lengthy process even when the possibility exists. In the meantime, clinical supervisors have a critical front-line role to play in helping their trainees work through, if not avoid, the kinds of barriers that I have experienced.

How can supervisors guide trainees in conceptualizing and implementing their work with poor clients, whose life circumstances and social experiences are often vastly different from their own? And how can they increase their own competence in this area? Harry Aponte (1994), a social worker and family therapist with a career-long commitment to poor families, explained that "therapy with the poor must have all the sophistication of the best psychological therapies. It must also have the insight of the social scientist and the drive of the community activist" (p. 9). Few of us, however, have received clinical training that integrated the development of our therapeutic skills with a sociocultural analysis of social class and an ability to incorporate and address the needs of poor communities. Without this foundation, supervisors who wish to integrate issues of class and poverty into their work with students (as well as in their own work) may not have a sense of where to begin.

I offer, therefore, five interrelated growing edges where therapists can take action with regard to their work with trainees and also their own continuing education (Smith, 2009). They are areas for learning that therapists should be ready to encounter and explore as poverty and social class gain salience within the context of their work. Incorporating these suggestions may be challenging at first, given that our own training likely did not address them. This does not, of course, constitute a reason not to go forward; this state of affairs merely parallels the position in which our field found itself years ago with regard to raising the racial awareness of practitioners a few years ago.

1. *Take action to supplement your own knowledge base with regard to social class and poverty.* Most often, neither graduate curricula nor ordinary life experience has prepared therapists for encounters with the deprivations, humiliations, and crises that characterize the lives of the poor, and I have described the many knowledge gaps and misinterpretations that characterized my introduction into a poor community. Similarly, Janna Smith (2000) discussed the ways in which therapists may be stunned by the realities of their poor clients' lives, ranging from the ever-present threat of homelessness to the economic and social isolation of poor urban neighborhoods to the "Kafkaesque nature of the welfare system" (p. 72). Describing poverty as a traumatizing, crisis-to-crisis existence, Smith also presented some of the psychological correlates of these experiences, such as constant, enormous shame that inspires periods of furious perfectionism

alternating with exhausted collapse. Writing of his work in community psychiatry, Dumont (1992) described the "whirlpool of poverty" (p. 4) that caught his clients in its currents of unemployment, racism, malnutrition, and violence. Dumont discussed his clients' internalization of societal attitudes toward the poor, and the psychological double-bind in which poor people find themselves as a consequence: the simultaneous experience of "both guilt (the feeling of having done something bad) and powerlessness (the feeling of being unable to do anything effective)" (p. 8).

Baker (1996) outlined the some of the stark differences between the occupational worlds of working-class and middle-class people, differences of which many therapists are unaware and may therefore misinterpret. "It may seem outrageous that people could be fired for being genuinely sick, be required to ask for permission and wait for a replacement in order to use the rest room, [or] be denied permission to make or receive personal phone calls," Baker explained (p. 19). By way of example, Baker cited a story of a therapist who initiated a hospitalization for a client who had recently filed a claim against her employer, and who now believed that she was being followed; the therapist diagnosed her as having paranoid delusions and the client was subsequently placed on medication. Union representatives later pointed out that employers often have workers followed under similar circumstances, and that it would be unusual if the client did not suspect that she was being followed.

Helpful resources exist by which therapists and their supervisors can deepen their understanding of social class, the circumstances faced by poor Americans, and the implications of both for clinical work. With regard to the former, publications associated with the nonprofit resource center Class Action (www.classism.org) provide a comprehensive, accessible overview of the parameters of social class. Their publications include the books *Class Matters* (Leondar-Wright, 2005) and *The Color of Wealth* (Lui, Robles, Leondar-Wright, Brewer, & Adamson, 2005), the second of which addresses the historical and present-day intersections of classism and racism. A second book with the same title, *Class Matters*, was compiled from a series of articles by correspondents of The *New York Times* (2005), and covers a wide range of class experiences derived from both rural and urban settings. Perhaps one of the most evocative treatments of social class is contained in the book *Where We Stand: Class Matters* (2000), by feminist scholar and social critic bell hooks. Telling readers "I have long struggled to make sense of class in my life" (p. viii), hooks goes on to explore the intersections of class with race and gender and the moral implications of contemporary class realities. The ethnographic studies referenced in Chapter 4 of this book will be useful in conveying a viewpoint derived from the experiences of women, men, and adolescents living in poverty.

2. *Take action to develop your awareness of social class identity, particularly so-cial class privilege.* When people with privileged identities begin to expand their awareness of oppression, they often find that the most intuitive part of the work is to feel sympathy for the plight of the oppressed, which is certainly appropri-ate. The more important and demanding part of the work, however, is to locate oneself within the larger system that advantages some groups as it disadvantages others, and to locate the attitudes and beliefs that support that system within oneself. Exploring a privileged identity for the first time can be challenging and painful under the best of circumstances; exploring class privilege presents added difficulties related to the absence of class awareness in American society. This exploration must go beyond sympathy or guilt regarding those who are impacted by classism, although those feelings are an understandable part of the process. Rather, comprehending classism and class privilege means identifying the policies, procedures, attitudes, beliefs, and taken-for-granted social mecha-nisms that place obstacles in the paths of poor and working-class people as they simultaneously advantage middle-class and wealthy individuals (Smith, 2008).

Chalifoux (1996) interviewed working-class women about their psycho-therapeutic experiences and concluded that when therapists and clients are from different class backgrounds, they often view basic life experiences and decisions quite differently. The women recounted, for example, that their therapists seemed to have difficulty incorporating clients' precarious financial circumstances into the therapeutic context, with one participant wondering why her therapist could not understand that "freedom of choice takes money" (p. 30). "I did not find that these therapists were particularly unsympathetic or knowingly unkind," Chalifoux clarified. "What I did find was that the therapists . . . were unaware of their own class values" (p. 32). Therapists can develop awareness of their class-related values and perspectives by applying the knowledge they acquire to their own everyday experiences and the class references contained therein. Some of these are readily apparent, such as the conspicuous wearing of designer logos and popular culture's fascination with the activities of owning-class people. Others are less obvious; Baker (1996) called into question the taken-for-granted American upward mobility dialogue that often devalues physical labor and the trade professions, asking, "Why is it better to be a therapist than a carpenter?" (p. 21). Negatively connoted expressions heard in everyday speech include *low-class* (and its opposite, *classy*), *low-rent*, and *trailer trash.*

Such considerations of class identity and privilege entail particular com-plexities for mental health professionals, as described by Baker (1996). She pointed out that although being a psychologist does not prevent one from being a person of color or a woman, it is not possible to become a psychologist and truly remain a member of the working class, given that the most defining aspects of class identity relate to occupation: "One may be from the working class, or even attempt to work in the interests of the working class, but as a therapist or psychologist one's relations to the world and the world of work are fundamentally different" (p. 16). Baker went on to point out that the implications of class transition are often ignored by psychotherapists with poor or working-class roots. This failure has important countertransferential implications, in that therapists who cannot acknowledge their own privileged status, or who have not dealt with the emotional issues that may accompany a change in class position, cannot fully appreciate their clients' experiences. Therapists also need to assess the degree to which the theories that guide their work reflect this awareness; Lott (2002) observed that "[p]sychological theories are preoccupied with people who are like those who construct the theories, that is, those in the middle class (and primarily European Americans)" (p. 100), resulting in perspectives that are not always relevant for clients living in poverty.

Becoming aware of one's class privilege in this way is analogous to other aspects of multicultural training with which therapists may be more familiar. For example, multicultural competence requires that White clinicians not only understand the damaging impact of racism on the well-being of people of color, but also that they address the advantageous effect that skin color privilege has had in their own lives. Peggy McIntosh's groundbreaking Wellesley College working paper on White privilege (1988) paved the way for countless White psychologists and others to begin unpacking the "invisible knapsack" of privileges that accrued to them merely through the accident of having been born with White skin. Although McIntosh's examination of White privilege contained many vital insights, perhaps the most powerful and viscerally moving portion for many White readers was her list of 46 concrete examples of unearned privileges that she enjoyed on a daily basis. Clearly, an in-depth analysis of class privilege is a complex undertaking, but a similar listing or other straightforward resource with regard to the privileges associated with class membership could serve as a springboard for such discussions between supervisors and supervisees.

A small number of authors in the social sciences and other fields have offered inventories and other training resources that, together, begin to make manifest the experience of class privilege. One of the earliest was a 1997 pamphlet called "The Invisibility of Upper Class Privilege" published by the Women's Theological Center (WTC) in Boston (available at www.thewtc.org/Invisibility_of_Class_Privilege.pdf). Citing McIntosh's work as their inspiration, the authors presented an extensive list of class privileges that included "I can hide family secrets and family failures behind the doors of my home" (WTC, 1997, p. 1) and "I have the freedom to be unaware of the living conditions of others" (p. 2). Yeskel and Leondar-Wright (1997) presented a four-module curriculum to guide personal exploration of classism and class privilege. The curriculum includes a class-background inventory exercise that, rather than presenting class privileges outright, derives them from a series of discussion prompts; a second workshop curriculum was offered by Leondar-Wright in 2005. Most recently, Liu, Pickett, and Ivey (2007) addressed counselors specifically as they developed a list of self-statements corresponding to White middle-class privilege. These statements included "I can be assured that I have adequate housing for myself and my family" and "My family can survive an illness of one or more members" (p. 205). The authors also presented a case example to illustrate the incorporation of class-related considerations within counseling practice.

Meriting special mention among materials for use by supervisors and trainees is a comprehensive new resource recently made available by the APA Task Force on Resources for the Inclusion of Social Class in Psychology Curricula (APA, 2008). This task force prepared a compendium of scholarly references, classroom exercises, course syllabi, and popular media resources related to issues of social class. It presents, therefore, an opportunity for a multidimensional exploration of class, classism, and poverty that should not be missed by mental health professionals and trainees interested in the fullest development of their multicultural and social justice competence.

3. *Actively support supervisees in processing a "realm of trauma."* When I was practicing in the community-based setting that I have described, I remember having the impression during my first year that the life stories of every single client whom I had seen were marked by tangible, life-altering, safety-threatening disruptions and crises—stints in the shelter system, the up-close witnessing of one or more murders, run-ins with the judicial system and/or incarceration itself, and physical victimization or assault. Suspecting that this must be an exaggeration, I checked my records and discovered that it was completely accurate. I was particularly struck by the fact that, often, these crises were not what brought the clients to counseling. Rather, they were simply features of life in the poorest communities, recounted during the taking of the client's history. To say the least, these had not been common milestones in the lives of the clients with whom I worked during the first decade of my career, spent in college counseling centers and independent practice. I was accustomed to working with clients whose presenting problems were largely relational, emotional, developmental, or psychological in nature; now I had clients who spoke of food running out and sleeping in cars.

Few psychologists have written about the personal experience and clinical implications of working with clients who live in poverty. One of the few who has is Neil Altman (1995), who described the unfamiliar "realm of trauma" (p.

1) that psychotherapists enter when they go to work in poor communities. In particular, Janna Smith (2000) described the trauma of poverty as having two overarching themes. The first of these involves the literal, dire, survival-oriented, day-to-day crises faced by poor families who are without basic resources and adequate protection from danger. The second is more psychological in nature:

> [W]hen poverty exists in a context of affluence, people tend to feel alienated, shamed, and angered by their marginalization. Attempting to survive in extreme circumstances, people without money make decisions which are difficult for outsiders to comprehend and thus are subject to simplistic maligning—a process which increases alienation. (p. 74)

Another part of this sense of shame, Smith went on to explain, derives from the humiliating, continuous involvement with bureaucracies that poverty necessitates. Poor families, she pointed out, are evaluated and re-evaluated for eligibility through a never-ending succession of office visits and unannounced inspections. Moreover, in my experience, these visits can be additionally frustrating in that they frequently prove fruitless in the end. Because necessary files cannot be located in the crowded office, or the appointments have fallen so far behind schedule that one's turn never comes, people find themselves constrained to repeat the entire process, often under time pressure and with children in tow. My other anecdotal observation is that these visits can be the occasion of overtly rude treatment, as welfare offices often seem understaffed by exhausted workers who themselves feel harassed from every direction.

These are not, typically, the situations faced by the hypothetical clients portrayed in graduate students' textbooks. Furthermore, as Altman (1995) observed, most therapists have been able to avoid specific knowledge and direct experience of poverty in their own lives. The result of this encounter, then, can be a personal and professional shock to the sensibilities of supervisees as they are faced with presenting problems and clients' narratives to which their training seems to bear little relevance, and that are moreover profoundly distressing on a human level. Beginning as well as more experienced clinicians can find themselves feeling disoriented, overwhelmed, and useless as clients leave their offices to resume the daily struggles that therapists may wonder if they themselves could surmount.

Supervisors can help supervisees stay oriented and engaged by emphasizing certain aspects of the process. The first is fairly concrete and involves pursuing missing information and knowledge regarding their poor clients' lives, which can help students feel less overwhelmed by the unfamiliar terrain of poverty. Psychologists are often not well-informed about the policies and procedures surrounding issues such as low-income housing and food-stamp eligibility; however, their colleagues who are social workers often are. These colleagues,

who may even be co-workers within the same clinic setting, can be valuable resources for learning about benefits and community issues. Needless to say, community members themselves are also excellent sources of knowledge; I became
acquainted with a senior citizens group in the community where I worked who
became my informal advisory board.

Second, supervisees need to understand that their feelings of helplessness
in the face of poor clients' struggles must be examined critically. Although the
survival-related obstacles faced by poor clients are indeed towering and life-
shaping, therapists can find them so disorienting that they fail to address sufficiently the emotional, existential, and self-reflective dimensions of clients' experiences—which are often what clients have come to talk about. As Janna Smith
(2000) explained, a therapist who works with poor clients "must witness an unremitting world, and experience her own grief and pain. When people have so
little and are suffering so much, it is hard not to feel both horrified and guilty.
Unrecognized, such feelings distort the therapist's judgment" (p. 86). As I mentioned, I have encountered versions of this stumbling block many times myself.

Third, the humanitarian distress that is engendered in many supervisees
through contact with poverty must be processed in supervision. Many supervisees will experiences stages of reaction characterized by disbelief, helplessness,
grief, and anger, for which supervisors need to listen actively. In my experience,
supervisees sometimes hesitate to fully explore these feelings with supervisors
because they are not certain that issues and feelings related to the sociocultural
context qualify as clinically relevant material, or that they believe that clinical
supervisors expect them to "just deal with it," as one student said to me. Phoebe
Schnitzer (1996), who has written of her clinical experiences in a poor community, characterized the way that these perceptions can play out:

> In a clinical seminar, beginning trainees were asked to identify which con-
> versations that they had with clients felt like "doing therapy" and which con-
> versations did not. Discussions of trauma or painful affect were seen as "real
> therapy," with past material taking precedence over present. . . . Often omitted
> altogether were matters of money and work, and matters of hardship and dis-
> crimination. (p. 580)

Beyond the sharing of these issues and feelings, what framework for analysis
can we offer supervisees? A social justice framework for psychological practice
integrates contextual considerations with individual issues, and the implementation of such a framework within supervision is the subject of the next section.

4. *Enact a social justice framework within your supervisory work.* The personal
is the political: This phrase was first heard in the 1970s during the Third Wave

of the women's movement, and if therapists-in-training have not grappled with its truth before working with people living in poverty, they will do so now. When supervisees go into poor communities to work, they witness through their clients the precariousness of life without health insurance; they observe the impact on poor communities of predatory businesses like check-cashing stores and "rent-to-own" furniture companies (Eckholm, 2006); they see firsthand the consequences of the environmental racism and classism that make poor communities the waste-dumping grounds for the nation (Bullard, 2005). For many supervisees, these revelations inspire more than sympathy for clients. They also inspire observations and questions about the social, cultural, and political systems that maintain these conditions. How it is that adequate health care is not available for all American families? Why does the minimum wage level allow an adult to work full-time and still live in poverty? Why are schools in poor communities overcrowded and underresourced at the same time that education is promoted as a pathway out of poverty for poor children (Kozol, 2005)?

Similar spoken and unspoken questions are often present in the supervisory context, whether the form of oppression in question is based on class, race, gender, sexual orientation, or physical ability. The pivotal supervisory decision is in choosing how to address them: If we talk about systems of oppression during clinical supervision, are we getting off-track? The decision to conceptualize and treat clients impacted by oppression *without consideration of oppression itself is a values-based, political choice,* as is the decision to do the opposite. The latter choice, which will I outline here, builds upon the social justice psychological perspective that I have elaborated previously. This perspective affirms that when we choose to leave oppression unacknowledged, we inadvertently support an unjust status quo by helping to obscure it.

At its most basic level, a social justice model for supervision makes room within the case conceptualization process for supervisees' observations, feelings, and questions about systemic sociocultural aspects and origins of client distress, and does not consider these conversations to be digressions from the clinical work. In so doing, this model for supervision can accomplish three interrelated ends. One is simply a more complete and accurate case conceptualization. Writing of their work with poor and marginalized women, Smyth, Goodman, and Glenn (2006) describe the nature of mental health issues among their clients:

> Much of poor and marginalized women's suffering represents the nexus of failed social policy, overstressed families or communities, individual vulnerabilities and illness, and poor judgment exercised at critical moments. . . . Yet, low-income women who present to the mental health system with symptoms of depression or anxiety are often offered treatment that assumes that with the right medication and increased insight achieved through counseling, their lives

will improve significantly. . . . Women then blame themselves for their suffering and are taught, once again, to feel ashamed of their situations and their
emotional distress. Eventually, the external brutalities of poverty may become
internalized as self-loathing. (p. 492)

The last sentence in this passage illustrates a second, related advantage of
social justice supervision. Not only can poor clients' circumstances and symptoms be understood more comprehensively when contextual elements are considered, supervisors and students who do so can better avoid unintentional col-
lusion with internalized oppression among these clients. The third advantage of
social justice supervision exists on a broader, more abstract level. If one agrees
that silence regarding injustice ultimately operates to perpetuate it, then the
explicit identification and labeling of sociocultural factors constitutes action in
the other direction. When supervisors and students reject strictly individualized
conceptualizations of the damage done by poverty, racism, and other forms of
oppression, they create a moment of alliance with socially just movement for all
people.

Importantly, a social justice model for supervision should *not* require that
supervisors provide elaborate responses regarding all issues and questions, or
even that absolute answers exist in every case. Writing about postmodern multicultural supervision, González (1997) described the effectiveness of a stance that
he called "supervisor-as-partial-learner" (p. 367). González further explained
this position as one of "informed uncertainty" (p. 367) that allowed him to work
with supervisees from within the context of his own style, cultural context, and
personal vision while providing equal space for the exploration of supervisees'
own questions and convictions. This stance has much in common with good
supervision generally, but is particularly relevant for supervision related to social justice issues. Interwoven issues of systemic inequity and personal identity
are complex, controversial, and anxiety-provoking, and many of us have had
little practice in exploring and articulating them. It is important that supervisors
honor and support students as they venture into this little-known territory, but
also that they not overwhelm students' exploration with their own views and
declarations.

5. *Actively advocate flexibility with regard to treatment approach.* Multicultural psychologists have long contended that the conventional roles and behaviors of psychological practice are "culture bound and potentially unhelpful
and oppressive to culturally different clients" (D. W. Sue et al., 1998, p. 81).
Certainly, poverty is not a true cultural designation, yet the parameters, landmarks, and challenges of life in poverty are far enough removed from middle-

class existence that therapists must be willing to use their mainstream-derived skills flexibly. Dumont (1992) observed that, within this chaotic terrain, "the 50-minute hour of passive attention, of pushing toward the past, of highlighting the shards of unconscious material in free association, just does not work" (p. 6). Janna Smith (2000) described the importance of flexibility around issues such as scheduling, pointing out that it is sometimes better to marvel with poor clients that they manage to come at all than insist on processing their "resistance." Phoebe Schnitzer (1996) observed that, in the clinic where she worked, poor clients communicated similar opinions via their attendance records:

> Clinical work within poor communities offers another perspective on the question of why "they don't come in": perhaps our poorest clients do not think their appointments are *worth* keeping. This possibility naturally leads to the question of how clinical methods can be rendered more meaningful to people in poor communities who are struggling with the practical issues of making ends meet. (p. 579)

It is one thing to agree in theory with multicultural psychologists and others who advocate flexibility in treatment approach; the fact is that there are few models of how to exercise that flexibility. Most supervisors and students have received conventional psychotherapeutic training, and there are few applied psychologists who are willing to openly present nontraditional approaches that they have used. Along with the guidance of multicultural, social, and community psychology theorists, participatory approaches to intervention development can help breach this gap. Most generally, such approaches derive from action research, which refers to "a cycle of inquiry involving *plan-act-observe-reflect*" (Herr & Anderson, 2005, p. 9). Participatory action approaches add to this cycle of inquiry by incorporating the collaboration of local community members. In this way, the best of psychologists' skills and the best of local wisdom can come together in the planning, launching, evaluation, modification, and re-launching of new therapeutic interventions. I will have more to say about this use of participatory action methodologies in the following chapter, but for now, I do not mean to suggest that every supervisor–supervisee pair must create brand-new interventions for use in particular communities. Rather, I hope to encourage supervisors to support their students in listening to, respecting, and incorporating what community members, local service providers, and clients themselves have to say about what works in their community—even if the answer does not sound precisely like a once-weekly 50-minute talk therapy hour.

## THE BROADER IMPLICATIONS OF
## SOCIALLY JUST PRACTICE AND SUPERVISION

Integrating issues of poverty and social class within psychology's multicultural/ social justice agenda is essential to the ability of psychologists to contribute their research, practice, and advocacy efforts toward greater equity and opportunity for poor Americans. Practitioners, supervisors, and their students have the opportunity to ally themselves with this movement by bringing these issues to the fore and making the supervisory context a space which refutes psychology's historical "invisibilizing" of poor people and lack of attention to social class issues (Lott, 2002). By contrast, "psychologists who are not participating in some manner in support of these movements may be, in the final analysis, part of the problem" (Sloan, 2003, p. 312).

# 6

# BEYOND PSYCHOTHERAPY: TRANSFORMING MENTAL HEALTH PRACTICE IN THE CONTEXT OF POVERTY

If you have come to help me, you are wasting your time. But if you have come because your liberation is bound up with mine, let us walk together.

—Lilla Watson

A social justice framework for mental health practice implies that oppression itself can function as a pathogen with regard to the emotional well-being of people in marginalized groups. This does not mean that a person who identifies as a member of a marginalized group cannot be appropriately diagnosed and treated within the context of conventional diagnostic nomenclature and psychological or medical techniques. It does, however, mean that when mental health practitioners work with poor clients, they are working with people whose psychological distress—as well as any interventions offered to them—must be understood within the context of their experiences of oppression. It requires us, therefore, to ground our understanding of poor clients' distress within "our knowledge of the depressogenic nature of poverty, inequality, and discrimination" (Belle & Doucet, 2003, p. 109).

In fact, such considerations oblige therapists to ask whether one can appropriately practice in the context of oppression *without* addressing oppression itself (Smith, Chambers, & Bratini, 2009). Such practice could be compared to a kind of "help" described by Paulo Freire (1970)—help that is offered by people with privilege to the oppressed in the absence of any acknowledgment of the sources and effects of oppression. Freire described this as *false generosity*. False generosity cloaks the extant power hierarchy in silence and protects it from challenge, with the "helpful" interaction therefore ultimately preserving and re-enacting power-over dynamics. Applying this concept to the therapeutic dyad, practice that is silent about oppression would re-enact the power differential between a middle-class therapist and his or her poor client.

The previous chapter presented treatment-related considerations for thera-pists, supervisors, and trainees whose practice takes place in the context of pov-erty, and suggested ways to make conventional psychotherapeutic practice more helpful and relevant when clients live in poverty. Taking this Freirean context as a point of departure, this chapter develops these considerations further with regard to our interventions themselves. How can practitioners, most of whom have received conventional mental health training, put their skills to use in other socially just ways in poor communities? Is psychotherapy the only tool in their toolbox? Certainly, multicultural approaches to counseling and psychotherapy are foundational to addressing this issue, because these approaches lay the philo-sophical groundwork for contextualized modifications of conventional thera-peutic technique. However, for practitioners who believe that oppression can be a pathogen, there is a horizon beyond the 50-minute insight-oriented talk-ther-apy hour, and in this chapter, I sketch out some of the landmarks in the territory ahead. In the first section, I will present a concept that can guide us in framing and evaluating the efficacy of socially just practice: psychopolitical validity. Fol-lowing that, I will profile some examples of socially just mental health practice along a continuum of increasing dissimilarity to conventional psychotherapy.

## ANOTHER WAY TO EVALUATE INTERVENTIONS: PSYCHOPOLITICAL VALIDITY

Before going on to present these new modalities for mental health practitioners, I will add another element to the backdrop for them. This element is Isaac Prilleltensky's concept of psychopolitically valid practice, which I mentioned briefly in Chapter 3 and which I believe complements feminist, social justice, and multicultural approaches to mental health theory and practice. Within APA's Multicultural Competencies, Guideline 5 states that "psychologists strive to apply culturally appropriate skills in clinical and other applied psy-chological practices" (APA, 2002, p. 47). The description of this guideline goes on to explain that "it is not necessary to develop an entirely new repertoire of psychological skills to practice in a culture–centered manner. Rather, it is helpful for psychologists to realize that there will likely be situations where culture–centered adaptations in interventions and practices will be more effec-tive" (APA, 2002, p. 47). Although this makes sense, psychologists have thus far been quite lenient with themselves with regard to adding new interventions to their repertoire. Although many psychologists would agree in concept that conventional psychotherapeutic roles and interventions can be oppressive to clients from marginalized groups, most of us still employ and train students to use primarily those techniques. Moreover, positioning this guideline within a social justice context, the aim becomes not just to use interventions that are "culture-centered" (the language here is diffuse) but to use ones that address positionality with regard to hierarchies of power and oppression.

Prilleltensky (2003) introduced a concept that can guide psychologists in understanding what might constitute such an intervention. Prilleltensky pointed out that psychologists have advanced their theoretical knowledge regarding oppression and liberation; the challenge is to more fully incorporate this knowledge into research and action. Toward this end, he suggested that we create and evaluate our actions according to a new type of validity: psychopolitical validity. To be psychopolitically valid, interventions and research must 1.) be informed by knowledge of oppression and power dynamics at every level (epistemic validity), and 2.) produce transformative action toward liberation in personal, interpersonal, and/or structural domains (transformative validity). How can the transformative psychopolitical validity of an intervention be gauged? Prilleltensky suggested the following questions as avenues for determining psychopolitical validity:

1. Do interventions promote psychopolitical literacy?
2. Do interventions educate participants on the timing, components, targets, and dynamics of best strategic actions to overcome oppression?
3. Do interventions empower participants to take action to address political inequities and social injustice within their relationships, settings, communities, states, and at the international level?
4. Do interventions promote solidarity and strategic alliances and coalitions with groups facing similar issues?
5. Do interventions account for the subjectivity and psychological limitations of the agents of change? (p. 200)

Prilleltensky (2003) addressed his comments to community psychologists, but they apply equally powerfully to mental health practitioners. What would it look like to act on our knowledge base in a psychopolitically valid way? The advisement that therapists apply multicultural knowledge, awareness, and skills to their psychotherapeutic interventions is critical—but what *else*? Are we limited to deploying the same tool from the same toolbox, even if in a more multiculturally sensitive way? Accepting first a contention made throughout this book—

that oppression itself is pathogenic—and second, that a social justice perspective means creating and offering psychopolitically valid interventions that address oppression, a number of new possibilities emerge. I see critical-consciousness-raising as a key underpinning of these, and I am again using Freire's (1970) language here. In Freire's (1970) work, *The Pedagogy of the Oppressed*, he argued that people's freedom from oppression involves an ongoing process of reflection on their sociohistorical context, an analysis that leads to "a critical comprehension of reality" (p. 47). Freire described *critical consciousness* as the process of comprehending one's existence in a sociohistorical context, and of understanding oneself to be a subject rather than an object to be defined by powerful others. This critical comprehension is facilitated by an egalitarian environment in which all involved—both teachers and students—can share and learn from each other in dialogue. However, "a mere perception of this reality," according to Freire, "will not lead to transformation" (p. 37); rather, action must flow from this new critical consciousness. The process and the action themselves then become the subject of reflection, leading to a continuous loop of action and reflection that Freire called *praxis*.

Freire called the literacy and consciouness-raising groups that he facilitated among Brazil's poor "culture circles," and many psychologists have been part of similar groups or workshops where multicultural issues and identity is explored. If oppression is pathogenic, why aren't such experiences, explicitly designed to facilitate critical consciousness, considered to be therapeutic *per se*? I will contend that they are, or at least merit investigation as such. Of course, psychologists already offer interventions like these in certain contexts. What I am suggesting is that 1.) we adopt psychopolitical validity as a social justice extension of multicultural competence, 2.) that we create and offer psychopolitically valid interventions systematically as a part of our professional repertoire, 3.) that we understand them to be therapeutic practices (and not just workshops or seminars or consultations that we do in addition to our therapeutic practice), and 4.) that we train our students to provide them just as we teach traditional techniques. This will require that psychologists expand their definitions of their own professional roles and functions beyond the individualistic medical model once and for all—which happens to be the model, as Albee put it, that is "supported by the ruling class because it does not require social change and major readjustments to the status quo" (Albee, 2000, p. 248).

This territory has been explored by practitioners and scholars who have already begun to transform their practice in ways that enhance psychopolitical validity. Some of these transformed practices are configured in the same way as conventional psychotherapy, but the therapist's role and technique within the dyad are very different. Others look nothing at all like psychotherapy. They reach out beyond the dyad to touch groups and communities, and they incorporate action for social justice within their process. I think of these practices as falling along a continuum of increasing dissimilarity to conventional psychotherapy. I conceptualize these gradations as beginning with *transformed psychotherapeutic practice.* These practices conform closely enough to conventional models of psychotherapy to go by that name, but important parameters of theory and technique have been modified in accord with feminist, multicultural, and/or social justice commitments. More dissimilar to conventional modalities are *co-created therapeutic practices.* These are practices designed to promote the emotional well-being of specific constituencies or communities that are developed collaboratively between mental health professionals and members of those communities, and they represent more radical departures from conventional psychotherapeutic techniques. Although they are therapeutic interventions in which mental health professionals are making use of their skills, they are not forms of psychotherapy. Most dissimilar to conventional psychotherapy are practice/actions through which practitioners create partnerships with groups of community members or representatives in a process of reflection and learning in which all grow and all participate in the creation of socially just action. I refer to these forms of practice/action as *community praxis,* again borrowing language from Paulo Freire (1970). As mentioned, Freire described *praxis* as a merging of reflection and action, as an action that emerges from and is inseparable from reflection, learning, and personal growth. These interventions invite mental health practitioners to engage in experiences that are not psychotherapy, yet are understood to be therapeutic nonetheless. The next section will begin the exploration of socially just treatment modalities with the category most similar to mainstream psychotherapy, transformed psychotherapeutic practice, using the specific example of relational-cultural therapy.

## TRANSFORMED PSYCHOTHERAPEUTIC PRACTICE: RELATIONAL-CULTURAL THERAPY AND MUTUALITY

Because socially just transformation of mental health practice has important roots in feminist approaches, I would like to ground its evolution in the publication of a small, pathbreaking, dynamo of a book called *Toward a New Psychology of Women,* written in 1976 by psychiatrist Jean Baker Miller. In it, she deconstructed the hierarchical relations between women and men and the subsequent devaluing of women as expressions of a culture that exalts power and can only see the less powerful as inferior and deviant. The activities, behaviors, and pursuits of dominants are seen as important, worthy, and "normal;" the activities, behaviors, and pursuits of subordinates are, by contrast, seen as trivial, menial, and dysfunctional (even when they happen to be necessary to the continuance of society). For example, women have historically been tasked with the maintenance of human relationships, something that men have just as much need for as do women. Yet, because caring for others and maintaining human connection is women's work, it is *de facto* not prioritized at the level of the "real" pursuits of men. Not only that, it is often pathologized via such characterizations as codependency and "women who love too much" (Norwood, 1990).

One of the flowerings of Miller's theorizing came in the founding of the Jean Baker Miller Training Institute at Wellesley College in 1995. Together with her colleagues there, Miller elaborated the theory and technique of *relational-cultural therapy*. Relational-cultural therapy is premised on, among other things, the subversion of the power-over dynamic inherent in the conventional therapeutic dyad. The model's central tenets are:

> People grow through and toward relationship throughout the life span.
> Movement toward mutuality rather than movement toward separation characterizes mature functioning.
> Relational differentiation and elaboration characterize growth.
> Mutual empathy and mutual empowerment are at the core of growth-fostering relationships.
> In growth-fostering relationships, all people contribute and grow or benefit; development is not a one-way street.
> Therapy relationships are characterized by a special kind of mutuality.
> Mutual empathy is the vehicle for change in therapy.
> Real engagement and therapeutic authenticity are necessary for the development of mutual empathy. (Jordan, 2000, p. 1007)

It is probably clear from this list that something very different happens in the room when a therapist works from a relational-cultural orientation: The therapist is not the only person helping, and the client is not the only person growing. This emphasis on mutuality is understood to be an integral component of the therapeutic experience: When a therapist has truly joined a client, according to this way of working, "something happens *in the therapist*: she is changed" (Miller & Stiver, 1997). When clients are able to see and experience the effect that they have had on the therapist, a sense of mutual connection and empathy is initiated through which people can heal from the sadness, shame, and self-blame that are the corollaries of isolation and disconnection.

Judith Jordan (2000) pointed out that not only can the conventional psychotherapeutic "blank screen" persona be unhelpful, it can actually initiate problems of its own:

> Nonengagement and relative anonymity of the therapist pose several problems to a model that holds mutual empathy as the main curative factor in therapy. The nonresponsiveness of the therapist often reinforces the patient's relational images of relational incompetence, of not mattering; it leads to unauthentic relating and locks patients into a sense that their feelings and thoughts do not matter. The therapist's distance also can become part of a mystification process by which the patient is free to idealize the therapist, and the therapist's power is artificially enhanced. (p. 1010)

Jordan (2000) went on to explain that none of this gives therapists license to be fully spontaneous and recklessly self-disclosing, nor are clients responsible for taking care of therapists or seeing to their growth. Rather, it is simply the case that during good therapeutic work, when each party is able to contribute and receive, healing happens for both: "Both people bring strengths, wisdom, gifts, troubles, and blind spots to this relationship. The therapist holds some special expertise in the area of mental suffering and relationships. Patients bring knowledge about themselves, wisdom about many matters, and even insights about the therapist that are invaluable" (p. 1011). Note the echoing of Freire (1970) here—the notion that personal growth is inherently facilitated by the dialectical process of connecting, sharing, and learning collaboratively.

A relational/cultural orientation dovetails with multicultural and social justice perspectives more broadly to create a prescription for therapeutic modalities that explicitly reject conventional roles and practices that reflect the cultural worldviews of privileged social classes. Foremost among these theorists is liberation psychologist Ignacio Martín-Baró (1994), who cited Freire extensively in his own writing and advised psychologists that the challenge in working with oppressed people was "not a matter of thinking for them or bringing them our ideas or solving their problems for them; it has to do with thinking and theorizing with them and from them" (p. 28). Elaborations of these themes along with suggestions for practice have been contributed by Ivey (1995); Utsey, Bolden, and Brown (2001); Prilleltensky and Nelson (2002); Vera and Speight (2003); Goodman et al. (2004); and D. W. Sue and S. Sue (2007). For all these theorists, transformed practice means offering interventions that privilege local culture as they incorporate action to dismantle barriers that clients face as the result of unjust social conditions.

By way of example, Lillian Comas-Diaz (2007) described *dichos* therapy, which uses Spanish proverbs to help connect Latino/a clients to their cultural ancestry as it guides them through negotiation of cultural conflicts. In "Earth therapy" (Duran, 2006, p. 122), Native communities create interventions to address the wounding of their land through mining, deforestation, and other aspects of colonization. Native ceremonial objects, such as pipes, bows, arrows, and baskets, are returned to their original homes as part of the healing of the Earth's traumatization. Blustein, McWhirter, and Perry (2005) adapted Isaac Prillelten-sky's theorizing to develop their emancipatory communitarian approach to vo-cational counseling:

> In school, prison, campus, or mental health agency settings, vocational psy-chologists would identify and seek to change unfair policies and practices, in-creasing, for example, the likelihood that students of a second language will receive additional educational resources; that women prisoners will receive needed educational and vocational planning services; that first generation, low-income college students will receive assistance to help them graduate; or that day-treatment patients diagnosed with major psychiatric problems will receive appropriate vocational rehabilitation services. These goals might be accom-plished through consultation, community outreach, program evaluation, and research at both the individual and system level, including active engagement with teachers, families, clinical staff, and administration. (p. 155)

As should be clear at this point, I believe that practitioners whose work takes place in the context of poverty should work in the tradition of these mental health professionals who modify their practices to fit the needs and social loca-tions of their clients, rather than expecting their clients to either make use of conventional interventions or not be served. In this way, I join Lisbeth Schorr (1999) in hoping for the appearance of "a new practitioner" (p. 421) to work in poor communities, a practitioner who works collaboratively with people and their families, who thoughtfully challenges the limits of her job description, and who works to understand people's stories and needs within their sociocultural context. Citing a program called Homebuilders as an example of how the new practitioner will work, Schorr gave an example of their practice:

> At a Homebuilders staff meeting I attended, a therapist told of appearing at the front door of a family in crisis, to be greeted by a mother's declaration that the one thing she didn't need in her life was one more social worker telling her what to do. What she needed, she said, was to get her house cleaned up. The Homebuilders therapist, with her special training and mind-set, responded by asking the mother, "Do you want to start with the kitchen?" (p. 421)

## CO-CREATED THERAPEUTIC EXPERIENCES

If we decide that, as "new" practitioners, we are willing to undertake this expan-sion of our roles and functions in collaboration with people in poor commu-nities, what might these new interventions look like? One avenue toward the development of new interventions is to involve the people themselves in their creation. Such an approach represents an opportunity for mental health professionals to address questions like these from a social and methodological stance that is less likely to merely reproduce existing forms of theory and practice that represent middle-class preconceptions of what is "normal" and what it means to be "helpful" to poor people. A methodological framework already exists for such collaborative undertakings, though it has rarely been applied to the development of therapeutic interventions: action research.

Most broadly, action research refers to "a cycle of inquiry involving *plan-act–observe–reflect*" (Herr & Anderson, 2005, p. 9). Adding a participatory element builds upon this orientation by incorporating the collaboration of local community members. These approaches have the potential to enhance psychopolitical validity by producing action and knowledge that contribute to social change. They also offer researchers and community members the opportunity "to 'research back', in the same tradition of 'writing back' or 'talking back' that characterizes much of the post-colonial or anti-colonial literature" (L. T. Smith, 1999, p. 7). A useful delineation of the action research spectrum was offered by Herr and Anderson (2005) based on their study of educators' initiatives to study their own practice. Based on this research, Herr and Anderson developed a "continuum of positionality" (p. 30) that described six possible locations for practitioners and researchers with regard to the research setting itself. These positionalities are specified by the insider/outsider status of the researcher with regard to the organizational setting where the research takes place: Insiders are researchers who are also practitioners within the setting, whereas outsiders are university or professional researchers who enter a particular setting to study it in collaboration with insiders and/or community members. Each position also intersects with a second dimension called *mode of participation*, or the degree to which local people are involved in the research; possibilities range from token or symbolic community participation to full collective action.

Herr and Anderson's continuum of positionalities begins with *insider* research, in which a practitioner studies his/her own practice in the tradition of narrative or case study research. Next is *insider in collaboration with other insiders*, where a team of insiders gathers to study an issue relevant to the setting's work, followed by *insiders in collaboration with outsiders*, in which such a team may invite outside researchers to participate or consult. Next on the continuum is the classic form of participatory action research (PAR), *a reciprocal collaboration* that is jointly initiated and implemented by true insider-outsider teams; *outsiders in collaboration with insiders* is, however, the more common version of PAR, wherein outsiders are the initiators of the project. The sixth category, *outsider studies insider*, approximates traditional university research but may contain participatory elements.

Action research suggests a direction for mental health professionals who, in keeping with a social justice perspective, would like to 1.) contradict the dominant/subordinate power relations inherent in traditional research paradigms, 2.) transform therapeutic practice in the context of oppression, and 3.) incorporate community knowledge into the creation of transformed interventions. It also invites the possibility that some form of action research to transform practice in keeping with social justice vision is within the reach of many practitioners working in community settings. Later in the chapter, I will have much more to say about PAR's potential in this regard, but even practitioners who are the only mental health professionals at their agencies, or who do not have latitude to engage in a full-fledged PAR undertaking, can study their own setting and practices and involve other members of the organization and the community to the extent possible. For therapists working in the context of oppression who wish to move beyond conventional, culture-bound interventions, such a framework can offer direction in the creation of more socially just practice to be implemented by the new practitioner.

## Examples of Co-Created Interventions

In 2003, I had the opportunity to collaborate with community members and colleagues from outside mental health in the creation and implementation of a socially just intervention in the community setting where I worked. The community-based organization (CBO) offered a variety of programs, including an alternative high school, general literacy classes, pre-college and career counseling, and a technology center—and with my arrival, psychological services yet to be determined. The CBO staff had perceived that many of their community members seemed in need of interventions that would address their emotional well-being, but were unsure exactly how such interventions should be configured. Their plan had been to hire a psychologist, and then provide an opportunity for him or her to help create a program of services.

I have described the process by which the conventional psychotherapeutic interventions in which I had been trained were revealed to be culture-bound and classist (Smith, 2005). One of the successful programmatic interventions that I did eventually provide was one that my training alone did not prepare me to develop or offer: It was created through a participatory process that included an educational programmer, a computer technologist/educator, the center's director, community members, and myself. These participants believed that the best psychological help for their community likely involved something other than, or in addition to, the provision of traditional talk therapy—yet none of us knew what that something was. To tackle this task, this team began a series of biweekly meetings to develop ideas for new psychological services. The team met over a 6-month period with the goal of service development; in addition, I had many informal conversations with community members about this topic when they were in the center.

Team members brought different perspectives to the table. Community members, who were part of a senior citizens group that met at the center, had deep knowledge of the community and its emotional pulse, as well as insight into the kinds of programming that community members might consider useful and relevant. The educational programmer was a community member himself and an indigenous counselor. The computer technologist taught us about the social justice movement within her field: The community technology center (CTC) movement, according to which CTCs are understood to be public space where the "digital divide"—the growing technological gulf that contributes to the social exclusion of poor people—is challenged by empowering community members to be change agents as they gain technological skills.

As we discussed our experiences at the CBO, some basic observations related to community needs began to crystallize. It was a community where people longed for lives with the ordinary options and opportunities that middle-class people enjoy—although that was perceived as an exotic, out-of-reach life that community residents could barely imagine. It was a community of young people who were confronted with a future that, to say the least, appeared to present few alternatives. ("What can I do?" said one 19-year-old in frustration. "I don't play sports, I don't play music, and I don't want to sell drugs.") It was a community where taken-for-granted pathways to career success were almost unknown, in that young people could grow up never having known anyone who went to college, or who went out to work every day, or who contributed to a savings account. It was a community where, in the midst of one of the greatest urban concentrations in the world, men and women of every age spoke of loneliness; the struggle to keep their heads above water in a constricted world of economic hardship isolated people from each other. Yet, the community elders believed that, for many community residents coming into our center, the idea of a lengthy personal discussion alone with a stranger was absurd and did not bear much relevance to their survival or progress.

Having identified these emotional, vocational, and practical concerns, we began to imagine how we might, from the resource base that existed in the center, offer a comprehensive program that would support whole-person emotional well-being as it facilitated sociocultural awareness and provided access to opportunities that were not naturally occurring in the community—we felt that, in the context of the multiple oppressions bearing down on community members, the three could not be separated. Ideally, we hoped to create a program that would help people bridge the gap of isolation that surrounded them, have a deeper understanding the impact of sociocultural forces in their lives, and envision and move toward different opportunities. We considered that educational attainment and the development of valued skills such as technical competency serves several purposes: It allows people to increase their own sense of efficacy, it provides a basis from which people can contribute to and connect with their communities, and it facilitates academic and career success. Finally, we shared a belief that the facilitation of critical consciousness—the ability to identify and analyze the social forces that impact one's self-concept and worldview—is an essential opportunity for people involved in the work of liberation.

The comprehensive program that grew out of these conversations was piloted in the form of a year-long internship. Interns, who could be of any age, would have the opportunity to build socioemotional and technical competencies, improve their connections within the community, and develop their personal, interpersonal, and social awareness. Within the center, they would have the opportunity to practice these skills under supervision, and receive a stipend from the center for their services as teaching assistants, outreach facilitators, and peer mentors. Five interns were in the pilot class: Three were students enrolled in the CBO's alternative high school and two were senior citizens from the community.

The interdisciplinary programming team worked closely with interns, both through supportive group and ongoing training experiences. Thematically, our plan was that the internship would incorporate six elements. First, concepts from *Freirean pedagogy*—critical consciousness, co-intentional education, the process of liberation—were foundational to the internship experience. The year began with readings selected from Freire's work, and the themes that emerged were woven throughout the experience. The second element involved *interdisciplinary learning and supervision*. The internship afforded participants the opportunity to work closely with professionals with expertise in technical fields and social science, and to observe these professionals collaborating with and learning from each other. *Communication and socioemotional skills workshops* were offered to contribute to general interpersonal ability as well as to interns' peer counseling, and program facilitation activities. Next, interns received *training in technical and computer literacy*, including new media, media literacy, and basic applications. Ongoing seminars were devoted to the exploration of *sociocultural identity and oppression*, wherein interns learned about the interactions between social constructions of identity and emotional well-being. Finally, a *group project* would culminate the internship. Over the course of the year, the intern group planned and conducted a project and presentation for the community that incorporated a community action/ social justice perspective.

Conceptually, our team envisioned these elements to work together according to a three-component model. These components, which overlap broadly, were *competence, community*, and *consciousness,* and we began to call them "the three C's." *Competence* referred to the provision of opportunities for the acquisition of socioemotional skills, technical literacy, and educational attainment; *consciousness,* to the promotion of self-, interpersonal, and sociocultural awareness; and *community,* to strengthening, sustaining, and building community at multiple levels, i.e., the community of a classroom, the local community within which the center is located, and larger communities outside the neighborhood.

By the end of the year, the interns had, among other things: learned to teach basic computer classes for community members; created and presented a community outreach program on sexual orientation called "Thinking Outside the Box"; and developed, written, filmed, and edited a video on local pollution and environmental racism that was eventually used by a city environmental group in their community presentations. Four of the interns completed GEDs (one had begun the internship with a high school diploma). All of the interns, including the senior citizens, applied for continuing education at the post-secondary level, with two acceptances by the year's end. Two of the interns had also secured new jobs, one opportunity growing directly out of contacts that the intern made during the filming of the video. At our internship graduation event, the interns spoke to a gathering of their friends and families about the experience and its personal outcomes. One of the elements that they captured in their words was the powerful contribution of critical consciousness to psychological well-being, with one of them commenting that reading passages from Freire's *Pedagogy of the Oppressed* had been like waking up from a dream.

This program, then, was generally informed by a psychological perspective, and included components that encouraged group process, community connection, and the development of critical consciousness—components that are not so different from the transformed therapeutic modalities described in the previous section. However, it also promoted emotional well-being through skill attainment and other components that lie well beyond the parameters of conventional therapeutic practice—the efficacy of which has been recently supported by Alisha Ali and her colleagues as they discovered that a community-based program designed to facilitate business skills also decreased depression (Ali, Hawkins, & Chambers, 2010). I recounted the example of the co-created CBO internship in an article in which two of my colleagues also described interventions that they had developed in collaboration with community members (Smith, Chambers, & Bratini, 2009). One of them, Debbie-Ann Chambers, told of her experiences working as a counselor in a CBO that served poor youth of color in East Harlem, New York City. Struggling for funding, the CBO had never finished the build-out of its facilities, so its interior featured no small private rooms of the sort that counselors typically use. In addition, local culture was such that the teenagers participating in the CBO's programming saw mental health services as highly stigmatized and culturally irrelevant.

Debbie could have simply concluded that the CBO was not prepared to offer counseling; they had no facilities and their clientele was not interested. It would have been easy and even reasonable to walk away from this setting as not suitable for psychological practice. Yet, with her expansive, contextualized conceptualization of emotional well-being, and her commitment to participatory approaches, Debbie was able to openly and explicitly follow the teenagers' cues to develop an intervention that sprang from their natural inclinations to express themselves through music and rhyming: a group experience that used poetry writing and reading as its format. Outlining the group's process, Debbie described a memorable moment that occurred when the group was faced with one member's anger toward a teacher:

> The group responded to this member by making a collaborative poem. . . . [T]his experience highlighted the importance of collaboration and valuing the contributions and knowledge of every member. Group members all spoke a sentence expressing their feelings, and in the end, when we reflected on what we had written, there was a euphoric feeling in the room that students connected to the fact that something had been jointly created to voice to their specific concerns. (p. 164)

Needless to say, an experience like this one looks very different from the ones that are typically offered under the auspices of mental health services— even more different than relational-cultural therapy. But was something therapeutic not happening there? Life in poverty brings with it an experience of social marginalization, exclusion, and voicelessness, and I believe that we need to explore the possibility that this intervention that the teenagers helped create, and that featured a creative process at its heart by which they could voice their own realities, was as healing as an intervention imported from White middle-class culture—if not more so.

## MORE DIFFERENT STILL: COMMUNITY PRAXIS

As mentioned, transformed psychotherapeutic practices like relational-cultural therapy and multicultural therapies are characterized by techniques that are vastly different from conventional dyads. In contrast to the relatively neutral, distant, and impersonal roles prescribed by traditional modalities, these therapists are engaging with their clients as individuals who are themselves affected by the therapeutic process, and are openly using culturally meaningful symbols and discussions of colonization as tools to promote healing. Co-created therapeutic experiences build on these approaches by adding a participatory dimension to the equation. In these experiences, therapists invite clients, community members, and others to work with them to develop interventions that are tailor-made for local community needs. These interventions may or may not conform to our expectations for therapeutic interventions. Debbie's intervention featured a group modality but was not a therapy group; my intervention was a year-long experience that included components that were process-oriented and could be construed as counseling-related or psychoeducational, but other components that were clearly not. My third co-author, Luci Bratini, ended up implementing PAR itself with the teenagers where she worked—which leads into the subject of this section. These are the interventions that actively comprise community-level involvement by mental health practitioners—experiences I call *community praxis.*

## An Example of Community Praxis: The ROAD Project

Through community praxis, mental health practitioners move another step farther away from the traditional psychotherapeutic dyad. In community praxis, practitioners are not so much offering interventions to people as they are engaging alongside community members in practice/actions that explicitly connect individual and community well-being to the larger sociocultural context. These practice/actions position mutual support, critical-consciousness-raising, and social action as contributors to individual and community well-being. Through community praxis, mental health practitioners are making use of their training and skills, but are mobilizing them in different ways—and more directly—in concert with their social justice intentions than in any other modality. Community praxis allows for a more explicit targeting of oppression as a pathogenic influence in the lives of marginalized groups, and has the potential to contribute to social action through its very process.

What does community praxis look like? Lisa Goodman and her colleagues (2007) contributed an outstanding description of such a practice/action in describing the ROAD (Reaching Out About Depression) project, at that time a 3-year-old project ongoing in Cambridge, Massachusetts. ROAD was organized around a core group of low-income women and a collaborating network of counseling and law school students, and had as its mission the discovery of alternative solutions for depression for women in the community. Goodman and the ROAD participants followed Belle and Doucet (2003) in conceptualizing poverty itself as depressogenic, and described the rationale behind ROAD as a mental health intervention this way:

> It is our contention that the dichotomy between structural and individual change is a false one. Instead, the two can and should work together dialectically. . . . Central to ROAD's design and development are the ideas that 1.) mental health arises not (only) from intrapsychic exploration but from peer support and political action activities; and 2.) psychological issues such as isolation, feelings of helplessness, or lack of agency can keep communities of people from organizing in the first place. Given the inextricability of psychological and political empowerment, sacrificing either one means sacrificing the other. (p. 266)

The core group developed and facilitated a series of workshops for the community addressing depression in the lives of poor women, the topics of which included motherhood, partner violence, and economic inequality. The resource team also met with ROAD workshop participants in their homes and advocated within the community on their behalf, with the goal of making these services unnecessary as the women became more able to engage in advocacy themselves.

The components of the program illustrated its operations with regard to individual, collective, and sociopolitical empowerment, the authors defining the latter as the ability to create social change in communities, and describing social action as a central part of ROAD. Goodman et al. (2007) summarized the individual psychological benefits of participation in ROAD as emerging from its warm atmosphere, the ability of participants to share their stories with each other, its critical-consciousness-raising elements, the skills that the women gained from the workshops, and the action of workshops toward the building of empowerment. One of the ROAD participants summed up the unique ability of ROAD to contribute meaningfully to the emotional well-being of the community and its people where traditional mental health services had failed:

> Mental health care providers can learn from ROAD that you have to consider people in their circumstances, as whole people. We're not just depressed, or depression-havers. We're people with lives and things in our lives that are affecting our health. You're talking about someone who is being forced to grovel. Talking about our mental health is not the same as someone who feels down sometimes. If you don't have a roof over your head, if you don't have your electric bill paid, then how are you going to take care of your mental health? There is not a traditional mental health strategy that gets at that. (p. 286)

Returning to the criteria for psychopolitical validity, it should become clear that, for the ROAD project, many of Prilleltensky's questions can be answered with a resounding "yes." Participation in ROAD clearly promoted psychopolitical literacy, educated participants with regard to actions to overcome oppression, and empowered participants to take action to address inequities and injustice within their relationships and their community.

I believe that a general model for mental health community praxis in the tradition of ROAD is located within the continuum of action research positionalities that I described earlier (Herr & Anderson, 2005). At that point, I was presenting the continuum for the purpose of describing approaches by which practitioners could collaborate with community members to create new interventions tailored to their needs. Now I would like to return to another point on the continuum—PAR—and present it in, perhaps, an unexpected light: as a community praxis intervention in and of itself (Smith & Romero, 2010).

## PAR as Practice

PAR is best known as a process of research, education, and action in which conventional distinctions between the researcher and the researched are challenged (Brydon-Miller, 1997). It is an approach through which academic or professional researchers do not conduct studies *on* communities (or youth or other groups of people); instead, they conduct studies *with* communities (or youth or other groups of people). This collaborative approach makes possible the production of knowledge and the expression of meaning that represents (because it comes from) lives and worldviews other than those characteristic of university settings and other elite locations. Practitioners and academic researchers therefore participate as co-researchers and co-seekers in PAR, a process that challenges everyone involved to create mutual engagement and to interrogate obstacles to that mutuality (echoes of relational-cultural theory here).

PAR teams must be prepared to engage in a personal struggle with deeply embedded beliefs about what constitutes knowledge as professionals are positioned as co-learners alongside their community colleagues (echoes of Freirean pedagogy again). By contradicting the relatively neutral and distant posture to which mental health professionals are traditionally trained, PAR counteracts the power-over dynamic that ultimately separates them from those with whom they work. Fields of practice such as public health and education have established traditions of action research, which includes community-based participatory research (CBPR) (e.g., Minkler & Wallerstein, 2002), and nonpracticing psychologists such as social psychologists have participated extensively in PAR (e.g., Lykes, 2000; Torre & Fine, 2005). Yet, these approaches are little-utilized by mental health practitioners.

The emergence of PAR as an intervention—as community praxis, more precisely—is perhaps not so unexpected if we review the basic premises presented thus far: the idea that the emotional well-being of people living in poverty cannot be understood outside the context of oppression, and the longstanding contention of feminist, multicultural, and social justice theorists that conventional roles and interventions employed by mental health practitioners are not well-suited for contextualized work, and in fact can reproduce oppressive relationships between dominant and subordinated group members. These premises require that we find a different way of putting our skills to work on behalf of people living in poverty. Goodman et al. (2007) made a similar point with regard to the women with whom they developed ROAD:

> What is needed instead is a response that simultaneously attends to poor women's psychological and material well-being as well as the structural barriers that inhibit their own efforts to bring about social change. . . . ROAD works to alleviate psychological symptoms through personal empowerment, combat the fragmentation of low-income women's communities through collective empowerment, and address damaging social conditions through sociopolitical empowerment. (p. 271)

Although ROAD was not PAR *per se*, PAR answers this same call for "what is needed," and provides conceptual and theoretical guidelines for doing so. As outlined, PAR in its conceptual foundations represents a general model for mutuality and collaboration, a space in which all contribute and all learn and all are changed. PAR inherently subverts some of the damaging consequences of poverty and classism such as social exclusion and voicelessness through the explicit sharing of power and voice. Involvement in a PAR experience incorporates all six principles articulated by Goodman et al. (2004) as foundational to feminist, multicultural, and social justice practice: ongoing self-examination, sharing power, giving voice, facilitating consciousness-raising, building on strengths, and leaving people with tools for social change.

In so doing, PAR invites practitioners to *ally* themselves with members of poor communities to create knowledge and action for social change. These alliances and actions also represent a way for us, as people affiliated with social power, to put those affiliations to use toward egalitarian, prosocial ends. As academics or practitioners associated with elite institutions, as professionals with highly esteemed letters after our names that encourage people to listen to us, we have a platform. Through PAR, we can make that platform available to people whose voices are *not* often heard within public or scholarly discourse. PAR then becomes a vehicle by which community members and young people can reach policymakers and the general public with their words and ideas—a vehicle by which they can challenge the limitations imposed on their participatory citizenship by sociocultural marginalization. The idea of PAR as practice builds on these possibilities by emphasizing the *process* by which PAR alliances imagine, develop, and implement initiatives—a process that can be transformative for all involved. PAR alliances correspond to practice/actions, therefore, that are psychopolitically valid and that encourage emotional growth.

The impact of the PAR experience on community participants' emotional growth is not just theoretical—it has been referenced within many descriptions of PAR (e.g., Smith & Romero, 2010). Law's (1997) PAR project was undertaken in collaboration with a group of parents of children with disabilities. Together, the team worked to identify local cultural, economic, and environmental factors that created challenges for these children. Near the project's conclusion, Law asked parents for their perceptions of the PAR experience. Her co-researchers reported that PAR had allowed them to express feelings, take action, and discover a sense of connection to other participants, diminishing their previous feelings of isolation. M. Brinton Lykes (1994, 1997, 2000) has participated in PAR teams with local people around the world. Describing a collaboration with Mayan women in rural Guatemala, Lykes (2000) observed that "[p]articipation has . . . been an opportunity not only for individual growth and development but also for sharing stories, comparing differing versions of survival, rethreading community wherein to develop a shared vision towards collective action for change" (p. 393). She reported that her co-researchers attributed enhanced self-esteem and self-confidence to their participation in PAR. Accordingly, Lykes (2009) has formulated a conceptualization of PAR within which psychosocial well-being is one of the primary components. Reflecting on his PAR involvements, Mexican activist Arturo Ornelas portrayed the PAR experience as one of deep personal healing through communion with others, writing,

> You begin by recognizing a need and knowing it well. Then you start taking action. Reflecting on that action with the others, maybe every day for a half hour or more, a dialogue starts about the need and about the action. . . . The Spanish for word for knowledge, *saber*, comes from the Latin *sabor*, meaning flavor. In order to know, you need to taste, to eat. In my culture, you cannot separate these things. . . . You are nourished by knowledge. You achieve intimacy by doing a deep analysis of your inner being and celebrating that analysis by dialoguing with others. It is an act of creation and re-creation. (Debbink & Ornelas, 1997, p. 19)

My colleague LeLaina Romero and I (2010) had the opportunity to experience the personal impact of PAR participation firsthand alongside our team of co-researchers from a poor community in New York City. Our co-researchers were a group of women who were residents of the community who also worked as peer educators on behalf of a CBO that provided outreach and referral services for local women with HIV/AIDS, substance abuse problems, and/or who were in abusive relationships. During the three years that the project was ongoing, our PAR team addressed the issue of community well-being, which eventually took the form of housing-related activism in light of a coming real-estate "revitalization" of the area, which threatened to sweep away longtime low-income residents of the community. At the two-year point in the project, we stopped to take stock of our experiences. LeLaina and I knew that our participation had had life-changing and career-changing consequences for us. How had our co-researchers experienced it? They agreed to sit together and speak about their experiences in a focus-group-style discussion, and it was recorded and transcribed for all of us to consider together.

The themes that emerged from the conversation included some that had to do with the process of PAR, and other that related to the personal "take-aways" from PAR. With regard to the process, it was clear that the women did not trust LeLaina or me at the outset, despite our many conversations about PAR and our professions of commitment to all that it stood for. "I felt like they were up to something," said one of the women, while another disclosed her internal dialogue upon meeting us: "Come on, man, what are *you* getting out of this?" The women also felt that the early sessions with us were boring: "We would come together and continue to come together, and like, no decisions were ever made." These reactions need not have surprised us, given social scientists' historic objectification, if not exploitation, of researched communities through the vehicles of their questions and checklists (Lykes, 1997). Moreover, we entered a poor community as middle-class women associated with an elite educational institution, and we entered a community of color as a White woman and a biracial woman who was often identified by community members as White. All these identities associated us with dominant social groups that have historically oppressed communities like the one where the project took place.

Despite these initially negative impressions, our co-researchers gave us the benefit of the doubt, and the women described the subsequent twists and turns in the long and winding road of PAR. They recalled the many times we stopped to check our own process, observing, for example, that the university co-researchers often preferred to talk rather than to *do*; reflecting on the increasing ease with which community co-researchers took leadership of meetings; and remembering how easy it was for all of us to feel hopeless about change in the face of powerful, well-financed social forces.

Our co-researchers emphatically affirmed that PAR had impacted their emotional well-being. Their words described the same benefits from PAR that Goodman et al. (2007) mentioned with regard to ROAD: personal empowerment, collective empowerment, and sociopolitical empowerment. According to the women, the PAR experience had increased their sense of self-worth and self-efficacy, it had enhanced their abilities to connect with and accept caring from significant others in their lives, and it left them with tools that enabled them to work for change both in their own lives and on behalf of their community. The women discussed the new feeling of the power of that they experienced as a collective, with one commenting:

> Like you can know that you're worthy, you know? How we [pause] . . . what's the word? How we, how we can make a difference, and how sticking together and being consistent and determined, the power that we have to make a change, you know what I'm saying?

PAR, the women explained, had made them feel that they had something to offer as role models to their families and the community, with one member sharing that she now felt like "a lifeboat." Another team member reported that her experiences in PAR had enabled her to reach out more comfortably to others and to listen in a different way:

> I see myself to be more conscious of other people's feelings, and more considerate, you know, and not just like so hard, 'cause before, you know, that's what I felt . . . now I know how to sit and listen to somebody, where before I'd be like, get over it.

Team members even related their PAR experience to their overall wellness including physical well-being, with one woman explaining,

> When I feel good and I'm part of something, I want to take care of myself a little more, you know? So my wellness, it's made me more conscious of my feelings, on my health, on what I eat. Just everything, it's had that big impact on every—you know, my whole well-being, everything.

In my work, I have observed that the impact of PAR on psychological well-being can play out in the very same way for youth. A group of counseling psychology graduate students and I offered PAR experiences for teenagers in four New York City public schools and one CBO, most of them lasting for one school year. In each of six groups (one school had two groups), two or three counseling psychology graduates students partnered with a group of 4 to 12 high school or middle school students to talk about and eventually study an issue of their choosing. The students ultimately created actions around these topics, which included photographic essays, surveys of the student community, and/ or presentations at the 2009 Teachers College Winter Roundtable conference in New York City. Topics chosen by the different groups ranged from community violence to gentrification to the need for student-friendly, student-centered guidance with regard to sexuality.

In focus groups held for them at the end of the year, our youth co-researchers spoke about the personal benefits that accrued to them over and above the experience of working on and presenting their projects. With regard to sociopolitical literacy, they spoke about the new insight, understanding, and agency that they now brought to their experience of the world. As one young man said, "Yo, like have I really been *seeing* this all the time? Have I been overlooking it since I was a child?" Another added,

> Well, now, I look at, I look at the big picture. Instead of just seeing a
> bunch of trash bags that haven't been picked up in like three days, I
> see a problem that needs fixing—and then through that problem, I see
> a solution.

They experienced a new ability to name and validate their own reality by giving voice to it, thereby simultaneously affirming the power of their own voices:

> We took pictures, photographic proof, that what we're saying is not
> lies, and we actually have some problems in the city, you know. And
> things that need to be changed. A community that needs change.

Along these lines, the kids were able to experience themselves as holders of wisdom and as sources of learning that they could share with others. As one of them said to his university co-researcher, a graduate student in counseling psychology, "I felt as if we were teaching *you*, we were giving you something, we were enlightening you, showing you the way of our community that maybe you haven't seen before, maybe you've overlooked." By talking about issues in PAR, some teenagers gained new perspectives on things closer to home:

> I realized that like it's not only me who grows through certain things,
> and I think, I know, I know how to understand it . . . like I go through
> a lot of verbal violence at home, like a lot of things are said to me that
> really hurt me, and like, I know how to deal with that now.

They also changed their ideas about what their futures might look like:

> I think this project—well, let's say we go to college and we got prob-
> lems in college. This project taught us how like to speak out 'cause,
> you know, if you don't say anything, things ain't gonna change. You say

something, things will change.

## Key Elements of PAR for Practitioners

The question of how to do PAR presents something of a contradiction in terms, in that it is a new, co-created endeavor every time that it happens. University and professional co-researchers can never know or plan in advance precisely how PAR projects will unfold, because at least half the answer to that question lies with community co-researchers as input from all team members eventually combines to give shape and direction to the work. Nevertheless, invaluable guidance is to be found in the writing of groundbreaking PAR researchers such as Patricia Maguire (1987), M. Brinton Lykes (1994; 1997; 2000), Cynthia Chataway (1997; 2001), Susan Smith (1997), Alice McIntyre (2000), and Michelle Fine (Cammarota & Fine, 2008; Fine & Torre, 2006). These authors share their accounts of joining with communities and youth to identify issues for study, create new knowledge, implement actions, and reflect on the process, and they do this without minimizing the challenges and pitfalls along the way.

In our PAR collaborations, my co-researchers and I have found that, as different as community praxis is from conventional mental health practice, many of our conventional skills have found ready application—we just needed to apply them in new ways. Writing about PAR as practice, LeLaina Romero and I proposed nine key elements of competence for practitioners hoping to participate in a PAR collaboration (Smith & Romero, 2010). These elements are not original with us; they are all generally derived from or analogous to elements of PAR as described by the foundational theorists listed above. Moreover, they are not only relevant for the practitioner or for university co-researchers—community researchers will make use of the skills that correspond to these elements, too. Our purpose in presenting them is simply to highlight key competencies and transformations that were especially important for us as practitioners making the transition to PAR, so that other mental health professionals can consider some of the dimensions along which they would need to adapt their skills if they were interested in doing the same.

1. The key elements begin with an appreciation for the gradual, complex process by which *trust* is built among team members. This is a process that must be examined within the team as it moves along, and not romanticized. Although practitioner or university co-researchers can reach levels of increasing trust and mutuality with community co-researchers, this does not cause differential connections to social power or disenfranchisement to disappear. A great PAR meeting that feels like "one big happy family" to university re-

searchers may or may not feel that way to community researchers; even when it does, the team must remain committed to attending to its own internal dynamics around race, class, gender, sexual orientation, and (dis)ability.

2. PAR is often a spiraling, nonlinear endeavor. Yet, in keeping with feminist and relational-cultural perspectives, practitioners must restrain their impulses to manage, streamline, or otherwise control the process as they enact a *power-sharing* approach to their participation with the team.

3. and 4. Practitioners must be proficient and comfortable with a *here-and-now orientation* and *transparency*, terms that we have borrowed from Yalom's (2005) theorizing about group psychotherapy facilitation. Specifically, practitioners should be able to actively process interpersonal dynamics as they occur, especially dynamics that involve them. Moreover, practitioners must be willing and able to use their own personhood within that work. Without transparency, practitioners will never move beyond their conventional, detached, power-over therapeutic stances; without the ability to spontaneously shift from content-related to process-related dialogue, interactions that could have been explored toward the building of trust will instead work against it.

5. PAR requires that practitioners continually work toward greater *awareness of their own sociocultural positionality*—in other words, toward understanding the social, professional, and interpersonal implications of their location at the intersections of class, race, gender, and other dimensions of identity. Furthermore, they should be able to put this awareness into words as part of the group's process. Most of us have not had training to develop this facility, and generally speaking, it is not a skill that ordinary life promotes. Many of us, therefore, should seek out specialized experiential training as part of our own continuing education. An outstanding source of such training is the national organization The People's Institute for Survival and Beyond (PISAB). PISAB's home is in New Orleans, but they organize training experiences all over the country, including their signature workshop, "Undoing Racism." More information can be found at the PISAB website at http://www.pisab.org/.

6. Based on their understanding of Freirean and liberatory perspectives, practitioners should be able to integrate *critical-consciousness-raising components* within the PAR process. These are experiential, didactic, and/or discussion-based components in which the team addresses the sociohistorical context in which their work takes place. Such efforts correspond to the team's ability to deconstruct cultural narratives that blame communities for their own oppression,

and thereby support individual community members' emotional well-being.

7. Practitioners should be able to move beyond an individual focus to embrace goals of *collective team efficacy*, which empowers team members both on their own behalf and on behalf of the community through a sense of solidarity. It also helps mitigate the feelings of hopelessness that can emerge when broad, entrenched social problems are considered head-on.

8. Practitioners and university co-researchers should be open to learning about the power of action, of doing in addition to speaking, thinking, interpreting, and otherwise intellectualizing. This interweaving of action and reflection is what Freire called *praxis*.

9. Practitioners' willingness to commit to *an expanded conceptualization of professional roles and practices* within a social justice framework is foundational to all of the foregoing. This framework departs radically from medical models of psychological treatment; requires mental health professionals to become flexible, active learners; and posits that all participants in the intervention will change and grow.

## CAN YOU IMAGINE?

I began this chapter with questions. I asked about ways that practitioners could make themselves most useful in poor communities—about ways they could use their skills to facilitate emotional well-being through psychopolitically valid practice/action. In response, I suggested a continuum of practice/actions that began with transformed feminist and multicultural psychotherapy, which I believe will continue to be important, helpful tools for practitioners' use in the context of poverty. However, new interventions that are co-created with community members may be even more powerful. Finally, community praxis represents the most psychopoliticially valid answer to the questions I raised, whether through projects like ROAD that are specifically designed to address emotional well-being, or through PAR projects that promote well-being as they raise critical consciousness, create knowledge, and promote social change. Can mental health professionals re-envision their practice to include practice/actions such as these? Are practitioners willing to venture so far outside their offices, and outside traditional mental health paradigms?

If one believes 1.) that oppression can function as a pathogen, 2.) that psychology as a field has an ethical obligation to include all people within the scope of its services, and 3.) that our practices should aim for psychopolitical validity,

I argue that the answer cannot be "no." When we, as practitioners, assume that our toolboxes will only contain certain tools, then we are deciding that our field will serve only people who find those tools culturally consonant, only people who have certain kinds of presenting problems, and only people who will work with us in settings where we can deploy those familiar interventions in a circumscribed way that is comfortable for us. Putting our knowledge and skills to work in a new set of practices may take us out of that comfort zone, but it does not take us out of our profession—rather, these new practices open up new vistas of professional contribution to the well-being of all segments of society:

> This is not a question of whether to abandon psychology; it is a question of whether psychological knowledge will be placed in the service of constructing a society where . . . the fulfillment of some does not require that others be deprived, where the interests of a few do not demand the dehumanization of all. (Ignacio Martín-Baró, 1994, p. 46)

# 7

# PARTING THOUGHTS ON POVERTY, HELP, SERVICE, AND ACTION

> When I give food to the poor, they call me a saint. When I ask why people are poor, they call me a Communist.
> —Dom Hélder Pessoa Câmara,
> Catholic archbishop of Olinda and Recife, Brazil

Throughout this book, I have presented perspectives on poverty and social class that, although they are certainly not new, represent new threads of discussion within mental health practice. In this chapter, I would like to leave mental health practitioners with some concluding conceptual fine points to add to this mix. They correspond to the further rethinking of poverty, help, service, and action in the context of economic injustice.

## POVERTY IS SOCIAL EXCLUSION

The first additional idea that I will introduce contributes a final note to the argument presented throughout the book for a shift in our thinking about poverty. I want to focus now on the fact that poor people are largely excluded from full participation in many mainstream social experiences. This can be seen as one of the consequences of poverty—or it can be brought to the forefront as one of the defining features of poverty. Such a perspective was foreshadowed nearly a century ago in Max Weber's social class theorizing (Burchardt, Le Grand, & Pichaud, 2002a), in which the action of dominant groups to exclude others to enhance their own privileged status was understood to be a primary operation of social class stratification: Subordinated groups *are* those who are excluded.

This premise corresponds to a way of conceptualizing the parameters of poverty called *social exclusion theory*, a perspective that is barely mentioned within American discourse but that has found broad acceptance in the United Kingdom and Europe in recent years; some British social workers have, in fact, described issues of social exclusion as the "very stuff" of their profession (Sheppard, 2006, p. 5; see also Pierson, 2002).

As recounted by Hilary Silver (1994), this theoretical perspective originated in French political debate of the 1960s within which the poor, as one of a number of vulnerable, unprotected social groups, began to be referenced as *les exclus*. Gradually, the discourse of exclusion made its way to other European countries, and in 1989, the Council of Ministers of Social Affairs of the European Community adopted a resolution to fight social exclusion and to work toward a "Europe of Solidarity" (p. 535). Silver listed some of the opportunities whose relative unavailability can constitute social exclusion:

> Consider just a few of the things that the literature says people may be excluded from: a livelihood; secure, permanent employment; earnings; property, credit, or land; housing; the minimal or prevailing consumption level; education, skills, and cultural capital; the benefits provided by the welfare state; citizenship and quality before the law; participation in the democratic process; public goods; the nation or the dominant race; the family and sociability; humane treatment, respect, personal fulfillment, and understanding. (p. 541)

Amartya Sen, the Nobel Prize–winning economist, is among those who have written of poverty in terms of social exclusion (Sen, 2000). Beginning with Aristotle, Sen outlined the history of thought surrounding poverty as "impoverished lives and not just . . . depleted wallets," noting along the way that economist Adam Smith himself had considered the suffering of the poor to derive from their lack of the ability to appear in public without shame. Accordingly, Sen emphasized that the social marginalization of poor people is a primary deprivation in itself, and that it moreover catalyzes other deprivations such as unemployment. A social exclusion perspective, then, underscores the *relational* aspects of poverty and their consequences, which place poor people outside the life of the community and outside full democratic participation in society more broadly. This focus on the relational features of poverty as a consequence of classism provides for a "broad approach of seeing poverty as the lack of freedom to do certain valuable things" (p. 5).

Burchardt, Le Grand, and Pichaud (2002b) proposed an operationalization of social exclusion in which these precluded, valuable opportunities fall along four dimensions: *consumption*, or the capacity to purchase goods and services; *production*, or participation in economically or socially valuable activities; *politi-*

*cal engagement*, or involvement in local or national decision-making; and *social interaction*, or integration with family, friends, and community. Barry (2002) pointed out that while social stratification, poverty, and social exclusion are closely intertwined, they are not synonymous, which has important implications. First, groups can be also excluded on the basis of race, ethnicity, or other identities. Second, although there will likely always be gradations of "haves" and "have-nots," the have-nots need not, *ipso facto*, be excluded from society—that is simply the way that our social structure operates. This observation does not mitigate the need to "raise the floor," in the words of Holly Sklar, Larissa Mykyta, and Susan Wefeld (2008)—the depth and extent of poverty in the United States dishonors us all. Yet, even once the floor is raised, we do not *have to* socially, culturally, or politically exclude people who have less.

Along these lines, Barry (2002) discussed the ways in which the sharing of common institutions, resources, and opportunities could support a more class-inclusive public life, noting the impact that that broader public provision and sharing of the basics would have in this regard: Social inclusiveness obviously increases when everyone in society has equitable access to education, health care, housing, and public transportation, and when those public opportunities are of sufficient quality that the vast majority of citizens wants to take advantage of them. Can we even imagine a class-inclusive society like that? For example, many of us in the middle and owning classes take for granted that we do not live next door to poor people or have poor people as close friends. What if we did? What if we reorganized our social and institutional world so that concentrated areas of poverty did not exist? Try to imagine a world where people who have less were represented throughout society. Of course, they would *not* be represented among those buying sky boxes at stadiums or the biggest diamonds at Tiffany's, but imagine that they were represented proportionately within civic organizations and legislative bodies. Imagine that their contributions to the smooth running of society were seen as dignified and valuable, and that their experiences and their ideas were respected, so that works by poor and working-class artists were studied alongside what we know as the "classics." By the way, this literature (e.g., Zandy, 1990), poetry (e.g, Daniels, 1990; Weynant, 2009), and music (consult Cornell University's Industrial Labor School's online library at http://www.ilr.cornell.edu/library/) does exist, but unless you happened to take a special class in working-class studies, you might never know it. (The same can be said, of course, about the art and literature of women, people of color, people with disabilities, and the queer community.)

If you cannot imagine such a society, there is a nation that comes close: Denmark. Denmark is a society where people who do different kinds of work are better represented throughout the nation's social structure. Because Denmark's citizens derive great security from the government's provision of essential benefits and services, people can pursue careers based on their interests or on the lifestyles that they choose for themselves. In every walk of life, Danes can feel that their contributions are respected and they are fully included within the social landscape:

> Garbage man Jan Dion says he's an 8 out of 10 in terms of happiness. He said he doesn't mind collecting garbage for a living, because he works just 5 hours in the morning and then can spend the rest of the day at home with family or coaching his daughter's handball team. Dion says no one judges his choice of career, and he actually loves what he does because he has many friends along his route. . . . Josef Bourbon, a carpenter's apprentice, is also happy with his choice of career and enjoys the work. "I think it's about building something, seeing what you've worked on the whole day—you can see what you've done," he said. (Weir & Johnson, 2007, pp. 1–2)

The example provided by Denmark can also help us imagine a society where the have-nots do not have so much less. On the October 22, 2009, episode of her television show, Oprah Winfrey told her viewers about research that showed that Danes have the highest levels of life satisfaction in the world, and she interviewed Danish people on the street to learn why they thought this was. She learned that Danes do not worry about homelessness, or lack of health care, or how they will take care of themselves in old age, because the country of Denmark provides for those things, along with free education, the addition of living expenses for college students, free child care, and a year's maternity leave for new parents. Oprah followed up by asking about the high taxes that Danes pay to support these services—was that not the downside to life in their country? "We don't mind," said one interviewee, "because we believe that we get a lot for them." "That's why we're happy!" added another woman. Oprah offered that some people would call that socialism. "We call it civility," was the reply.

Our exclusion of poor people constitutes a unique source of harm to them. Many varieties of deprivation that accrue to families living in poverty have been presented thus far, but at this point I would like to juxtapose that discussion with evidence provided by social scientists who have examined the effects of social exclusion in the laboratory. Psychologists Jean Twenge, Roy Baumeister, and their colleagues have studied social exclusion through the use of experimental paradigms in which participants are excluded or rejected by peers, or given bogus feedback indicating that they would have lonely future lives. The experience of exclusion was consistently associated with strikingly unfavorable results throughout nearly a decade of research: Excluded participants behaved more aggressively (Twenge, Baumeister, Tice, & Stucke, 2001); they made more high-risk, self-defeating decisions; and they procrastinated more (Twenge, Catanese, & Baumeister, 2002). They gave up sooner on frustrating tasks and increased their consumption of unhealthy foods (Baumeister, DeWall, Ciarocco, & Twenge, 2005).

Exclusion even affected people's ability to think clearly, as participants who were told that they would be alone in life showed decrements on logic and reasoning tasks (Baumeister, Twenge, & Nuss, 2002). These cognitive decrements were not just the result of having received bad news: Participants who received other kinds of negative future predictions, such as suffering accidents or injuries, did not show the same impairments. In one study, socially excluded participants were more likely to agree that "Life is meaningless," to have a distorted sense of time, to avoid emotional language, and to face away from mirrors, prompting Twenge, Catanese, and Baumeister (2003, p. 409) to hypothesize that social exclusion produces a kind of "inner numbness" that may relate to suicidality. Most recently, Campbell et al. (2006) investigated the neural substrates of social exclusion using magnetoencephalography (MEG). As participants responded to mathematical tasks presented on a screen, MEG was used to assess the neural activity of those assigned to either a social exclusion or a control condition. The socially excluded participants showed lower levels of neural activity in brain areas consistent with the nature of the task, leading the authors to suggest that social exclusion may have "a powerful influence on top-down processing during relatively demanding cognitive tasks" (p. 133).

Of course, laboratory-induced effects cannot be overgeneralized with regard to natural events and their consequences, and experiences of social exclusion encountered on an individual, occasional basis are different from those that derive from one's ongoing group membership or social location. However, although we can readily see that the social exclusion experienced by the poor is not precisely the same as that produced by these experimental situations, it is also difficult to reject *completely* the idea that any of this research evidence is applicable. It does not require a lengthy stretch of the imagination to surmise that one's exclusion from the company and activities of mainstream society—from the lives that are represented everywhere in the news, on television, and in dominant cultural narratives—could contribute to self-defeating behavior, unhealthy styles of living, and inner numbness that further compromise poor people's abilities to find peace of mind and pathways out of poverty. The harm that is exacted by social and cultural exclusion dovetails with Bourdieu's conceptualization of symbolic violence toward the oppressed, and with Freire's explanation of the process by which marginalized groups internalize their own oppression. Furthermore, the unexamined observation of these consequences among the poor by class-privileged people contributes to victim-blaming interpretations: why aren't they more persistent? Why don't they exercise more? Certainly, the voices of the poor themselves support the existence of poverty's destructive relational dimensions, as conveyed evocatively by the writer Dorothy Allison (1994):

> The inescapable impact of being born in a condition of poverty that this society finds shameful, contemptible, and somehow deserved, has had dominion over me to such an extent that I have spent my life trying to overcome or deny it. . . . We were not noble, not grateful, or even hopeful. We knew ourselves despised. (p. 15)

Life on the socioeconomic margins, then, is characterized by experiences that correspond to the notion that we psychologically exclude the poor from *real* society, from the portion of humanity that we belong to, as Susan Fiske's (2007) neurological data suggested in Chapter 3. Not only do their experiences of us support this notion, but so does our conduct toward them. As a nation, we seem generally content to provide substandard schooling for their children. We argue endlessly about the national importance of funding health care for their families, and we dump our trash in their communities. Although we certainly want the working poor to show up for work in the places where we expect to make use of their services, we are not sufficiently concerned about their ability to live on their earnings to sustain national dialogue regarding a living wage. I am not suggesting that anyone thinks these circumstances are favorable or good. It is simply that mainstream society does not seem noticeably bothered or hindered by them at all—as though these are just the givens of life for some people, for people we have relegated to the margins. What the social exclusion research emphasizes is that the very fact that we stand by and allow people to be so relegated is a form of violence all its own.

### "HELPING" THE POOR

Altruistic motives are readily seen among mental health professionals. For example, every year at national conventions, members of the American Psychological Association participate in volunteer efforts in poor communities in the host city. In 2006, APA volunteers worked for a day with Habitat for Humanity to construct houses in New Orleans (Dingfelder, 2006). Yet the offering of help by relatively privileged people to people who live in the context of oppression is not an uncomplicated matter, even when it is offered by people whose professional function is to help, and this is the next conceptual angle that I would like to reframe.

In a clinical context, unexamined attitudes that mental health professionals may have regarding the poor can be expected to influence their efforts to help in powerful ways. Altman (1995) described how a therapist encountering the poor "frequently enters, psychologically, a realm of trauma and loss that she may have been able to avoid, to some degree, in her own life" (p. 1). Furthermore, Altman (1995) illuminated some of the snares associated with unexplored class and race identities for those who persevere despite the difficulties: "I had an identification with my father as a 'white knight' who would ride into the ghetto with his big car and rescue the inhabitants. Work in the ghetto allowed me to feel special and admirable" (p. 4). Therapists must be aware, according to Altman (1995), of the potential for such motivations, which can engender behaviors and attitudes that reinforce the one-down position to which society relegates poor clients by "perpetuating a myth . . . that the therapist is high-minded, healthy, altruistic, and giving, while the patient is sick, needy, and dependent" (p. 7). Aponte (1994) pointed out a related pitfall in the form of therapists whose efforts to be helpful to poor clients actually constitute attempts to replace the client's views, beliefs, and lifestyle with the therapist's own; Aponte cautioned therapists that they are to "serve, not colonize" (p. 11).

Practitioners' inclination to deliver help to poor clients via an attitude adjustment or skills training would be understandable, given the thrust of much of the psychological research on poverty. That research leaves us, after all, with a picture of the poor as people in need of instruction in such areas as parenting skills, language stimulation, healthy lifestyle coaching, anger management techniques, and medication compliancy, and the creation of such programming is the stuff of conventional social service provision and grant-writing. Moreover, my point is not that there is anything wrong with any of these services when they are needed. After all, when a family needs something, like coats, and a coat drive brings them, then that coat drive was a truly valuable thing in their lives. When a family is hungry, a soup kitchen is of undeniable value. Rather, my concerns are in two related areas: First, what is the larger meaning and impact of interventions that constitute handouts—whether what is being handed out is a coat, soup, or parenting skills? This question does not refer to the impact on the receivers of such handouts, which is the way it is usually asked, as in the oft-repeated saying about giving a man a fish as opposed to teaching him to fish. I am interested in the impact and meanings for the so-called helpers. Second, we know that poverty causes damage and deprivation at every level. How can our "help" go beyond handouts to encompass action directed toward social inequity, the cause of the causes?

Paulo Freire theorized about the troubling contradictions at the heart of conventional notions of help. Freire's *Pedagogy of the Oppressed* (1970) was written as just that, a pedagogy—a philosophy of teaching, especially when teachers are working in the context of oppression. But what Freire had to say to teachers can be extended to would-be helpers of many kinds, including mental

health professionals. This is not my idea. I was lucky enough to have a professor in graduate school who assigned *Pedagogy of the Oppressed* to his students in
a course on group psychotherapy. This was Jack Corrazzini, a psychologist who
was teaching at Virginia Commonwealth University and was the director of its
counseling center. One of our tasks in his class was to figure out what *Pedagogy
of the Oppressed* had to do with being a group therapist. The bottom line was
this: When you set out to be helpful to another person, particularly in a context
where there is a power differential between yourself and the helpee, *you need to
check yourself first*. If you do not, you may not only end up being unhelpful, you
may actually serve to perpetuate the helpee's one-down position—his or her
oppression.

What are we checking *for* within ourselves? I have already mentioned the
kind of "help" that Freire described as false generosity, which is assistance offered by people with privilege to the oppressed in the absence of any acknowl-
edgement of the context of oppression. Within such transactions, I, as a helper
coming from a relatively privileged social location, offer the helpee some benefit
of my position, knowledge, or purchasing power. It may well be that the benefit
is truly needed and that the helpee is grateful to receive it. However, what goes
unaddressed in this transaction is an entire subtext regarding the hierarchical
differences in our positions and how the transaction preserves it. In the case of
group therapy, when the leader interacts with group members from the veiled,
authoritative, one-up posture provided by conventional roles, this power dynamic is preserved. When the leader instead positions the group process itself
as the engine of change, and facilitates members' ownership of it, the power
dynamic is challenged. Here, the unexamined, self-serving handouts of Freire's
false generosity are seen as analogous to a therapist's "handout" of expert help to
clients, in that the therapist has ultimately preserved her position in the group
as the all-knowing, superior other rather than to ally herself with her clients'
liberation.

When people live in poverty, "helpful" transactions can consist of these met-
aphorical handouts as well as material ones. The unacknowledged subtext, then,
extends to the causes of the causes of the need, why the need continues to exist,
and why I would rather spend a day in a soup kitchen than take part in action to
eradicate it. Why do so many people need coats? Why do so many people need
soup? Why do schoolchildren in poor communities need remedial programs?
And what is the meaning of my location within a system that contributes to
those outcomes for other people but not for me?

Charitable transactions can fog my view of the structural elements of poverty
so that I never have to think about any of those questions. This is accomplished in
two related ways. First, charity leads me to avert my gaze from structural elements
and focus on the individual, the specific, and the concrete. These elements are

thereby tacitly construed within the transaction as the essence of the problem—or rather, their lack is the problem, and remedying that lack is the answer. So perhaps I give money to a hunger organization or participate in a fundraiser to purchase new baseball uniforms or computers for a school in a poor neighborhood. Again, there is nothing wrong with these actions *per se* and no doubt whatsoever that the schoolchildren will benefit significantly from having new computers. The point is that I have configured the problem to be primarily one of supplying specific resources without also asking why a fundraiser has to take place for these children to have the school equipment that they need. Configuring the problem in this way creates a reassuring fog around those challenging structural questions: It's a question of computers! *That's* easy enough to solve. The second way that charity functions is that, if I ever do happen to see through the fog to glimpse some unfairness of things, charity gives me a way to separate myself from it. Even if I notice that the playing field is not exactly even, I have created an experience of myself as a charitable, caring helper. I am one of the good guys. My head now rests more easily on my pillow and I proceed uninterruptedly with my life on the up-side of an inequitable status quo.

Checking yourself, then, means asking yourself, how and why do I want to help—and what *is* help, anyway? When the context is one of oppression, charity is not the final answer. As Freire explained, true generosity consists of

> fighting to destroy the causes which nourish false charity. False charity constrains the fearful and subdued, the 'rejects' of life to extend their trembling hands. True generosity lies in striving so that these hands—whether of individuals or entire peoples—need be extended less and less in supplication, so that more and more they become hands which work, and, working, transform the world. (p. 29)

Martin Luther King, Jr., who was assassinated weeks before the march on Washington, D.C., that would launch his Poor People's Campaign, expressed the very same perspective:

> On the one hand, we are called to play the Good Samaritan on life's roadside, but that will be only an initial act. One day we must come to see that the whole Jericho Road must be transformed so that men and women will not be constantly beaten and robbed as they make their journey on life's highway. True compassion is more than flinging a coin to a beggar. It comes to see that an edifice which produces beggars needs restructuring. (1967, p. 1)

I feel the need to state this one final time: I am not dismissing the usefulness of charitable giving that supplies people with resources that they need. In fact, *in the short term*, such giving is literally vital to the survival of many poor families.

I also do not doubt in the least that sincere altruism is behind such efforts. I just think that charity is the easy part of the work. It does not require us to do or say anything risky or controversial. It does not require us to look at ourselves. And it returns immediate dividends in that it portrays us to ourselves as benevolent and dissociated from systems of oppression, a gratifying notion that allows us to more fully enjoy our own good fortune. These are ways that, *in the long term*, charity is part of the problem.

Along these lines, we need to ask ourselves what it means that our nation allows so much of the provision of necessary resources for poor families to depend upon private philanthropy. One of my friends here in New York told me about a back-to-school tradition in her Manhattan neighborhood: All the parents shop for supplies such as soap and boxes of tissue and bring them to the local public schools. Why have we left it to affluent parents to make sure that children at school have soap? Why does it take black-tie galas hosted by movie stars to bring the basics to American communities?

Many of our social service agencies depend entirely upon giving and grantmaking by wealthy donors. One of the upshots of this configuration is that the philosophical and political framework in which such services are offered then necessarily becomes one that reflects the interests of owning-class people. Many people who go to work for community-based organizations find this out to their great disappointment, when the nonprofit organization whose website sounded so inspirational turns out to perpetuate the same kinds of classist and racist stereotypes that operate elsewhere in society. Even grassroots activists who receive funding are likely to find themselves increasingly motivated to tailor their messages and their services to suit the visiting grantmakers who now pay the bills. Relying upon donors also leaves these vital services in a precarious position: during an economic downturn, those donors may well decide to hold on to that money—and the doors can close overnight. I collaborated with a CBO that provided shelter and support for homeless and otherwise vulnerable gay and transgender youth, and one Wednesday, we were informed that Friday would be the last day of operation. What would happen to those kids the following week? No one could say.

When we start to consider *change* in addition to charity—change that would address poverty itself so that there would not be so many people in need of charity—a comfortable, unexamined stance is not available. Thinking about being part of change, rather than part of the status quo, requires us to go beyond the gratifying posture of the compassionate altruist. It requires us to ask questions of ourselves and others that people who currently enjoy relative socioeconomic privilege do not usually wish to consider. Questions like, why isn't there a national movement, an *uprising*, in support of a living wage? Why is national discourse regarding the provision of basic health care for all families able to be derailed again and again? Why are we content to allow American schoolchildren in poor communities—*our* children—to go without the same teaching staff and computers and gym classes that other children have? In New York City and Detroit, two cities with the lowest median incomes in the United States (U.S. Census Bureau, 2007), the high school *graduation* rates were 45.2% and 24.9% respectively (Einhorn, 2008). Where are the rest of those kids? Why aren't we causing a ruckus at town hall meetings because our nation's young people are allowed to drift away from schools and into the streets? We have no place in our legal economy for all these youngsters, so we make beds for them in our prisons, with the U.S. prison population having exploded by an additional 700% between the years of 1969 to 1999 (Reiman, 2007). This is, of course, assuming that they live that long—San Francisco district attorney Kamala Harris found that, in her city, over 94% of all the young people who die from homicide are high school dropouts (Harris, 2009). What kind of country do we want to live in?

Some economically privileged people do raise these questions. An organization called Resource Generation supports young, progressive adults in using inherited wealth for social change (Redington, 2009). One of its organizers, Karen Pittelman, used her $3 million trust fund to establish a foundation for low-income women activists (Pittelman, 2005). Similarly, Responsible Wealth is an organization comprised of business leaders and wealthy individuals in the top 5% of national wealth and/or income who advocate for economic justice in the form of fair taxes and corporate accountability. They have taken such actions as lobbying the governor of Connecticut to balance the budget by raising *their* tax rates rather than cutting human services, and by organizing in support of a public health care option (United for a Fair Economy, 2009). In association with Responsible Wealth, Chuck Collins, Mike Lapham, and Scott Klinger (2004) published "I Didn't Do It Alone," a paper that presents the accounts of successful, wealthy people who realize that their fortunes were not created in a vacuum—in addition to their own hard work, their accumulation of wealth was supported by the U.S. economic and tax structure, low-wage workers around the world, race and gender privilege, and luck. Like Ben Cohen of Ben and Jerry's Ice Cream, these individuals are willing to be accountable:

> I always worked on the idea that 50% of the money that I get goes back to the community in the form of advocating for progressive social change—to change the system, so that we don't end up with as many people in poverty. . . . I've got this quote up on my wall, "If we had justice, we wouldn't need charity." So I use 50% of the money I get to try to achieve that. (p. 35)

Warren Buffett, one of the world's wealthiest men, challenged other attendees at a $4,600-per-plate fundraiser to consider the structural advantages built in to the American tax system for the benefit of members of his social class. "The

400 of us here pay a lower part of our income in taxes than our receptionists do, or our cleaning ladies, for that matter," said Buffett, explaining that his tax rate was 17.7% as opposed to the 30% rate paid by his secretary. "If you're in the luckiest 1% of humanity," he continued, "you owe it to the rest of humanity to think about the other 99%" (Bawden, 2007).

There are class-privileged people, then, who provide examples of movement toward Freire's conception of true generosity: people who, though they may be involved in charitable undertakings, are also willing to speak out about structural elements of economic injustice and contribute to social change. Such help may therefore coincide with charitable help-dispensing, but it goes beyond charity to comprise commitment and action toward economic equity. This understanding can be applied to mental health practice as well. Transformed psychotherapeutic practice, co-created interventions, and community praxis, as described in the previous chapter, are examples of professional activities that better correspond to Freire's conceptualization of authentic generosity than does the conventional expert dispensing of "help." In conventional dyads, existing structural dynamics remain unchallenged, resulting in "helpful" interactions that re-enact power-over dynamics between a relatively class-privileged therapist and a poor client. Transformed psychotherapeutic practice, co-created interventions, and community praxis, to varying degrees, subvert these dynamics by explicitly locating the work within a social, cultural, historical, and political context. In this way, in addition to supporting people in making creative, responsible use of the life chances and options that are available to them, these approaches help people interpret and analyze broad sociocultural conditions rather than internalizing them as personal failings. All three of them may also, and community praxis certainly does, comprise the creation and implementation of actions that can ally practitioners with people and communities as they work together for economic justice.

None of this contradicts people's ability to make the most of their circumstances, or to take action to improve their own lives. As therapists and counselors, of course we believe that people's purposeful actions can improve their lives. This question, therefore, is not an *either-or* proposition, as in 1.) either structural oppressions like classism and racism are real, or 2.) people's responsibility to act is real. It is instead a *both-and* issue—both are real. As therapists, we want to support people in taking purposeful action, and we also want to support them in interpreting the cultural context that has shaped their starting points, as well as the kinds of obstacles and options that they have (and do not have) in their social class baskets. Without doing the former, we imply that people can only be victims, not survivors and thrivers. Without doing the latter, we tacitly encourage poor people to locate the blame for classism, poverty, racism, and their consequences within themselves—an unwarranted, overwhelming, and destructive burden that pits people against themselves, their families, and their communities.

Mental health practitioners can also apply liberatory considerations to the political and economic contexts in which they and other social scientists practice and earn their livings, contexts which exemplify the power-over relationships that Freire described. In particular, the poverty industry—the business of studying, managing, counseling, and otherwise "serving" poor people—is an enterprise that provides paychecks to the personnel of innumerable charities, food pantries, social service providers, nonprofit administrators, and philanthropic organizations, as well as tax writeoffs for the corporations and wealthy individuals who support them. Poor people almost never have representation in the decisions made by this industry, whose financial growth has outpaced the U.S. gross domestic product; the GDP grew by 37% between 1994 and 2004, while indices of financial health for public charities rose during that time by 56% (Urban Institute, 2007). In her analysis of the workings of such organizations (and of the welfare system itself), Funicello (1993) illuminated the classist assumptions and profit motives behind our preference for "serving" the poor rather than providing direct income support and otherwise changing the system:

> Poor folks just can't be trusted—not like someone with a salary well above the median. When did honesty become a class trait? . . . Repeatedly poor mothers would say, just give me the money and I'll feed my own kids. One common reaction to the notion of giving mothers money directly has always been, "If you give them money, how do you know they'll spend it on food?" I'd have to ask . . . if you give it to the hunger organizations, how do you know they won't spend it on their Christmas parties? (p. 146)

Funicello went on to point out that government agencies and nonprofit organizations are often the sponsors of social science research on poverty, research that is no less subject to the biases of the funder than were studies funded by the tobacco industry that attested to the safety of cigarettes. One might juxtapose this comment with the observation that relatively few psychological explorations of poverty are conducted via an analysis of the reproduction of power and privilege. Rather, we prefer to focus our attentions on documenting and proposing palliatives for the many problems, symptoms, and deprivations that poor people experience, and which we and other social service providers might expect to find employment in cataloging and remedying.

## WHAT IS RESEARCHABLE VERSUS WHAT IS GOOD

In addition to its revised definitions of poverty and help, the development of contextualized, socially just mental health praxis presents suggests another area for conceptual amendment: how do we describe and assess these interventions and their impact in this era of empirically validated practice? How can we evaluate a process that encompasses both individual and community experience and/or privileges participants' own evaluations of outcomes and/or is essentially time-unlimited? Our socialization as professionals and as social scientists will have left many of us believing implicitly that any endeavor that does not lend itself to conventional quantitative assessment is inherently flawed or somehow not "real" practice at all. Others of us who hold out the possibility that such practices are of value may nevertheless be stumped by the prospect of evaluating them, whether as clinicians called upon to justify their practices, members of a grant-writing team seeking funding, or faculty members hoping to publish.

Lisa Goodman, Katya Fels Smyth, and Victoria Banyard (2010) presented this dilemma as they wrote about "the conflation of what is researchable using specific quantitative research methods with what is good or useful" in the context of poverty (p. 20). They emphasized that the actions and interventions that are most useful to the emotional well-being of poor communities are not circumscribed, manualizeable treatments but actions that involve complex, evolving processes and outcomes. This creates a potentially paradoxical situation for practitioners: either engage in the practices that seem most contextually, theoretically, and practically appropriate to the context of poverty, or engage in the practices that seem most researchable according to the paradigms that our field recognizes and rewards. It is like the old joke: A police officer approaches a man searching the ground around a streetlight for his keys. "Oh, is this where you lost them?" asks the officer, coming over to help him. "No," answers the man, "but the light is better here."

An elaboration of this position was offered by Smyth and Lisbeth Schorr in a 2009 working paper, part of a series published by the John F. Kennedy School of Government at Harvard University. In their paper, the authors wrote of innovative human services programs that are contextualized and multifaceted in their assistance to marginalized families and communities. The authors called these the "What It Takes" programs. Discovering that such programs exist, wrote Smyth and Schorr, is the good news; the bad news is that these programs are struggling to survive due to the narrow definitions of "success" and "evidence" and "proof" imposed upon them by funders and policymakers. They quoted one program director's reflections on this no-win situation:

> [The] kind of rigid, narrow accountability that funders are demanding is of questionable validity . . . [and will force] programs [to] keep doing only what worked yesterday, instead of what works today. Scientific evaluations generally require staff to standardize interventions and deliver them consistently over long periods of time, regardless of individual needs, cultural considerations, or changes in circumstances. In contrast, [our program] aims to be flexible, innovative, and culturally competent. And so the very qualities that staff and families believe make the program effective are the qualities that make measurement difficult. (Smyth & Schorr, 2009, p. 6)

The upshot, according to Smyth and Schorr (2009), is that we lack ways of evaluating the effectiveness of innovative programs and/or are likely to overlook them completely if they do not correspond to familiar measurement models. Moreover, as these programs fight to survive, they are often forced to distort, de-emphasize, or eliminate the very components that made them successful in the first place as they attempt to comply with funders who require experimental manipulations and quantitative data in exchange for continued support. Smyth and Schorr proposed a new, expanded evaluative paradigm for programmatic use when conventional approaches are not appropriate. This expanded model would

1. emphasize theories of change and logical connections between actions and outcomes,
2. incorporate methods such as case studies and other qualitative approaches,
3. allow for systemic complexity,
4. privilege intentional programmatic adaptations,
5. seek to generate sufficient evidence quickly enough to allow for continuous improvements,
6. create actions according to consensus approaches,
7. allow projects to draw upon existing knowledge (rather than independently establish relationships between all inputs and outputs), and
8. allow programs to establish outcomes that are meaningful to their work.

The authors maintained:

We are among those who value the push toward greater accountability. This is a time when we need more than ever to know whether what we are paying for actually translates into changed lives. Debates about which results matter, which matters can be measured, and whether it counts if you can't count it are important and worth having. But the discussions have largely been dominated by those who advocate a limited definition of evidence in the pursuit of decisive determinants of efficacy. (p. 220)

These authors and others (Berwick, 2008; McCall & Green, 2004) are calling for a sea change in our thinking about process, outcome, and evaluation—one that will inspire many psychologists and mental health professionals to instinctively shrink back. As psychologists, we have been socialized within a profession that looks most often to the hard sciences and medicine for inspiration, hoping to share some of the respectability, relative certitude, and third-party payments that those fields enjoy. As a result, we feel most intellectually fit and ready to meet our peers when we are speaking the language of randomized clinical trials, independent and dependent variables, empirical data, statistical

analyses, and evidence-based practice. This is fine when conventional methodological features such as these are appropriate to our projects—but what about
when they are not? For those of us employed in traditional academic or clinical
settings, the choice can feel like, either abandon the project or prepare to be
seen as some kind of professional lightweight. As someone whose professional
commitments have often taken her outside the circumscribed and highly esteemed arena of conventional methodology and toward projects in the vein of
the "What It Takes" programs, I sometimes feel that my work is not fully translatable within the professional worlds of my colleagues. It is worth noting that
no one has ever said this to me directly (yet)—it is the result of my own fears
about venturing outside dominant paradigms of "real" research and scholarship.
Schorr and Yankelovich (2000) commented that discussions of these paradig-
matic differences can sometimes feel like religious quarrels, which waste the
time and energy of all involved:

> Many new approaches now are becoming available for evaluating whether
> complex programs work. What they lack in certainty they make up for in rich-
> ness of understanding that builds over time and across initiatives. Quarrels over
> which method represents "the gold standard" make no more sense than arguing
> about whether hammers are superior to saws. The choice depends on whether
> you want to drive in a nail or cut a board. (p. 2)

To re-imagine psychological and mental health practice in ways that align
us with the movement of marginalized groups towards social equity, we also
need to take part in the re-imagining of programmatic outcomes, evidence,
and evaluation. On these points, Smyth, Schorr, Goodman, and Banyard have
strengthened a dialogue that represents the confluence of many other voices
calling for methodological transformation. It has roots in the epistemological
foundations of PAR, in that they lead mental health professionals to question
and expand dominant-culture paradigms of knowledge production. It contains
echoes of what David Bakan (1967) called psychology's inclination toward
"methodolatry," or the narrow privileging of methodology to the extent that
our selection of methods ends up dictating the phenomena that we investigate.
It also calls to mind Linda Tuhiwai Smith's (1999) exposition of decolonized
methodology, which offers researchers and community members the opportunity to "research back" in the tradition of "writing back" or "talking back" (p. 7).
As Goodman, Smyth, and Banyard (2010) summarized:

> To the extent that some of the most innovative and context-sensitive ap-
> proaches to mental health may be the poorest fit for evaluation using controlled
> clinical trials, we risk continuing to privilege interventions that are more easily

studied by traditional methods over interventions that may be more effective and meaningful, but less responsive to these traditional tools—to the detriment of impoverished individuals and families (p. 21).

## ADVOCACY FOR ECONOMIC JUSTICE IS ADVOCACY FOR PSYCHOLOGICAL WELL-BEING

Thus far I have supported an expanded view of poverty that emphasizes social exclusion; a redefinition of help as going beyond charity to change; and an extension of program evaluation methodologies to allow for a more complex estimation of what works for people and communities in poverty. I will conclude the chapter by affirming the call from social justice psychologists such as Toporek, Lewis, and Crethar (2009)to broaden the scope of mental health practice to incorporate advocacy while bringing a special focus to economic injustice. As practitioners, we can reshape our work to integrate this stance; as professors and supervisors, we can incorporate considerations of class and poverty within our teaching and research; as a field, we can advocate for economic justice.

One of the easiest things that we can do to participate in policy advocacy on behalf of poor and working-class people is to join the subcommittees or task forces within our professional organizations that maintain a focus on issues of social class and poverty. The work of APA's Task Force on Socioeconomic Status, for example, has been referenced several times in the course of the present discussion. The Task Force led to the establishment of the APA Office on Socioeconomic Status, and members of that office's listserv receive regular poverty-related policy updates and notification of events and opportunities for advocacy. This is a convenient way for professionals to keep up with national developments related to poverty and social class, and to participate in collective petitioning or letter-writing campaigns targeting specific initiatives. Relatedly, the National Association of Social Workers has a Specialty Practice Section on Social and Economic Justice and Peace, and participates in such initiatives as Half in Ten, a partnership among organizations whose goal is to reduce the number of people living in poverty by half in the next 10 years. These groups serve an important function in bringing social class and poverty to the attention of the mental health professions, and also in providing an organizational nexus for practitioners who would like to facilitate their profession's movement in support of economic justice. Other simple strategies include making sure that when possible, our conferences and activities patronize companies that have fair trade policies—companies who insure that workers throughout the production cycle are paid a fair wage. Currently, coffee, chocolate, and wine are just a few of the products that can be purchased from fair trade organizations (to learn more, visit the websites of the Fair Trade Federation at http://www.fairtradefederation.org/ and the Fair Trade Labeling Organizations International at http://www.fairtrade.net/).

Given what we know about the impact of social exclusion and poverty on emotional well-being, such advocacy complements the general goals of professional mental health organizations: Advocating for the eradication of poverty and the greater inclusion of the poor *is* advocating for psychological well-being, given that over half of Americans are likely to spend at least a year below the poverty line at some point during their lives (Hacker, 2006). It also creates an avenue by which we can, together, target the causes of the causes, to again use Michael Marmot's language. Lott and Bullock (2007) described some of the poverty-related structural issues upon which we could have a collective influence, such as the need for universal access to health care, support for food assistance through mandated school breakfast programs, and the reform of TANF (Temporary Assistance to Needy Families). Lott and Bullock analyzed this federal welfare program's biased emphasis on women's marital status as a requirement for the receipt of aid, and critiqued its consequences as a "work-first" initiative as humiliating and punitive:

> Welfare programs can be geared toward providing families with the resources they need to become financially secure—health care, transportation, housing, nutritious food, vocational training or other educational opportunities, and quality child care. . . . Currently, applicants are often humiliated and told to seek help from family or friends, diverted from completing formal applications, sanctioned with full or partial benefit reductions for small infractions, and threatened with being removed from the welfare rolls when time limits are met regardless of need.

We could also speak up when workers' rights are undermined. Former U.S. labor secretary Robert Reisch cited national poll data indicating that a majority of working Americans would like to have a union if they could—a finding that does not fit with the current low levels of unionization that now exist among that private-sector workers (Reisch, 2009). Why are workers not joining unions if they want them? Reisch (2009) explained that

> those who try to form a union, according to researchers at MIT, have only about a 1 in 5 chance of successfully doing so. The reason? Most of the time, employees who want to form a union are threatened and intimidated by their employers. And all too often, if they don't heed the warnings, they're fired, even though that's illegal. I saw this when I was secretary of labor over a decade ago. We tried to penalize employers that broke the law, but the fines

are minuscule. Too many employers consider them a cost of doing business. (p. 15)

"This isn't right," concluded Reisch, and I expect that many of us—as a profession that supports every person's right to a voice—would agree. What is the social justice significance of the decline of unions? Eighty-year-old coal miner Joe Johnson recalled the days before the advent of the United Mine Workers Association:

> I worked in water up to my knees for a dollar a day loading coal by hand, and if I said anything about it the boss would tell me, "If you don't like it, there's a barefoot man waiting outside ready to take your job." (Couto, 1993, p. 167)

Poor working people without the opportunity to organize have none of the resources that command consideration from the rest of us. They do not have money, they do not own property, they do not control resources, they do not hire or fire other people, they do not hold political office, and they do not represent a powerful demographic to marketers or other trend-watchers. They simply do all the work that the rest of us need them to do and which we do not want to do ourselves. They clean offices and dry-clean clothing and trim meat and take care of the elderly along with all the other unexciting low-wage work that carries society along. *We depend upon them*—without them, our lives would come to a standstill.

We value our own opportunities to organize to advance our interests through the APA, the ACA, the NASW, and other professional associations. I encourage these groups to collectively call out class-based discrimination that stands in the way of other people's right to do so, and to support legislation like the Employee Free Choice Act, which penalizes companies that interfere with worker's rights.

Finally, it seems natural for organizations like ours to stand up in support of a living wage. Noting that "people who play by the rules shouldn't lose the game" (p. 150), Bane and Ellwood (1994) explained that our wage and tax policies mean that many low-wage workers are worse off than they would be on welfare, not only in terms of income, but also with regard to medical and food assistance. Moreover, we expect poor single mothers to take on not only this no-win situation, but to somehow secure child care as well. Unlike nations like the United Kingdom, this country has not yet been able to sustain a living wage dialogue on a on a national level. However, individual cities such as Santa Fe, San Francisco, and Brookline, Massachusetts, have successfully raised their minimum wages above the federal level, the result of grassroots campaigning by churches, university and high school students, community-based organizations, and labor unions in each locality. One of the earliest of these successes was in Baltimore:

Workers in some of Baltimore's homeless shelters and soup kitchens had noticed something new and troubling about many of the visitors coming in for meals and shelter: they happened to have full-time jobs. In response, local religious leaders successfully persuaded the City Council to raise the base pay for city contract workers to $6.10 an hour from $4.25, the federal minimum at the time. The Baltimore campaign was ostensibly about money. But to those who thought about it more deeply, it was about the force of particular moral propositions: first, that work should be rewarded, and second, that no one who works full time should have to live in poverty. (Gertner, 2006, p. 2)

Gertner, a *New York Times* reporter, asked a Catholic monsignor in Santa Fe if the decision to throw his support behind living wage reforms had been a difficult one:

"It was a no-brainer," he said. "You know, I am not by nature a political person. I have gotten a lot of grief from some people, business owners, who say, 'Father, why don't you stick to religion?' Well, pardon me—this is religion. The Scripture is full of matters of justice. How can you worship a God that you do not see and then oppress the workers that you do see?" (p. 28)

I hope that by now I have established a premise for my belief that, as psychologists, social workers, counselors, and therapists, we could give the same response regarding the establishment of our professional commitment to economic justice. Why don't we stick to mental health? Well, pardon me—this *is* mental health. Contributing our work toward the evolution of a more just society where all families have enough, toward a more democratic society where every person has a voice, and toward a more humane society where no one is kept on the outside looking in, is promoting mental health. Psychologists can't solve these problems by themselves—but, then again, no one person or profession can, so that's not what the choice is about. Through our practice, theory, research, and advocacy, we have a unique role to play in ending social exclusion. The choice is about whether or not we will step up and play our part.

# REFERENCES

Acosta, O., & Toro, P. A. (2000). Let's ask the homeless people themselves: A needs assessment based on a probability sample of adults. *American Journal of Community Psychology, 28*, 343–366.

Adler, N. E., Boyce, T., Chesney, M. A., Cohen, S., Folkman, S., Kahn, R. L., Syme, S. L. (1994). Socioeconomic status and health: The challenge of the gradient. *American Psychologist, 49*, 15–24.

Affleck, D. C., & Garfield, S. L. (1961). Predictive judgment of therapists and duration of stay in psychotherapy. *Journal of Clinical Psychology, 17*, 134–137.

Albee, G. W. (1969). Who shall be served? *Professional Psychology, 1*, 4–7.

Albee, G. W. (1996). Revolutions and counterrevolutions in prevention. *American Psychologist, 51*, 1130–1133.

Albee, G. W. (2000). The Boulder Model's fatal flaw. *American Psychologist, 55*, 247–248.

Albee, G. W., & Gulotta, T. P. (1997). Primary prevention's evolution. In G. Albee & T. Gulotta (Eds.), *Primary prevention works* (pp. 3–22). Thousand Oaks, CA: Sage.

Albelda, R. Badgett, M. V. L., Schneebaum, A., & Gates, G. J. (2009). Poverty in the lesbian, gay, and bisexual community. Retrieved September 25, 2009, from the website of the Williams Institute at http://www.law.ucla.edu/williamsinstitute/pdf/LGB-PovertyReport.pdf

Aldarondo, E. (2007). *Advancing social justice through clinical practice*. Mahwah, NJ: Lawrence Erlbaum Associates.

Ali, A., Hawkins, R. L., & Chambers, D. A. (2010). Recovery from depression among clients transitioning out of poverty. *American Journal of Orthopsychiatry, 80*(1), 26–33.

Allen, L., & Britt, D. (1983). Social class, mental health, and mental illness. In R. Felner, L. Jason, J. Moritsugu, & S. Farber (Eds.), *Preventative psychology: Theory, research, and practice* (pp. 149-160). New York: Pergamon.

Allison, D. (1994). *Skin*. Ithaca, NY: Firebrand.

Altman, N. (1995). *The analyst in the inner city*. Hillsdale, NJ: Analytic Press.

Anyon, J. (2005). *Radical possibilities*. New York: Routledge.

American Psychological Association. (2000). Resolution on poverty and socioeconomic status. Retrieved August 12, 2005, from http://www.apa.org/pi/urban/povres.html

American Psychological Association. (2002). Multicultural guidelines on education and training, research, practice, and organizational development for psychologists. Retrieved July 6, 2009, from http://www.apa.org/pi/multiculturalguidelines/formats.html

American Psychological Association. (2006). T*ask Force on Socioeconomic Status (SES): Final report, August 2006.* Washington, DC: Author.

American Psychological Association. (2008). Report of the task force on resources for the inclusion of social class in psychology curricula. Retrieved December 16, 2007, from http://www.apa.org/pi/ses/

Aponte, H. J. (1994). *Bread and spirit: Therapy with the new poor.* New York: Norton.

Argyle, M. (1994). *The psychology of social class.* London: Routledge.

Ayoub, C., O'Connor, E., Rappolt-Schlictmann, G., Vallotton, C., Raikes, H., & Chazan-Cohen, R. (2009). Cognitive skill performance among young children living in poverty: Risk, change, and the promotive effects of Early Head Start. *Early Childhood Research Quarterly, 24*(3), 289–305

Badgett, M. V. L., Lau, H., Sears, B., & Ho, D. (2007). *Bias in the workplace: Consistent evidence of sexual orientation and gender identity discrimination.* Retrieved September 25, 2009, from http://www.law.ucla.edu/williamsinstitute/publications/Bias%20 in%20the%20Workplace.pdf

Bakan, D. (1967). *On method: Toward a reconstruction of psychological investigation.* New York: Jossey-Bass.

Baker, N. L. (1996). Class as a construct in a "classless" society. In M. Hill & E. D. Rothblum (Eds.), *Classism and feminist therapy: Counting costs* (pp. 13–24). New York: Harrington Park.

Bane, M. J., & Ellwood, D. T. (1994). *Welfare realities.* Cambridge, MA: Harvard University Press.

Banyard, V. L. (1995). "Taking another route": Daily survival narratives from mothers who are homeless. *Journal of Community Psychology, 23,* 871–891.

Banyard, V. L., & Graham-Bermann, S. A. (1998). Surviving poverty: Stress and coping in the lives of housed and homeless mothers. *American Journal of Orthopsychiatry, 68,* 479–489.

Barefoot, J. C., Peterson, B. L., Dahlstrom, W. G., Siegler, I. C., Anderson, N. B., & Williams, R. B., Jr. (1991). Hostility patterns and health implications: Correlates of Cook-Medley Hostility scale scores in a national survey. *Health Psychology, 10,* 18–24.

Barnes, A. (2004). Race, schizophrenia, and admission to state psychiatric hospitals. *Administration and Policy in Mental Health and Mental Health Services Research, 31,* 241–252.

Barry, B. (2002). Social exclusion, social isolation, and the distribution of income. In J. Hill, J. Le Grand, & D. Piachaud (Eds.), *Understanding social exclusion* (pp. 13–29). New York: Oxford.

Baum, O. E., Felzer, S. B., D'Zmura, T. L., & Shumaker, E. (1966). Psychotherapy, dropouts, and lower socioeconomic patients. *American Journal of Orthopsychiatry, 36,* 629–635.

Baumeister, R. F., DeWall, C. N., Ciarocco, N. J., & Twenge, J. M. (2005). Social exclusion impairs self-regulation. *Journal of Personality and Social Psychology, 88,* 589–604.

Baumeister, R. F, Twenge, J. M., & Nuss, C. K. (2002). Effects of social exclusion on cognitive processing: Anticipated aloneness reduces intelligent thought. *Journal of Personality and Social Psychology, 83,* 817–827.

Bawden, T. (2007). *Buffett blasts system that lets him pay less tax than secretary.* Retrieved September 14, 2009, from http://www.timesonline.co.uk/tol/money/tax/article1996735.ece

Beeghley, L. (2008). *The structure of social stratification in the United States.* Boston: Allyn and Bacon.

Belle, D. (1990). Poverty and women's mental health. *American Psychologist, 45,* 385–389.

Belle, D., & Doucet, J. (2003) Poverty, inequality and discrimination as sources of depression among women. *Psychology of Women Quarterly, 27,* 101–113.

Belle, D., Doucet, J., Harris, J., Miller, J., & Tan, E. (2000). Who is rich? Who is happy? *American Psychologist, 55,* 1160–1161.

Berrick, J. D. (1995). *Faces of poverty.* New York: Oxford.

Berwick, D. M. (2008). The science of improvement. *JAMA, 299*(10), 1182–1184.

Black, L. L., & Stone, D. (2005). Expanding the definition of privilege: The concept of social privilege. *Journal of Multicultural Counseling and Development, 33,* 243–255.

Blazer, D. G., Kessler, R. C., McGonagle, K. A., & Swartz, M. S. (1994). The prevalence and distribution of major depression in a national community sample: The National Comorbidity Survey. *American Journal of Psychiatry, 151,* 983–989.

Blustein, D. L., Chaves, A. P., Diemer, M. A., Gallagher, L. A., Marshall, K. G., Sirin, S., & Bhati, K. S. (2002). Voices of the forgotten half: The role of social class in the school-to-work transition. *Journal of Counseling Psychology, 49*(3), 311–323.

Blustein, D. L., McWhirter, E. H., & Perry, J. C. (2005). An emancipatory communitarian approach to vocational development: Theory, research, and practice. *The Counseling Psychologist, 33,* 141–179.

Bogle, J. (2006). *The battle for the soul of capitalism.* New Haven, CT: Yale University Press.

Bourdieu, P. (1984). *Distinction: A social critique of the judgment of taste.* Cambridge, MA: Harvard University Press.

Bowley, G. (2009). With big profit, Goldman sees big payday ahead. Retrieved October 19, 2009, from http://www.nytimes.com/2009/07/15/business/15goldman.html?_r=1

Boyd-Franklin, N., & Bry, B. H. (2000). *Reaching out in family therapy.* New York: Guilford Press.

Bradley, R. H., & Corwyn, R. F. (2002). Socioeconomic status and child development. *Annual Review of Psychology, 53,* 371–399.

Bradley, R. H., Corwyn, R. F., McAdoo, H. P., & Coll, C. G. (2003). The home environments of children in the United States, Part I: Variations by age, ethnicity, and poverty status. *Child Development, 72,* 1844–1867.

Brown, D. B., & Parnell, M. (1990). Mental health services for the urban poor: A systems approach. In M. P. Mirkin (Ed.), *The social and political contexts of family therapy* (pp. 215–236). Boston: Allyn & Bacon.

Brown, G. W., & Moran, P. M. (1997). Single mothers, poverty, and depression. *Psychological Medicine, 27,* 21–33.

Brown, L. S. (1990). The meaning of a multicultural perspective for theory-building in feminist therapy. *Women & Therapy, 9*(1), 1–21.

Bruce, M.L., Takeuchi, D.T., & Leaf, P.J. (1991). Poverty and psychiatric status. *Archives of General Psychiatry, 48,* 470–474.

Brydon-Miller, M. (1997). Participatory action research: Psychology and social change. *Journal of Social Issues, 53*, 657–666.

Bullard, R. D. (2005). *The quest for environmental justice.* San Francisco: Sierra Club.

Bullock, H. E. (1995). Class acts: Middle-class responses to the poor. In B. Lott & D. Maluso (Eds.), *The social psychology of interpersonal discrimination* (pp. 118–159). New York: Guilford Press.

Bullock, H. E., Wyche, K. F., & Williams, W. R. (2001). Media images of the poor. *Journal of Social Issues, 57*, 229–246.

Burchardt, T., Le Grand, J., & Piachaud, D. (2002a). Introduction. In J. Hill, J. Le Grand, & D. Piachaud (Eds.), *Understanding social exclusion* (pp. 1–12). New York: Oxford.

Burchardt, T., Le Grand, J., & Piachaud, D. (2002b). Degrees of exclusion: Developing a dynamic, multidimensional measure. In J. Hill, J. Le Grand, & D. Piachaud (Eds.), *Understanding social exclusion* (pp. 30–43). New York: Oxford.

Cammarota, J., & Fine, M. (2008). Youth participatory action research. In J. Cammarota & M. Fine (Eds.), *Revolutionizing education* (pp. 1–12). New York: Routledge.

Campbell, W. K., Krusemark, E. A., Dyckman, K. A., Brunell, A. B., McDowell, J. E., Twenge, J. M., Clementz, B. A. (2006). A magnetoencephalography investigation of neural correlates for social exclusion and self-control. *Social Neuroscience, 1*, 124–134.

Cardwell, D. (2005). Transit strike: Race bubbles to the surface in stand-off. Retrieved September 14, 2009, from http://select.nytimes.com.

Carr, S. C., & Sloan, T. S. (Eds.). (2003). *Poverty and psychology.* New York: Kluwer Academic/Plenum Press.

Carter, R. T. (1995). *The influence of race and racial identity in psychotherapy: Toward a racially inclusive model.* New York: Wiley.

Caughy, M. O., & Ocampo, P. J. (2006). Neighborhood poverty, social capital, and the cognitive development of African American preschoolers. *American Journal of Community Psychology, 37*, 141–154.

Centers, R. (1949). *The psychology of social classes.* Princeton, NJ: Princeton University Press.

Chalifoux, B. (1996). Speaking up: White working class women in therapy. In M. Hill, & E. D. Rothblum (Eds.), *Classism and feminist therapy.* (pp. 25–34). New York: Harrington Park.

Chaney, K. (1994). Shifting horizons: Navigating a life. In J. Penelope (Ed.), *Coming out of the class closet* (pp. 173–180). Freedom, CA: Crossing Press.

Chataway, C. J. (1997). An examination of the constraints on mutual inquiry in a participatory action research project. *Journal of Social Issues, 53*, 747–765.

Chataway, C. J. (2001). Negotiating the observer-observed relationship: Participatory action research. In D. L. Tolman & M. Brydon-Miller (Eds.), *From subjects to subjectivities: A handbook of interpretive and participatory methods* (pp. 239–255). New York: New York University Press.

Clawson, R. A., & Trice, R. (2000). Poverty as we know it: Media portrayals of the poor. *Public Opinion Quarterly, 64*, 53–64.

Collins, C., Lapham, M., & Klinger, S. (2004). *I didn't do it alone: Society's contribution to individual wealth and success.* Retrieved October 29, 2009, from http://www.responsiblewealth.org/press/2004/notalonereportfinal.pdf

Collins, C., & Yeskel, F. (2005). *Economic apartheid.* New York: New Press.

Comas-Diaz, L. (2007). Ethnopolitical psychology. In E. Aldarondo (Ed.), *Advancing social justice through clinical practice* (pp. 91–118). Mahwah, NJ: Lawrence Erlbaum.

Conger, J. J. (1988). Hostages to fortune: Youth, values, and the public interest. *American Psychologist, 43,* 291–300.

Connelly, M. (2005). Opportunity and advancement: A nationwide poll (graphic). Retrieved September 29, 2009, from http://www.nytimes.com/packages/html/national/20050515_CLASS_GRAPHIC/index_03.html

Corak, M. (Ed.) (2004). *Generational income mobility in North America and Europe.* Cambridge, UK: Cambridge University Press.

Correspondents of the New York Times. (2005). *Class matters.* New York: Henry Holt.

Couto, R. A. (1993). The memory of miners and the conscience of capital. In S. L. Fisher. (Ed.), *Fighting back in Appalachia* (pp. 165–194). Philadelphia: Temple University Press.

Cozzarelli, C., Wilkinson, A. V., & Tagler, M. J. (2001). Attitudes toward the poor and attributions for poverty. *Journal of Social Issues, 57,* 207–228.

Crossley, N. (2008). Social class. In M. Grenfell (Ed.), *Pierre Bourdieu: Key concepts* (pp. 87–99). Stockfield, UK: Acumen.

Crowe, E. C, Connor, C. M. D., & Petscher, Y. (2009). Examining the core: Relations among reading curricula, poverty, and first through third grade. *Journal of School Psychology, 3,* 187–214.

Cushman, P. (1990). Why the self is empty. *American Psychologist, 45,* 599–611.

Daniels, J. (1990). *Punching out.* Detroit, MI: Wayne State University Press.

Daniels, J. (1995). Humanistic interventions for homeless students: Identifying and reducing barriers to their personal development. *Journal of Humanistic Education and Development, 33,* 164–172.

Daniels, J., D'Andrea, M., Omizo,, M., & Pier, P. (1999). Group work with homeless youngsters and their mothers. *Journal for Specialists in Group Work, 24,* 164–185.

Davis, A. (1983). *Women, race, and class.* New York: Vintage.

Davis, B., & Frank, R. (2009). *Income gap shrinks in slump at the expense of the wealthy.* Retrieved October 19, 2009, from the http://online.wsj.com/article/SB125254156520197777.html

Davis, P. (1995). *If you came this way.* New York: Wiley.

Debbink, G., & Ornelas, A. (1997). Cows for campesinos. In S. E. Smith, D. G. Willms, & N. J. Johnson (Eds.), *Nurtured by knowledge* (pp. 13–33). New York: Apex.

Democratic Underground. (2008). Poverty is not an adventure. Posted by nadine_mn August 20, 2008, to the Democratic Underground general discussion board. Retrieved April 5, 2010, from http://www.democraticunderground.com/discuss/duboard.php?az=view_all&address=389x3826143

DeNavas-Walt, C., Proctor, B. D., & Smith, J. C. (2009). Income, poverty, and health insurance coverage in the United States: 2008. Retrieved September 27, 2009, from http://www.census.gov/prod/2009pubs/p60-236.pdf

Denny, P. A. (1986). Women and poverty: A challenge to the intellectual and therapeutic integrity of feminist therapy. *Women & Therapy, 5,* 51–64.

DeParle, J. (2009). *Hunger in U.S. at a 14-year high.* Retrieved April 8, 2010, from http://www.nytimes.com/2009/11/17/us/17hunger.html

Dingfelder, S. (2006). A hand in rebuilding New Orleans: APA volunteers helped build houses in the upper Ninth Ward. *Monitor on Psychology, 37*, 48.

Dumont, M. P. (1992). *Treating the poor: A personal sojourn through the rise and fall of community mental health.* Belmont, MA: Dymphna Press.

Duneier, M. (1999). *Sidewalk.* New York: Farrar, Strauss, & Giroux.

Duran, E. (2006). *Healing the soul wound.* New York: Teachers College Press.

Eckholm, E. (2006). *Study documents 'ghetto tax' being paid by the urban poor.* Retrieved January 14, 2008, from http://www.nytimes.com/2006/07/19/us/19poor.html

Edin, K., & Kefalas, M. (2005). *Promises I can keep.* Berkeley: University of California Press.

Ehrenreich, B. (2001). *Nickel and dimed: On (not) getting by in America.* New York: Henry Holt.

Einhorn, E. (2008). *Study shows New York City has one of the nation's sorriest graduation rates.* Retrieved September 14, 2009, from http://www.nydailynews.com/ny_local/education/2008/04/01/2008-04-01_study_shows_new_york_city_has_one_of_the.html

Ellwood, M. J., & Bane, D. T. (1994). *Welfare realities.* Cambridge, MA: Harvard Press.

England, P. (2008). Devaluation and the pay of comparable male and female occupations. In D. B. Grusky (Ed.), *Social stratification* (pp. 834–838). Philadelphia: Westview Press.

Evans, G. W. (2004). The environment of childhood poverty. *American Psychologist, 59,* 77–92.

Evans, L. (1994). Dykes of poverty: Coming home. In Penelope, J. (Ed.) *Coming out of the class closet* (pp. 161–172). Freedom, CA: Crossing Press.

Farber, B. A., & Azar, S. T. (1999). Blaming the helpers: The marginalization of teachers and parents of the urban poor. *Journal of Orthopsychiatry, 69,* 515–528.

Ferrie, J. (Ed.) (2004). *The Whitehall II study.* Retrieved October 14, 2009, from http://www.ucl.ac.uk/whitehallII/findings/Whitehallbooklet.pdf

Fine, M. (1990). "The public" in public schools: The social construction/constriction of moral communities. *Journal of Social Issues, 46,* 107–119.

Fine, M., Torre, M. E., Boudin, K., Bowen, I., Clark, J., Hylton, D., Martinez, M., "Missy," Roberts, R. A., Smart, P., & Upegui, D. (2001). *Changing minds: The impact of college in a maximum security prison.* Retrieved January 2, 2010, from http://web.gc.cuny.edu/che/changingminds.html

Fine, M., Burns, A., Payne, Y. A., & Torre, M. E. (2004). Civics lessons: The color of class and betrayal. *Teachers College Record, 106,* 2193–2223.

Fine, M., & Torre, M. E. (2006). Intimate details: Participatory action research in prison. *Action Research, 4,* 253–269.

Fine, M., & Weis, L. (1999). *The unknown city: The lives of poor and working-class young adults.* New York: Beacon Press.

Fine, M., & Weis, L. (2003). *Silenced voices and extraordinary conversations.* New York: Teachers College Press.

Fischer, C. S., Hout, M., & Stiles, J. (2006). What Americans had: Differences in living standards. In C. S. Fischer & M. Hout (Eds.), *Century of difference: How America changed in the last 100 years* (pp. 137–161). New York: Russell Sage Foundation.

Fiske, S. T. (2007). On prejudice and the brain. *Daedalus, 136,* 156–160.

Fletcher, B. (2004). How race enters class is the United States. In M. Zweig (Ed.), *What's class got to do with it?* (pp. 35–44). Ithaca: Cornell University Press.

Fouad, N. A., & Brown, M. T. (2000). The role of race and class in development: Implications for counseling psychology. In S. D. Brown & R. W. Lent (Eds.), *Handbook of counseling psychology* (3rd ed., pp. 379–408). New York: Wiley.

Fouad, N. A., McPherson, R. H., Gerstein, L., Blustein, D. L., Elman, N. S., Helledy, K. I., & Metz, A. J. (2004). Houston 2001: Context and legacy. *The Counseling Psychologist, 31*, 15–77.

Freire, P. (1970). *The pedagogy of the oppressed.* New York: Continuum.

Fulmer, M. (2008). Can a family eat on $100 a week? Retrieved September 25, 2009, from http://articles.moneycentral.msn.com/CollegeAndFamily/RaiseKids/CanA-FamilyEatOn100AWeek.aspx?page=1

Funicello, T. (1993). *Tyranny of kindness.* New York: Atlantic Monthly Press.

Furnham, A. (2003). Poverty and wealth. In S. C. Carr & T. S. Sloan (Eds.), *Poverty and psychology* (pp. 163–183). New York: Kluwer Academic/Plenum Press.

Gallo, L. C., & Matthews, K. A. (2003). Understanding the association between socio-economic status and physical health: Do negative emotions play a role? *Psychological Bulletin, 129*, 10–51

Gerst, H. H., & Mills, C. W. (1948/2007). *From Max Weber: Essays in sociology.* New York: Routledge.

Gertner, J. (2006). What is a living wage? Retrieved September 22, 2009, from http://www.nytimes.com/2006/01/15/magazine/15wage.html

Gilbert, D. (2008). *The American class structure in an age of growing inequality.* Los Angeles: Pine Forge Press.

Gluckman, A., & Reed, B. (1997). *Homo economics.* New York: Routledge.

Goodman, L. A., Glenn, C., Bohlig, A., Banyard, V., & Borges, A. (2009). Feminist relational advocacy: Processes and outcomes from the perspective of low-income women with depression. *The Counseling Psychologist, 37*(6), 848–876.

Goodman, L. A., Liang, B., Helms, J. E., Latta, R. E., Sparks, E., & Weintraub, S. (2004). Training counseling psychologists as social justice agents: Feminist and multicultural perspectives. *The Counseling Psychologist, 32*(6), 793–837.

Goodman, L. A., Litwin, A., Bohlig, A., Weintraub, S. R., Green, A., Walker, J., White, L., & Ryan, N. (2007). Applying feminist theory to community practice: A multilevel empowerment intervention for low-income women with depression. In E. Aldarondo (Ed.), *Advancing social justice through clinical practice* (pp. 265–290). Mahwah, NJ: Lawrence Erlbaum.

Goodman, L. A., Smyth, K. F., & Banyard, V. (2010). Beyond the 50-minute hour: Increasing control, choice, and connections in the lives of low-income women. *American Journal of Orthopsychiatry, 80*(1), 3–11.

Goodman, P. S. (2009). Foreclosures force ex-homeowners to turn to shelters. Retrieved October 19, 2009, from http://www.nytimes.com/2009/10/19/business/economy/19foreclosed.html?pagewanted=1&em

González, R. C. (1997). Postmodern multicultural supervision. In D. R. Pope & H. L. K. Coleman (Eds.), *Multicultural counseling competencies: Assessment, education, training, and supervision* (pp. 350–386). Thousand Oaks, CA: Sage.

Graff, H., Kenig, L., & Radoff, G. (1971). Prejudice of upper class therapists against lower class patients. *Psychiatric Quarterly, 45*, 475–489.

Grenfell, M. (Ed.) (2008). *Pierre Bourdieu: Key concepts.* Stockfield, UK: Acumen.

Grossman, J. (2006). Fair labor standards act of 1938: Maximum struggle for a minimum wage. Retrieved June 26, 2009, from http://www.dol.gov/oasam/programs/history/flsa1938.htm

Grusky, D. B. (2008). *Social stratification.* Philadelphia: Westview.

Grusky, D. B., & Ku, M. C. (2008). Gloom, doom, and inequality. In D. B. Grusky (Ed.), *Social stratification* (pp. 2–28). Philadelphia: Westview Press.

Hacker, J. S. (2006). *The great risk shift: The new insecurity and the decline of the American dream.* New York: Oxford University.

Halbfinger, D. M., & Holmes, S. A. (2003, March 30). Military mirrors working class Americans. Retrieved July 5, 2009, from http://www.nytimes.com/2003/03/30/international/worldspecial/30DEMO.html?scp=1&sq=military mirrors the work

Hargreaves, S. (2009). Hunger hits Detroit's middle class. Retrieved August 18, 2009, from http://money.cnn.com/2009/08/06/news/economy/detroit_food/index.htm?postversion=2009080610

Harris Interactive. (2005). *Negative attitudes to labor unions show little change in past decade.* Retrieved October 18, 2007, from www.harrisinteractive.com

Harris, K. (2009). Truancy costs us all. Retrieved October 30, 2009, from http://www.sfgate.com/cgi-bin/article.cgi?f=/c/a/2009/10/14/ED6V1A4HQQ.DTL

Harvard Mahoney Neuroscience Institute. (2009). The stress of poverty affects childhood brain development. Retrieved January 2, 2010, from http://www.hms.harvard.edu/hmni/On_The_Brain/Volume15/HMS_OTB_Winter09_Vol15_No1.pdf

Heesacker, M., Wester, S. R., Vogel, D. L., Wentzel, J. T., Mejia-Millan, C. M., & Goodholm, C. R. (1999). Gender-based emotional stereotyping. *Journal of Counseling Psychology, 46*, 483–495.

Heflin, C. M., Siefert, K., & Williams, D. R. (2005). Food insufficiency and women's mental health: Findings from a 3-year panel of welfare recipients. *Social Science and Medicine, 61*, 1971–1982.

Heiman, M. K. (1996). Race, waste, and class: New perspectives on environmental justice. *Antipode 28*(2). Retrieved April 5, 2010, from http://www.ejnet.orgj

Heitler, J. B.. (1973). Preparation of lower-class patients for expressive group psychotherapy. *Journal of Consulting and Clinical Psychology, 41*, 251–260.

Helms, J. (Ed.). (1990). *Black and white racial identity: Theory, research, and practice.* Westport, CT: Greenwood.

Henry, D. (2006). Worker vs. CEO pay: Room to run. Retrieved April 5, 2010, from http://www.businessweek.com/magazine/content/06_44/c4007010.htm

Henry, P. J., Reyna, C. E., & Weiner, B. (2004). Hate welfare but help the poor: How the attributional content of stereotypes explains the paradox of reactions to the destitute in America. *Journal of Applied Social Psychology, 34*, 34–58.

Heppner, M. J., & O'Brien, K. (2006). Women and poverty: A holistic approach to vocational interventions. In W. B. Walsh & M. J. Heppner (Eds.), *Handbook of career counseling for women* (pp. 75–102). Mahwah, NJ: Erlbaum.

Heppner, M. J., & Scott, A. B. (2004). From whence we came: The role of social class in our families of origin. *The Counseling Psychologist, 32*, 596–602.

Herr, K., & Anderson, G. L. (2005). *The action research dissertation*. Thousand Oaks, CA: Sage.

Hill, M., & Rothblum, E. D. (Eds.). (1996). *Classism and feminist therapy: Counting costs*. New York: Harrington Park.

Hobfoll, S. E., Ritter, C., Lavin, J., Hulsizer, M. R., & Cameron, R. P. (1995). Depression prevalence and incidence among inner-city pregnant and postpartum women. *Journal of Consulting and Clinical Psychology, 63*, 445–453.

Hollingshead, A. B., & Redlich, F. G. (1958). *Social class and mental illness*. New York: Wiley.

hooks, b. (1981). *Ain't I a woman: Black women and feminism*. Boston: South End.

hooks, b. (1984). *Feminist theory: From margin to center*. Cambridge, MA: South End.

hooks, b. (2000). *Where we stand: Class matters*. New York: Routledge.

Hoyt, S. K. (1999). Mentoring with class. In A. J. Murrell & F. J. Crosby (Eds.), *Mentoring dilemmas: Developmental relationships within multicultural organizations* (pp. 189–210). Mahwah, NJ: Erlbaum.

Humphreys, K., & Rappaport, J. (1993). From the community mental health movement to the war on drugs: A study in the definition of social problems. *American Psychologist, 48*, 892–901.

Inclan, J., & Ferran, E. (1990). Poverty, politics, and family therapy: A role for systems theory. In M. P. Mirkin (Ed.), *The social and political contexts of family therapy* (pp. 193–214). Boston: Allyn & Bacon.

Ivey, A. (1995). Psychotherapy as liberation. In J. Ponterotto, J. Cassas, L. Suzuki, & C. Alexander (Eds.), *Handbook of multicultural counseling* (pp. 53–72). Thousand Oaks, CA: Sage.

Ivey, A. E., D'Andrea, M., Ivey, M. B., & Simek-Morgan, L. (2002). *Counseling and psychotherapy: A multicultural perspective* (5th ed.). Boston: Allyn & Bacon.

James, S. E., Johnson, J., & Raghavan, C. (2003). The violent matrix: A study of structural, interpersonal, and intrapersonal violence among a sample of poor women. *American Journal of Community Psychology, 31*, 129–141.

Javier, R. A., & Herron, W. G. (2002). Psychoanalysis and the disenfranchised: Countertransference issues. *Psychoanalytic Psychology, 19*, 149–166.

Johnston, D. C. (2006). Tax cheats called out of control. Retrieved August 21, 2009, from http://www.nytimes.com/2006/08/01/business/01tax.html

Jones, E. (1974). Social class and psychotherapy: A critical review of research. *Psychiatry, 37*, 307–320.

Jordan, J. V. (2000). The role of mutual empathy in relational/cultural therapy. *Journal of Clinical Psychology, 56*, 1005–1016.

Juntunen, C. L., Cavett, A. M., Clow, R. B., Rempel, V., Darrow, R. E., & Guilmino, A. (2006). Social justice through self-sufficiency: Vocational psychology and the transition from welfare to work. In R. L. Toporek, L. H. Gerstein, N. A. Fouad, G. Roysircar, & T. Israel (Eds.), *The handbook for social justice in counseling psychology* (pp. 294-310). Thousand Oaks, CA: Sage Publications.

Kaiser Commission. (2006). Who are the uninsured? Retrieved June 25, 2009, from http://www.kff.org/uninsured/upload/7553.pdf

Karon, B. P., & VandenBos, G. R. (1977). Psychotherapeutic technique and the economically poor patient. *Psychotherapy: Theory, Research and Practice, 14*, 169–180.

King, M. L., Jr. (1967). Beyond Vietnam—A time to break silence. Speech delivered in New York City on April 4, 1967. Retrieved October 15, 2009, from http://www.americanrhetoric.com/speeches/mlkatimetobreaksilence.htm

Kleinfield, N. R. (2006). Living at an epicenter of diabetes, defiance and despair. Retrieved September 26, 2009, from http://www.nytimes.com/2006/01/10/nyregion/nyregionspecial5/10diabetes.html?pagewanted=1&_r=1

Koch, W. (2009). Homelessness in suburbs, rural areas increases. *USA Today*, Nation section. Retrieved July 9, 2009 from the http://www.usatoday.com/news/nation/2009-07-09-homeless_N.htm?loc=interstitialskip

Kozol, J. (2005). *The shame of the nation.* New York: Crown.

Krieger, N. (2004). Embodiment: A conceptual glossary for epidemiology. *Journal of Epidemiolology and Community Health, 59*, 350–355.

Krieger, N., Williams, D. R., & Moss, N. E. (1997). Measuring social class in U.S. public health. *Annual Review of Public Health, 18*, 341–378.

Law, M. (1997). Changing disabling environments through participatory action research. In S. E. Smith, D. G. Willms, & N. J. Johnson (Eds.), *Nurtured by knowledge: Learning to do participatory action–research* (pp. 34-58). New York: Apex.

LeBlanc, A. N. (2003). *Random families.* Scribner: New York.

Lee, V. L., & Burkam, D. T. (2002). *Inequality at the starting gate.* Washington, DC: Economic Policy Institute.

Legal Momentum. (2003). *Reading between the lines: Women's poverty in 2003.* Retrieved October 18, 2007, from http://www.legalmomentum.org/womeninpoverty.pdf

Leondar-Wright, B. (2005). *Class matters.* Gabriola Island, Canada: New Society Publishers.

Leonhardt, D. (2005). The college dropout boom. Retrieved March 26, 2010, from http://www.nytimes.com/2005/05/24/national/class/EDUCATION-FINAL.html?_r=1&scp=1&sq=david%20leonhardt%20college%20dropout&st=cse

Leonhardt, D., & Fabrikant, G. (2009). Rise of the super-rich hits a sobering wall. Retrieved October 19, 2009, from the http://www.nytimes.com/2009/08/21/business/economy/21inequality.html

Liu, W. M. (2001). Expanding our understanding of multiculturalism: Developing a social class worldview model. In D. B. Pope-Davis & H. L. K. Coleman (Eds.), *The intersection of race, class, and gender in counseling psychology* (pp. 127–170). Thousand Oaks, CA: Sage Publications.

Liu, W. M. (2002). The social class-related experiences of men: Integrating theory and practice. *Professional Psychology: Research and Practice, 33*(4), 355–360.

Liu, W. M., Ali, S., Soleck, G., Hopps, J., Dunston, K., & Pickett, T. (2004). Using social class in counseling psychology research. *Journal of Counseling Psychology. 51*, 3–18.

Liu, W. M., Pickett, T., & Ivey, A. E. (2007). White middle-class privilege: Social class bias and implications for training and practice. *Journal of Multicultural Counseling and Development, 35*, 194–206.

Liu, W. M., Soleck, G., Hopps, J., Dunston, K., & Pickett, T. (2004). A new framework to understand social class in counseling: The social class worldview model and modern classism theory. *Multicultural Counseling and Development, 32*, 95–122.

Lorde, A. (1984). *Sister outsider: Essays and speeches.* Trumansburg, NY: Crossing Press.

Lorion, R. P. (1973). Socioeconomic status and traditional treatment approaches reconsidered. *Psychological Bulletin, 79*, 263–270.

Lorion, R. P. (1974). Patient and therapist variables in the treatment of low-income patients. *Psychological Bulletin, 81*, 344–354.

Lott, B. (2002). Cognitive and behavioral distancing from the poor. *American Psychologist, 57*, 100–110.

Lott, B., & Bullock, H. E. (2007). Psychology and economic injustice. Washington, DC: APA.

Lott, B., & Saxon, S. (2002). The influence of ethnicity, social class and context on judgments about U. S. women. *Journal of Social Psychology, 142*, 481–499.

Lui, M., Robles, B., Leondar-Wright, B., Brewer, R., & Adamson, R. (2005). *The color of wealth.* Boston: The New Press.

Lustig, D. C., & Strauser, D. R. (2007). Causal relationships between disability and poverty. *Rehabilitation Counseling Bulletin, 50*, 194–202.

Lykes, M. B. (1994). Terror, silencing, and children. *Social Science and Medicine, 38*, 543–552.

Lykes, M. B. (1997). Activist participatory research among the Maya of Guatemala: Constructing meaning from situated knowledge. *Journal of Social Issues, 53*, 725–746.

Lykes, M. B. (2000). Possible contributions of a psychology of liberation: Whither health and human rights? *Journal of Health Psychology, 5*, 383–397.

Lykes, M. B. (2009, May). PAR as life project. Presentation at Qualitative Methods as Social Critique, a conference at CUNY Graduate Center, New York, NY.

Maguire, P. (1987). *Doing participatory research: A feminist approach.* Amherst: University of Massachusetts.

Marable, M. (2000). *How capitalism underdeveloped Black America.* Chicago: South End.

Marmot, M. (2006). *The status syndrome.* New York: Holt.

Marmot, M., & Wilkinson, R. G. (Eds.). (2006). *The social determinants of health.* Oxford, UK: Oxford University Press.

Martín-Baró, I. (1994). *Writings for a liberation psychology.* Boston: Harvard Press.

Marymount University (1999). The consumer and sweatshops. Retrieved on April 8, 2010, from http://www.marymount.edu/news/garmentstudy/overview.html

Mathematica Policy Research. (2010). Hunger in America 2010: A national report. Retrieved April 8, 2010, from http://feedingamerica.issuelab.org/research/listing/hunger_in_america_2010_national_report

Mays, V. (2000). A social justice agenda. *American Psychologist, 55*(3), 326–327.

Mazumder, B. (2005). The apple falls even closer to the tree than we thought. In S. Bowles, H. Gintis, & M. O. Groves (Eds.), *Unequal chances* (pp. 80–99).

McCall, R. B., & Green, B. L. (2004). Beyond the methodological gold standards of behavioral research: Considerations for practice and policy. *Social Policy Report, 18*, 3–19.

McIntosh, P. (1988). *White privilege and male privilege: A personal account of coming to see correspondences through work in women's studies.* Wellesley, MA: Working Paper Series, Wellesley College.

McIntyre, A. (2000). *Inner-city kids: Adolescents confront life and violence in an urban community.* New York: New York University Press.

McLoyd, V. C. (1998). Socioeconomic disadvantage and child development. *American Psychologist, 53*, 185–204.

Miller, A. B., & Keys, C. B. (2001). Understanding dignity in the lives of homeless persons. *American Journal of Community Psychology, 29*, 331–354.

Miller, M., & Serafin, T. (2006). The 400 richest Americans. Retrieved September 14, 2009, from http://www.forbes.com/lists/2006/54/biz_06rich400_The-400-Richest-Americans_land.html

Miller, J. B. (1976). *Toward a new psychology of women.* Boston: Beacon Press.

Miller, J. B., & Stiver, I. P. (1997). *The healing connection.* Boston: Beacon Press.

Minkler, M., & Wallerstein, N. (2002). *Community-based participatory research for health.* New York: Jossey-Bass.

Minuchin, P. (1995). Children and family therapy: Mainstream approaches and the special case of the multicrisis poor. In R. H. Mikesell, D. Lusterman, & S. H. McDaniel (Eds.), *Integrating family therapy* (pp. 113–124). Washington, DC: American Psychological Association.

Minuchin, P., Colapinto, J., & Minuchin, S. (1998). *Working with families of the poor.* New York: Guilford Press.

Miranda, J., Azocar, F., Organista, K. C., Dwyer, E., & Areane, P. (2003). Treatment of depression among impoverished primary care patients from ethnic minority groups. *Psychiatric Services, 54*, 2, 219–225.

Miranda, J., & Green, B. L. (1999). The need for mental health services research focusing on poor young women. *Journal of Mental Health Policy and Economics, 2*(2), 73–80.

Mirkin, M. P. (1990). *The social and political contexts of family therapy.* Boston: Allyn & Bacon.

Mohr, J., Israel, T., & Sedlacek, W. E. (2001). Counselors' attitudes regarding bisexuality as predictors of counselors' clinical responses. *Journal of Counseling Psychology, 48*, 212–222.

Moreira, V. (2003). Poverty and psychopathology. In S. C. Carr & T. S. Sloan (Eds.), *Poverty and psychology* (pp. 69–86). New York: Kluwer Academic/Plenum Press.

Moskowitz, M. (1996). The social conscience of psychoanalysis. In R. M. Pérez Foster, M. Moskowitz, & R. A. Javier (Eds.), *Reaching across boundaries of culture and class* (pp. 21–46). Northvale, NJ: Aronson.

Mufson, S. (2010). Massey Energy has litany of critics, violations. Retrieved April 8, 2010, from http://www.washingtonpost.com/wp-dyn/content/article/2010/04/06/AR2010040601531.html

Naranyan, D. (2000). *Voices of the poor: Can anyone hear us?* New York: Oxford.

Naranyan, D., Chambers, R., Shah, M. K., & Petesch, P. (2000). *Voices of the poor: Crying out for change.* New York: Oxford.

National Center for Public Policy and Higher Education. (2002). *Losing ground: A national status report of the affordability of American higher education.* Retrieved June 26, 2009, from http://www.highereducation.org/reports/losing_ground/ar.shtml

National Coalition for the Homeless. (2005). *Who is homeless? NCH Fact Sheet #3.* Retrieved June 26, 2009, from http://www.ncchca.org/files/Homeless/NCH_Who%20is%20Homeless_07.pdf

National Low Income Housing Coalition. (2005). NLIHC releases 2005 housing affordability report. Retrieved September 27, 2009, from http://www.nlihc.org/detail/article.cfm?article_id=2614&id=48

National Poverty Center (2006). *Poverty in the United States.* Retrieved May 12, 2010, from http://www.npc.umich.edu/poverty

Newman, K. S. (1999). *No shame in my game.* New York: Vintage.

Newman, K. S., & Chen, V. T. (2008). *The missing class: Portraits of the near poor in America.* New York, Beacon.

*New York Times.* (2006). Editorial: The Sago mine disaster. Retrieved September 28, 2009, from http://www.nytimes.com/2006/01/05/opinion/05thu1.html

Norwood, R. (1990). *Women who love too much.* New York: Pocket.

Oliver, M. L., & Shapiro, T. M. (1997). *Black wealth/White wealth.* New York: Routledge.

Passel, J. S., & Cohn, D. (2009). A portrait of unauthorized immigrants in the United States. Retrieved October 9, 2009, from http://pewhispanic.org/files/reports/107.pdf

Pavkov, T. W., Lewis, D. A., & Lyons, J. S. (1989). Psychiatric diagnoses and racial bias: An empirical investigation. *Professional Psychology: Research and Practice, 20*(6), 364–368.

Penelope, J. (Ed.) (1994). *Out of the class closet.* Freedom, CA: Crossing Press.

Pérez Foster, R. M. (1996). What is a multicultural perspective for psychoanalysis? In R. M. Pérez Foster, M. Moskowitz, & R. A. Javier (Eds.), *Reaching across boundaries of culture and class* (pp. 3–20). Northvale, NJ: Aronson.

Pierson, J. (2002). *Tackling social exclusion.* London: Routledge.

Pittelman, K. (2005). *Classified: How to stop hiding your privilege and use it for social change.* New York: Soft Skull Press.

Pogge, T. (Ed.) ( 2007*). Freedom from poverty as a human right.* New York: Oxford.

Ponterotto, J. G., Casas, J. M., Suzuki, L. A., & Alexander, C. M. (2001). *Handbook of multicultural counseling.* Thousand Oaks, CA: Sage.

Prilleltensky, I. (1989). Psychology and the status quo. *American Psychologist, 44*, 795–802.

Prilleltensky, I. (1994). *The morals and politics of psychology.* Albany: State University of New York Press.

Prilleltensky, I. (1997).Values, assumptions, and practices: Assessing the moral implications of psychological discourse and action. *American Psychologist, 52*, 517–535.

Prilleltensky, I. (2003). Understanding, resisting, and overcoming oppression: Toward psychopolitical validity. *American Journal of Community Psychology, 31*, 195–201.

Prilleltensky, I. (2008). The role of power in wellness, oppression, and liberation: The promise of psychopolitical validity. *American Journal of Community Psychology, 36*, 116–136.

Prilleltensky, I., & Nelson, G. (2002). *Doing psychology critically: Making a difference in diverse settings.* New York: Palgrave.

Quadagno, J. (1994). *The color of welfare.* New York: Oxford University Press.

Raffo, S. (Ed.) (1997). *Queerly classed.* Chicago: South End Press.

Rainwater, L. (1970). Neutralizing the disinherited. In Allen, V. L. (Ed.), *Psychological factors in poverty* (pp. 9–28). Chicago: Markham.

Ramachandran, N. (2005). Despite good economic news, wages don't keep pace. Retrieved April 5, 2010, from www.usnews.com/usnews/biztech/articles/051226/26wage.htm

Rank, M. R. (1994). *Living on the edge.* New York: Columbia University Press.

Rank, M.R. (2004). *One nation, underprivileged.* New York: Oxford University Press.

Redington, P. (2009). Helping the rich. Retrieved October 29, 2009, from http://www.wiretapmag.org/stories/44623/.

Reid, P. T. (1995). Poor women in psychological research: Shut up and shut out. In N. R. Goldberger & J. B. Veroff (Eds.), *The culture and psychology reader* (pp. 184–204). New York: New York University Press.

Reiman, J. (2007). *The rich get richer and the poor get prison.* New York: Pearson.

Reisch, R. (2009). The union way up. Retrieved September 25, 2009, from http://www.latimes.com/news/opinion/la-oe-reich26-2009jan26,0,1124419.story

Rhode, D. (2004). Access to justice: Connecting principles to practice. *Georgetown Journal of Legal Ethics, 17*(3), 369–422.

Ringen, S. (April, 2009). Poverty—The Rowntree project revisited. Paper delivered at the Kennedy School of Government, Harvard University. Retrieved June 1, 2009, from http://users.ox.ac.uk/~gree0074/documents%20en/pov07

Robinson, E. (2005, September 9). No longer invisible. *Washington Post.* Retrieved April 5, 2010, from www.washingtonpost.com

Rodney, W. (1982). *How Europe underdeveloped Africa.* Washington, DC: Howard University.

Ryan, W. (1971). *Blaming the victim.* New York:

Saez, E. (2009). Striking it richer. Retrieved September 25, 2009, from http://elsa.berkeley.edu/~saez/saez-UStopincomes-2007.pdf

Salomon, A., Bassuk, S. S., & Brooks, M. G. (1996). Patterns of welfare use among poor and homeless women. *American Journal of Orthopsychiatry, 66*, 510–525.

Sampson, E. (1993). Identity politics: Challenges to psychology's understanding. *American Psychologist, 48*, 1219–1230.

Saris, R. N., & Johnston-Robledo, I. (2000). Poor women are still shut out of mainstream psychology. *Psychology of Women Quarterly, 24*, 233–235.

Schnitzer, P. K. (1996). "They don't come in!" Stories told, lessons taught about poor families in therapy. *American Journal of Orthopsychiatry, 66*, 572–582.

Schorr, L. B. (1999). Fighting poverty and building community: Learning from programs that work. *American Journal of Orthopsychiatry, 69*, 420–423.

Schorr, L. B., & Yankelovich, D. (2000). What works to better society can't be easily measured. Retrieved October 14, 2009, from http://articles.latimes.com/2000/feb/16/local/me-64711

Schubert, J. D. (2008). Suffering/symbolic violence. In M. Grenfell (Ed.), *Pierre Bourdieu: Key concepts* (pp. 183–198). Stockfield, UK: Acumen.

Scott, J. (2005). Life at the top in America isn't just better, it's longer. In *The New York Times* & B. Keller (Eds.), *Class Matters* (pp. 27–50). New York: Times Books.

Seeman, T. E., Crimmins, E., Huang, M. H., Singer, B., Bucur, A., Gruenwald, T., et al. (2004). Cumulative biological risk and socioeconomic differences in mortality: MacArthur studies of successful aging. *Social Science and Medicine, 58*, 1985–1997.

Sen, A. K. (2000). *Social exclusion: Concept, application, and scrutiny.* Manila, Philippines: Office of Environmental and Social Development, Asian Development Bank.

Sen, A. K. (2008). From income inequality to economic inequality. In D. B. Grusky (Ed.), *Social stratification* (pp. 235–248). Philadelphia: Westview Press.

Shaiken, H. (2007). Unions, the economy, and employee free choice. Retrieved March 26, 2010, from http://www.sharedprosperity.org/bp181.htm

Sharkey, J. (2006). For the super-rich, it's time to upgrade the old jumbo jet. Retrieved September 28, 2009, from http://www.nytimes.com/2006/10/17/business/17megajets.html

Sheppard, M. (2006). *Social work and social exclusion.* Hampshire, England: Ashgate.

Sherman, L. (2009). World's happiest places. Retrieved October 26, 2009, from http://www.forbes.com/2009/05/05/world-happiest-places-lifestyle-travel-world-happiest.html

Shipler, D. K. (2004). *The working poor.* New York: Vintage.

Siassi, I., & Messer, S. B. (1976). Psychotherapy with patients from lower socioeconomic groups. *American Journal of Psychotherapy, 30*, 29–40.

Siefert, K. A., Bowman, P. J., Heflin, C. M., Danziger, S. H., & Williams, D. R. (2000). Social and environmental predictors of maternal depression in current and recent welfare recipients. *American Journal of Orthopsychiatry, 70*, 510–522.

Siefert, K., Heflin, C. M., Corcoran, M. E., & Williams, D. R. (2001). Food insufficiency and the physical and mental health of low-income women. *Women & Health, 32*, 159–177.

Silver, H. (1994). Social exclusion and social solidarity: Three paradigms. *International Labour Review, 133*, 531–578.

Sklar, H., Mykyta, L., & Wefeld, S. (2008). *Raise the floor.* Boston: South End Press.

Sloan, T. S. (2003). Poverty and psychology: A call to arms. In S. C. Carr & T. S. Sloan (Eds.), *Poverty and psychology* (pp. 301–314). New York: Kluwer Academic/Plenum Press.

Smith, J. M. (2000). Psychotherapy with people stressed by poverty. In A. N. Sabo & L. Havens (Eds.), *Real world guide to psychotherapy practice* (pp. 71–92). Cambridge MA: Harvard University Press.

Smith, L. (2005). Classism, psychotherapy, and the poor: Conspicuous by their absence. *American Psychologist, 60*, 687–696.

Smith, L. (2008). Positioning classism within psychology's social justice agenda. *The Counseling Psychologist, 36*, 895–924.

Smith, L. (2009). Enhancing training and practice in the context of poverty. *Training and Education in Professional Psychology, 3*, 84–93.

Smith, L., Allen, A., & Bowen, R. (2010). Expecting the worst: Exploring the associations between poverty and misbehavior. *Journal of Poverty, 14*, 33–54.

Smith, L., Baluch, S., Bernabei, S., Robohm, J., & Sheehy, J. (2003). Applying a social justice framework to college counseling practice. *Journal of College Counseling, 6*, 3–13.

Smith, L., Chambers, D. A., & Bratini, L. (2009). When oppression is the pathogen: The participatory development of socially just mental health practice. *American Journal of Orthopsychiatry, 79*, 159–168.

Smith, L., Foley, P. F., & Chaney, M. P. (2008). Addressing classism, ableism, and heterosexism within multicultural-social justice training. *Journal of Counseling and Development, 86*, 303–309.

Smith, L., & Redington, R. (in press). Class dismissed: Making the case for the study of classist microaggressions. In D.W. Sue (Ed.), *Microaggressions and Marginality: Manifestations, Dynamics, and Impact.* New York: Wiley.

Smith, L., & Romero, L. (2010). Psychological interventions in the context of poverty: Participatory action research as practice. *American Journal of Orthopsychiatry, 80*(1), 12–25.

Smith, L. T. (1999). *Decolonizing methodologies.* New York: Zed Books.

Smith, S. E. (1997). Deepening participatory action research. In S. E. Smith, D. G. Willms, & N. J. Johnson (Eds.), *Nurtured by knowledge* (pp. 173–263). New York: Apex.

Smyth, K. F., Goodman, L., & Glenn, C. (2006). The full-frame approach: A new response to marginalized women left behind by specialized services. *American Journal of Orthopsychiatry, 76*, 489–502.

Smyth, K. F., & Schorr, L. B. (2009). A lot to lose: A call to rethink what constitutes evidence in finding social interventions that work. Malcolm Wiener Center for Social Policy at Harvard Kennedy School of Government, working paper series.

Sousa, L., & Rodrigues, S. (2009). Linking formal and informal support in multiproblem low-income families: The role of the family manager. *Journal of Community Psychology, 37*, 649–662.

Speight, S. L., & Vera, E. M. (2004). A social justice agenda: Ready or not? *The Counseling Psychologist, 32*, 109–118.

Stapleton, D. C., O' Day, B. L., Livermore, G. A., & Imparato, A. J. (2006). Dismantling the poverty trap: Disability policy for the twenty-first century. *The Milbank Quarterly, 84*, 701–732.

Stout, L. (1996). *Bridging the class divide.* New York: Beacon.

Strickland, B. R. (2000). Misassumptions, misadventures, and the misuse of psychology. *American Psychologist, 55*(3), 331–338.

Sue, D. W. (1978). Eliminating cultural oppression in counseling: Toward a general theory. *Journal of Counseling Psychology, 25*, 419–428.

Sue, D. W. (2001). Multidimensional facets of cultural competence. *The Counseling Psychologist, 29*, 790–821.

Sue, D. W., Capodilupo, C. M., Torino, G., Bucceri, J. M., Holder, A., Nadal, K., & Esquilin, M. E. (2007). Racial microaggressions in everyday life: Implications for counseling. *American Psychologist, 62*, 27–286.

Sue, D. W., Carter, R. T., Casas, J. M., Fouad, N. A., Ivey, A. E., Jensen, M., LaFromboise, T., Manese, J. E., Ponterotto, J. G., & Vazquez-Nutall, E. (1998). *Multicultural counseling competencies.* Thousand Oaks, CA: Sage.

Sue, D. W., & Kirk, B. A. (1975). Asian-Americans: Use of counseling and psychiatric services on a college campus. *Journal of Counseling Psychology, 22,* 84–86.

Sue, D. W., & Sue, S. (1972). Ethnic minorities: Resistance to being researched. *Professional Psychology, 3,* 11–17.

Sue, D. W., & Sue, S. (2007). *Counseling the culturally diverse.* New York: Wiley.

Sue, S., & Lam, A. G. (2002). Cultural and demographic diversity. In J. C. Norcross (Ed.), *Psychotherapy relationships that work: Therapist contributions and responsiveness to patients* (pp. 401–422). New York: Oxford University Press.

Sullivan, P. (2009a). Too rich to worry? Not in this downturn. Retrieved October 19, 2009, from http://www.nytimes.com/2009/10/03/your-money/03wealth.html

Sullivan, P. (2009b). All this anger against the rich may be unhealthy. Retrieved October 19, 2009, from http://www.nytimes.com/2009/10/17/your-money/17wealth. html?pagewanted=2&nl=your-money&emc=your-moneyema4

Swick, K. J. (2008). Empowering the parent child relationship in homeless and other high risk parents and families. *Early Childhood Education, 36,* 149–153.

Tait, V. (2005). *Poor workers' unions.* Chicago: South End Press.

Thomas, K. S., Nelesen, R. A., Ziegler, M. G., Natarajan, L., & Dimsdale, J. E. (2009). Influence of education and neighborhood poverty on pressor responses to phenylephrine in African-Americans and Caucasian Americans. *Biological Psychology, 1,* 18–24.

Thompson, C. L. (1989). Psychoanalytic psychotherapy with inner city patients. *Journal of Contemporary Psychotherapy, 19,* 137–148.

Tompsett, C. J., Toro, P. A., & Guzicki, M. (2006). Homelessness in the United States: Assessing changes in prevalence and public opinion, 1993–2001. *American Journal of Community Psychology, 37,* 47–61.

Toporek, R. L., Gerstein, L. H., Fouad, N. A., Roysircar, G., & Israel, T. (2006). *Handbook for social justice in counseling psychology.* Thousand Oaks, CA: Sage.

Toporek, R. L., Lewis, J. A. & Crethar, H. (2009). Promoting systemic change through the ACA advocacy competencies. *Journal of Counseling and Development, 87,* 260–268.

Torre, M. E., & Fine, M. (2005). Bar none: Extending affirmative action to higher education in prison. *Journal of Social Issues, 61,* 569–594.

Transgender Law Center (2009). State of transgender California. Retrieved September 25, 2009, from http://www.transgenderlawcenter.org/pdf/StateofTransCAFINAL.pdf

Trevithick, P. (1998). Psychotherapy and working-class women. In I. B. Seu & M. C. Heenan (Eds.), *Feminism and psychotherapy* (pp. 115–134). Thousand Oaks, CA: Sage.

Twenge, J. M., Baumeister, R. F., Tice, D. M., & Stucke, T. S. (2001). If you can't join them, beat them: Effects of social exclusion on aggressive behavior. *Journal of Personality and Social Psychology, 81,* 1058–1069.

Twenge, J. M., Catanese, K. R., & Baumeister, R. F. (2002). Social exclusion causes self-defeating behavior. *Journal of Personality and Social Psychology, 83,* 606–615.

Twenge, J. M., Catanese, K. R., & Baumeister, R. F. (2003). Social exclusion and the deconstructed state: Time perception, meaninglessness, lethargy, lack of emotion, and self-awareness. *Journal of Personality and Social Psychology, 85,* 409–423.

Uchitelle, L. (2009). Still on the job but at half the pay. Retrieved October 19, 2009, from http://www.nytimes.com/2009/10/14/business/economy/14income. html?scp=2&sq=half%20as%20much&st=cse

United for a Fair Economy. (2009). Responsible wealth. Retrieved September 14 , 2009, from http://www.faireconomy.org/issues/responsible_wealth

United States Bureau of the Census. (2006). Income, poverty, and health insurance coverage in the United States: 2005. Retrieved October 9, 2009, from http://www.census.gov/prod/2006pubs/p60-231.pdf

United States Bureau of the Census. (2007). Income, poverty, and health insurance coverage in the United States: 2006. Retrieved September 14, 2009, from http://www.census.gov/prod/2007pubs/p60-233.pdf

United States Bureau of the Census. (2008). Household income rises, poverty rate unchanged, number of uninsured down. Retrieved October 20, 2009, from http://www.census.gov/Press-Release/www/releases/archives/income_wealth/012528.html

United States Department of Health and Human Services. (2007a). The 2007 HHS poverty guidelines. Retrieved on April 5, 2010, from http://aspe.hhs.gov/poverty/07poverty.shtml

United States Department of Health and Human Services. (2007b). HHS: What we do. Retrieved on April 5, 2010, from http://www.hhs.gov/about/whatwedo.html/

United States Department of Justice. (2008). Prison statistics. Retrieved June 25, 2009, from http://www.ojp.usdoj.gov/bjs/prisons.htm

United States Department of Labor. (2009). Employment situation summary. Retrieved October 19, 2009, from http://www.bls.gov/news.release/empsit.nr0.htm

United States Environmental Protection Agency, Region 4. (2001). *Martin Country Coal Corporation Task Force Report, October 2001.* Retrieved June 26, 2009, from http://www.epa.gov/region4/waste

Urban Institute. (2007). *The nonprofit sector in brief.* Retrieved April 5, 2010, from http://www.urban.org/UploadedPDF/311373_nonprofit_sector.pdf

Urbina, I. (2006, April 2). Keeping it secret as the family car becomes a home. *The New York Times,* National Desk.

Urbina, I. & Cooper, M. (2010). Deaths at West Virginia mines raise issues about safety. Retrieved April 8, 2010, from http://www.nytimes.com/2010/04/07/us/07westvirginia.html?fta=y

Utsey, S. O., Bolden, M. A., & Brown, A. L. (2001). Visions of revolution from the spirit of Frantz Fanon. In J. G. Ponterotto, J. M. Casas, L. A. Suzuki, & C. M. Alexander (Eds.), *Handbook of multicultural counseling* (pp. 311–336). Thousand Oaks, CA: Sage.

Vera, E. M., & Speight, S. L. (2003). Multicultural competence, social justice, and counseling psychology: Expanding our roles. *The Counseling Psychologist, 31*(3), 253–272.

Vollers, M. (1999). Razing Appalachia. Retrieved March 26, 2010, from http://motherjones.com/politics/1999/07/razing-appalachia

Weeden, K. A., Kim, Y., Di Carlo, M., & Grusky, D. B. (2008). Is the labor market becoming more or less gradational? In D. B. Grusky (Ed.), *Social stratification* (pp. 249–265). Philadelphia: Westview Press.

Weinger, S. (1998). Poor children "know their place": Perceptions of poverty, class, and public messages. *Journal of Sociology and Social Welfare, 25*, 100–118.

Weininger, E. B. (2005). Foundations of Pierre Bourdieu's class analysis. In Wright, E. O. (Ed.), *Approaches to class analysis*. (pp. 82–118). Cambridge: Cambridge University Press.

Weir, B., & Johnson, S. (2007). Denmark: The happiest place on earth. Retrieved October 26, 2009, from http://abcnews.go.com/2020/story?id=4086092&page=1&page=1

Weis, L., & Fine, M. (Eds.). (1993). *Beyond silenced voices*. Albany: State University of New York Press.

Weynant, K. (2009*). Stealing dust*. Georgetown, KY: Finishing Line Press.

Wilkinson, R. G. (1996). *Unhealthy societies: The afflictions of inequality*. New York: Routledge.

Wilkinson, R. G. (2006). *The impact of inequality*. New York: New Press.

Williams, D. R., Takeuchi, D. T., & Adair, R. K. (1992). Socioeconomic status and psychiatric disorder among Blacks and Whites. *Social Forces, 71*, 179–194.

Women's Theological Center. (1997). *The invisibility of upper class privilege*. [Brochure]. Boston, MA: Author. Retrieved December 10, 2007, from http://www.thewtc.org/Invisibility_of_Class_Privilege.pdf

Working Poor Families Project. (2006). Still working hard, still falling short. Retrieved September 25, 2009, from http://www.workingpoorfamilies.org/nat_report/nat_report2.html

Wright, E. O. (1996). *Class counts*. New York: Cambridge University Press.

Wright, E. O. (2005). *Approaches to class analysis*. New York: Cambridge University Press.

Vogel, L. C., & Marshal, L. L. (2001). PTSD symptoms and partner abuse: Low income women at risk. *Journal of Traumatic Stress, 14*, 569–584.

Yalom, I. D. (2005). *The theory and practice of group psychotherapy*. New York: Basic Books.

Yeskel, F. and Leondar-Wright, B. (1997). Classism curriculum design. In M. Adams, L. A. Bell, & P. Griffin (Eds.), *Teaching for diversity and social justice* (pp. 232–260). New York: Routledge.

Yoshikawa, H., & Seidman, E. (2001). Multidimensional profiles of welfare and work dynamics: Development, validation, and associations with child cognitive and mental health outcomes. *American Journal of Community Psychology, 29*, 907–936.

Zandy, J. (1990). *Calling home: Working class women's writings*. New Brunswick, NJ: Rutgers University Press.

Zweig, M. (2000). *The working class majority*. Ithaca, NY: Cornell University Press.

# INDEX

Acosta, O., 54
Action research, 110. *See also* Participatory
    action research (PAR)
Activism, 137
Adair, R. K., 45
Adamson, R., 22, 23, 91
Adler, N. E., 45
Advocacy, 25
    for economic justice, 143–46
    individual and systemic, 62
Advocacy Research Team, 63
Affleck, D. C., 57
Albee, G. W., 44, 49–50, 51–52, 53, 56, 57,
    58, 104
Albelda, R., 23
Aldarondo, E., 63
Alexander, C. M., 83
Ali, A., 113
Ali, S., 62
Allen, A., 33
Allen, L., 47
Allison, D., 32, 132
Altman, N., 59, 94, 95, 133
Altruism, 132–34
American Counseling Association, 61
American Medical Association (AMA), 25
American Psychological Association (APA),
    84, 94
    multicultural competencies, guidelines
        for, 61, 102–3
    Resolution on Poverty and SES, 60–61
    Task Force on SES, 11, 18, 143
Anderson, G. L., 99, 109, 117
Anderson, N. B., 46
Annie E. Casey Foundation, 28
Anyon, J., 35

Aponte, H., 59, 86, 90, 133
Applied psychology, 44, 56–63
Areane, P., 45
Argyle, M., 8
Ayoub, C., 47, 48
Azar, S. T., 47
Azocar, F., 45

Badgett, M. V. L., 23
Bail, 37
Bakan, D., 142
Baker, N. L., 10, 91, 92, 93
Baluch, S., 25
Bane, D. T., 21
Bane, M. J., 33, 145
Banyard, V., 45, 54, 63, 140, 142
Barefoot, J. C., 46
Barnes, A., 41
Barry, B., 129
Bassuk, S. S., 45, 47
Baum, O. E., 57
Baumeister, R. F., 130–31
Bawden, T., 138
Beeghley, L., 21
Belle, D., 36, 45, 55, 101, 115–16
Bernabei, S., 25
Berrick, J. D., 65, 73, 78
Berwick, D. M., 141
Bhati, K. S., 62
Bias(es), 6–7. *See also* Classism
Black, L. L., 62
Blazer, D. G., 45
Blighted neighborhoods, 68–69
Blustein, D. L., 61, 62, 63, 108
Bogle, J., 29, 42
Bohlig, A., 63, 115–16, 118, 120

# ABOUT THE AUTHOR

**Laura Smith** is an assistant professor in the department of counseling and clinical psychology at Teachers College, Columbia University. Dr. Smith was formerly the director of training of the APA-accredited predoctoral internship program at Pace University, the founding director of the Rosemary Furman Counseling Center at Barnard College, and the director of psychological services at the West Farms Career Center, where she provided services within a multifaceted community-based organization in the Bronx. Her research interests include social class and poverty, the influence of classism on psychological theory and service, the development of socially-just models of community-based psychological practice, and participatory action research (PAR) in schools and communities.